DID I HEAR YOU RIGHT?

Stephen P. McCue

A collection of outrageous quotes by Democrat leaders and their supporters in their relentless quest for power in the 21st century.

DEFIANCE PRESS
& PUBLISHING

Did I Hear You Right?

ISBN-13: 978-1-963102-60-4 (Paperback)
ISBN-13: 978-1-963102-59-8 (eBook)

Published by Defiance Press & Publishing, LLC

Bulk orders of this book may be obtained by contacting Defiance Press & Publishing, LLC. www.defiancepress.com.

Public Relations Dept. – Defiance Press & Publishing, LLC
281-581-9300

Defiance Press & Publishing, LLC
281-581-9300
info@defiancepress.com

Dedication

To my family: For our many lively discussions about politics around the dining room table.

To my sons, Jack and Kevin: The path ahead may be rough at times. Always stay true to your values, and you'll find your way.

Table of Contents

Preface

As you make your way through this book, you may find yourself asking, "Why would someone *say* that?" Of course, we don't know for sure what was going through the mind of the individual in question at the time, but as you proceed, the following words may help explain the motivation behind many of the quotes featured in this work.

- Arrogance
- Corruption
- Deceit
- Forgetfulness
- Greed
- Hatred
- Honesty
- Hypocrisy
- Ignorance
- Insensitivity
- Intolerance
- Pandering
- Power
- Racism
- Retaliation
- Ridicule
- Socialism

You may notice that I did not include the media as a source for quotes. This was intentional because the mainstream media alone would likely provide enough material to fill multiple volumes, and I wanted to keep this work relatively brief. You will find that I frequently share my opinion about the quotes and the speakers. I do so knowing that your interpretation may be very different from mine, and I do not presume that my opinion should be taken as the definitive view in any way. I share it primarily to engage the reader, speculate about the intent behind the quote, and, whenever possible, poke a little fun at the speaker. Whenever it seemed helpful, I've also tried to provide a bit of context for the quote. Some quotes are accompanied by descriptions that are relatively thorough while other quotes more or less speak for themselves. Some of the featured quotes refer to serious issues affecting our country and were chosen to highlight potential dangers in Democrat ideology. Others are more lighthearted or even ridiculous and may simply leave the reader scratching their head. In the end, I hope you will agree that collectively, the word that probably describes them best is *outrageous*.

–Stephen McCue

Chapter 1

Political Candidates

"Be a politician: no training necessary."
–Will Rogers

"I'd nominate any gay to the Supreme Court, or lesbian or bisexual or transgendered person to the Supreme Court, as long as they were ready to uphold Roe v. Wade."

–Dennis Kucinich, July 14, 2003

Ohio Congressman Dennis Kucinich made this comment as a Democrat presidential candidate. At the time, seven of the Democrat presidential candidates were competing with each other to win the endorsement of the gay and lesbian lobbying group The Human Rights Campaign. In an apparent attempt to one-up the other candidates, who were still debating the merits of issues like gay marriage, Kucinich took the conversation to a whole new level with this comment. I don't claim to be a Constitutional scholar, but it seems like a president should give more consideration to a Supreme Court justice's overall qualifications rather than whether or not they pass a litmus test on abortion.

"I actually did vote for the $87 billion before I voted against it."

–John Kerry, March 16, 2004

Kerry made this famous comment during his 2004 presidential campaign. He had already been criticized for his record of flip-flopping on issues. He was referring to an $87 billion supplemental appropriation for military operations in Afghanistan and Iraq. When he was asked why he voted against the funding, Kerry tried to defend his action by responding with the quote above. The comment did not help his case.

"Because the truth is, we still live in two different Americas: one for people who have lived the American Dream and don't have to worry, and another for most Americans who work hard and still struggle."

–John Edwards, July 28, 2004

Edwards made this remark during his speech to the Democrat National Convention as John Kerry's vice-presidential running mate in the 2004 presidential race. Although the Kerry/Edwards ticket lost the election to Bush/Cheney, two years later, Edwards appeared to be the Democrat party's frontrunner for the next presidential nomination. That's when one of the most disgusting scandals in American political history began. Senator Edwards met and started an affair with a movie producer named Rielle Hunter. In December 2006, Edwards formally announced his plans to seek the Democrat Party's nomination for president. That month, he also hired Hunter to serve as a videographer for his campaign, which allowed the two to continue to meet in secret. Although Edwards' wife Elizabeth discovered their affair, John insisted to her that it had ended. On March 22, 2007, John and Elizabeth Edwards held a press conference to announce that Elizabeth's breast cancer had returned and was incurable. Continuing his affair with Hunter, John learned in May 2007 that she was pregnant with his child.

In October 2007, the *National Enquirer* published a story claiming Edwards was having an affair. Then in December 2007, the *National Enquirer* published a picture of a pregnant Hunter. After unsuccessfully trying to convince Hunter to have an abortion, Edwards drummed up a plan to have one of his former campaign officials, Andrew Young, who was also married, claim paternity of Hunter's baby.

After disappointing performances in the Iowa caucuses and the New Hampshire and South Carolina primaries, Edwards decided to suspend his presidential campaign on January 30, 2008. Almost two years later, Edwards admitted that he was the father of Hunter's baby. After the truth was finally exposed, Elizabeth filed for divorce but sadly died from cancer later that year.

On June 3, 2011, a federal grand jury returned a six-count indictment of the former US Senator and presidential candidate. According to the indictment, during his presidential campaign Edwards conspired to accept and receive more than $900,000 in campaign contributions in an effort to protect and advance his candidacy from disclosure of an extramarital affair and the resulting pregnancy.

Edwards was eventually acquitted on one count, and a mistrial was declared when the jury deadlocked on the remaining five counts. Little did we know at the time how symbolic Edwards' reference to "two different Americas" during his 2004 convention speech was. It could represent the two different personas he carefully managed in the years to come. There was his public image of the clean-cut family man who inspired hope in his supporters—and the real John Edwards, who was desperately trying to keep the door closed to the skeletons in his closet.

"You've got the first sort of mainstream African-American who is articulate and bright and clean and a nice-looking guy. I mean, that's a storybook, man."

–Joe Biden, January 31, 2007

In this classic line, Biden's attempt to praise one of his colleagues exposed his own racism. After his "storybook" reference in 2007, Biden seemed to contradict himself in 2023 during his commencement speech at Howard University, one of the nation's largest historically Black colleges and universities, when he said, "We know that American history has not always been a fairytale. From the start, it's been a constant push and pull for more than 240 years between the best of us, the American ideal that we're all created equal, and the worst of us, the harsh reality that racism has long torn us apart. It's a battle that's never really over."

Biden's original statement referring to Senator Barack Obama was made on the day he declared his candidacy for president. Obama declared his own candidacy for president ten days later. This was not the first time Biden had exposed his racist tendencies. On June 17, 2006, Biden was recorded saying, "You cannot go to a 7-Eleven or a Dunkin Donuts unless you have a slight Indian accent. I'm not joking."

"Number one, there is not a single military man in this audience who will tell this senator he can get those troops out in six months if the order goes today. Let's start telling the truth. Number one, you take all the troops out. You better have helicopters ready to take those 3,000 civilians inside the Green Zone where I have been seven times and shot at. You better make sure you have protection for them or let them die number one. So, we can't leave them there. And it's going to take a minimum 5,000 troops to

10,000 just to protect our civilians. So, while you're taking them out, Governor, take everybody out."

–Joe Biden, July 23, 2007

Biden was responding to a comment from Governor Bill Richardson about the withdrawal of American troops from Iraq during a Democrat presidential debate. In addition to his dubious claim of being shot at, Biden's remark was also noteworthy because his advice turned out to be a prophetic warning about America's disastrous withdrawal from Afghanistan under his watch fourteen years later. Months after assuming the presidency in 2021, Joe Biden ordered the withdrawal of all American forces from Afghanistan in what became a debacle. He truly should have taken his own advice in 2007. Not only did Biden withdraw American troops before he decided to withdraw American civilians and Afghani allies, but he also surrendered our main airbase in the country and instead ordered flights to leave from Kabul Airport, which was a far less secure location. During the chaotic withdrawal, there were fewer than 2,500 American troops on the ground to coordinate the departure, and Biden ultimately left approximately 9,000 American civilians and approximately 78,000 Afghan allies who had worked for the American government behind in Afghanistan.

"I remember landing under sniper fire. There was supposed to be some kind of greeting ceremony at the airport, but instead, we just ran with our heads down to get into the vehicles to get to our base."

–Hillary Clinton, March 17, 2008

Clinton, who was running for president at the time of this statement, was referring to a trip she and her daughter Chelsea made to Bosnia in 1996 when she was First Lady. A video later showed Clinton and her daughter walking from the plane and being greeted with a small ceremony in which an eight-year-old Muslim girl read a poem to her. There were no signs of danger. Clinton later acknowledged her error, saying "So I made a mistake. That happens."

"You go into some of these small towns in Pennsylvania, and like a lot of small towns in the Midwest, the jobs have been gone now for twenty-five years and nothing's replaced them...So it's not surprising then that they get bitter, they cling to guns or religion, or antipathy to people who aren't like them, or anti-immigrant sentiment, or anti-trade sentiment as a way to explain their frustrations."

–Barack Obama, April 6, 2008

Presidential candidate Barack Obama made this comment during a fundraising event in, of all places, San Francisco. One gets the impression that his audience there are his real constituency and the sad folks in rural Pennsylvania and the Midwest are just poor, misguided individuals who still believe in antiquated concepts like religion. Ten years later, on September 7, 2018, former President Barack Obama gave another speech to an audience at the University of Illinois Urbana-Champaign, during which he said, "Each time we painstakingly pull ourselves closer to our founding ideals, that all of us are created equal, endowed by our Creator with certain inalienable rights...somebody somewhere has pushed back. The status quo pushes back...More often it's manufactured by the powerful and the privileged who want to keep us divided and keep us angry and keep us cynical because that helps them maintain the status quo and keep their power and keep their privilege." If Obama counts himself among the "powerful and privileged who want to keep us divided and keep us angry and keep us cynical," then I absolutely agree with him.

"I'm told Chuck Graham, state senator, is here. Stand up, Chuck, let 'em see you. Oh, God love you. What am I talking about? I tell you what, you're making everybody else stand up though, pal."

–Joe Biden, September 9, 2008

Biden made this statement during the 2008 presidential race as he was introducing Missouri State Senator Chuck Graham during a campaign rally. Graham had been using a wheelchair ever since he was involved in a car accident in high school, which was apparently unbeknownst to his friend Joe Biden.

"We are five days away from fundamentally transforming the United States of America."

–Barack Obama, October 30, 2008

Obama made this statement five days before the 2008 presidential election. Statements like this present a strong case that Barack Obama had mixed feelings at best about our country. After all, one does not typically propose to fundamentally change something he loves. I believe wholeheartedly in American exceptionalism and our unique place in the history of the world. I'm not so sure Obama would agree.

On April 4, 2009, President Obama told an audience in France, "I believe in American exceptionalism, just as I suspect that the Brits believe in British exceptionalism and the Greeks believe in Greek exceptionalism."

On June 19, 2013, he told an audience in Germany, "We are also citizens of the world."

At both the start of his presidency and its end, Obama traveled the world and repeatedly referenced American mistakes and flaws in relation to the country he was visiting. Some critics have described these international trips as "Obama's apology tour." No one, myself included, would argue that America today or in its past is perfect. However, it should not be the role of the President of the United States to continuously point out our shortcomings on the world stage. Doing so only reduces our prestige and influence around the globe.

We must remember that since our foundation, people around the world have looked to the United States as a land of hope and opportunity. As the most successful democracy in the history of the world, we should focus on our freedom and our many blessings. Among their other responsibilities, I don't think it's too much to ask our president to be our head cheerleader as well. Obama's "apologies" have only served to diminish our reputation both here and abroad. I prefer to think of our great country the way Ronald Reagan did it in a 1964 speech. It is simply put—"The last best hope of man on earth"—and I don't apologize for that.

"I still have a picture on my mantel, and it is a picture my mother had before that, a picture of my grandfather. And my Aunt Bea has walked by that picture at least a thousand times remarked that he, her father, my Papaw, had high cheekbones like all of the Indians do."

–Elizabeth Warren, May 2, 2012

Warren, who was running for US Senator from Massachusetts at the time she said that, was explaining why she was identified as a minority in the *Association of American Law Schools* desk book between 1985 and 1996. Critics also accused Warren of using her alleged Native American ancestry to help her attain a teaching position at Harvard Law School, which touted her at the time as their first woman of color. In a 1984 cookbook called *Pow Wow Chow*, which was edited by Warren's cousin, she published five recipes under the title "Elizabeth Warren, Cherokee."

In an apparent attempt to clear the air about her ancestry claims once and for all, Warren agreed to release the results of a DNA test in October 2018. The data showed that there was high confidence that Warren had a Native American ancestor between six and ten generations ago, meaning she could be as little as 1/1024th Native American. According to a report in the *Washington Examiner*, "Geneticists estimate that the average European-American has genes that are 98.6% European, .19% African, and .18% Native American. By comparison, Warran's genes might be just 0.09% Native American. On average, if you have a European background, she's probably less Native American than you or I."

A few months after releasing the DNA test results, Warren apologized to the Cherokee Nation, stating "I am not a person of color; I am not a citizen of a tribe." Days later, on February 9, 2019, she announced her candidacy for president. Warren's campaign quickly came under attack from President Donald Trump, who mockingly referred to her as Pocahontas. After an unsuccessful campaign that included a third-place finish in her home state of Massachusetts, Warren suspended her campaign on March 5, 2020.

"I traveled the world."

–Hillary Clinton, September 9, 2015

During her presidential campaign, Clinton delivered a speech at the Brookings Institute where she tried to tout her accomplishments. During her tenure as Secretary of State, Clinton made many headlines for having traveled a total of 956,733 miles around the world. As the Associated Press observed, "If diplomatic achievements were measured by the number of countries visited, Hillary Rodham Clinton would be the most accomplished secretary in history."

Aside from an extensive travel record, however, her colleagues and voters alike all seemed to have trouble identifying any significant accomplishments by Clinton. Another presidential candidate, Republican Carly Fiorina, said it best. "Like Hillary Clinton, I too have traveled hundreds of thousands of miles around the globe. But unlike her, I have actually accomplished something. Mrs. Clinton, flying is an activity, not an accomplishment."

Apparently, Hillary doesn't quite understand what accomplishments are. In March 2023, she interviewed Secretary of Transportation Pete Buttigieg during a Clinton Global Initiative meeting at Vanderbilt University. During the conversation, she cited Buttigieg's accomplishments by saying, "You are the first openly gay cabinet member." Apparently, being gay is also now considered an accomplishment.

"We're going to put a lot of coal miners and coal companies out of business."

–Hillary Clinton, March 13, 2016

Clinton's comment was made during the 2016 presidential race at a town hall event in Columbus, Ohio, which also included Senator Bernie Sanders, another candidate for the Democrat party's nomination. Clinton's comment was widely denounced by voters in coal-producing states like West Virginia.

On May 2, 2016, Clinton held a small group discussion with voters in Williamson, West Virginia. During the discussion, she spoke with Bo Copley, a foreman and maintenance planner who had lost his job at a coal company. Copley told Clinton, "I just want to know how you can say you're going to put a lot of coal miners out of jobs, and then come in here and tell us how you're going to be our friend. Those people out there don't see you as a friend." Clinton apologized to Copley and called her previous remarks a "misstatement." In the 2008 West Virginia Democrat primary Clinton defeated Barack Obama in every county, winning 67% to 26%. Eight years later and two months after her town hall remark, Bernie Sanders defeated Clinton in the 2016 West Virginia Democrat primary 51.4% to 35.8%.

"You know, to be grossly generalistic, you could put half of Trump's supporters into what I call the basket of deplorables, right? They're racist, sexist, homophobic, xenophobic, Islamophobic, you name it."

–Hillary Clinton, September 9, 2016

The Democrat nominee for president made this comment at an LGBT fundraiser in New York City. Clinton went on to lose her bid for president to Donald Trump on November 8, 2016.

On September 7, 2018, former President Barack Obama delivered a speech at the University of Illinois at Urbana-Champaign urging the audience to vote in the midterm election that November. In the speech, Obama said, "We won't win people over by calling them names or dismissing entire chunks of the country as racist, or sexist, or homophobic."

"I look forward to going into the office of Attorney General every day suing him...and then going home."

–Letitia James, July 19, 2018

James made this comment during her campaign for New York State Attorney General. Unfortunately, malicious use of the law against former President Donald Trump has sadly become commonplace. Leaders on the Left have made their feelings clear. If they don't like you and your politics, they will ruin you.

James was running for Attorney General of New York, the chief law enforcement officer of the state. Individuals in that role have tremendous power and a tremendous responsibility to exercise that power carefully. While pursuing justice, prosecutors are supposed to begin with an alleged crime and then start an investigation. In this case and others involving Donald Trump, it appears that prosecutors have started with an individual and investigated them extensively to find a crime. That's not the way the law is supposed to be enforced, but apparently, James and her colleagues don't care. On September 21, 2022, James filed a lawsuit against Donald Trump alleging financial fraud.

"Since learning about how that phrase was being used to push back on that activism, I have stopped using it in that context."

–Pete Buttigieg, April 4, 2019

Presidential candidate Pete Buttigieg was referring to the phrase "All lives matter" and the fact that it was deemed offensive by the Black community. It's pretty sad when a politician is so worried about offending one specific constituency that he vows to avoid a phrase that is indisputable.

"If you look at my immediate reaction after the election, I refused to concede. It was largely because I could not prove what had happened, but I knew from the calls that we got that something happened...I feel comfortable now saying I won."

–Stacey Abrams, April 28, 2019

Abrams was referring to her loss to Brian Kemp in Geogia's 2018 gubernatorial election. Following her loss, Fair Fight Action, an organization founded by Abrams, filed a lawsuit alleging discriminatory and suppressive election practices in Georgia. On September 30, 2022, the case was decided in favor of Georgia Secretary of State Brad Raffensperger and the State Elections Board.

After losing her second campaign for governor again to Brian Kemp in November 2022 in an election that resulted in record voter turnout, Abrams claimed that it is possible to see an increase in voter turnout while still having voter suppression. In January 2023, a federal court ruled against Fair Fight Action's remaining claims against Georgia Secretary of State Brad Raffensperger, and Abrams' organization was ordered to pay $231,303.71 in legal fees.

On October 3, 2022, Abrams referred again to the 2018 gubernatorial election during an appearance on CNN, this time saying, "I have never denied the outcome...I have never been unclear about the fact that I did not win the race."

On August 14, 2023, Fani Willis, District Attorney of Fulton County, Georgia, indicted Donald Trump for violating sixteen Georgia statutes. The charges included racketeering and conspiracy. Following the indictment, Willis said, "Trump and the other defendants charged in this indictment refused to accept that Trump lost, and they knowingly and willfully joined a conspiracy to unlawfully change the outcome of the election in favor of Trump." With these two cases in mind, it should come as no surprise why many believe there is a two-tiered system of justice in America today.

"We could afford to take in a heartbeat another two million (per year). The idea that a country of 330 million cannot afford people…is absolutely bizarre…I would also move to increase the number of immigrants able to come."

–Joe Biden, August 8, 2019

Presidential candidate Joe Biden made this comment during a campaign stop in Des Moines Iowa hosted by the Asian & Latino Coalition Political Action Committee. He promised the audience that he would reverse many of President Trump's immigration policies. One wonders what exactly Biden meant when he said we can "afford" two million migrants. Did he mean we have plenty of available housing for them? Did he mean we have plenty of schools ready and able to teach them in their native languages?

Did he mean states like New York, which has an estimated debt of $329 billion, can afford to spend an additional $9.9 billion to serve a million new migrants in 2023?

Ellis Island in New York Harbor served as America's largest and most active federal immigrant processing station between 1892 and 1954. During the 62 years it was in operation, it processed approximately 12 million migrants.

According to US Customs and Border Protection, as of May 2023, there were no less than 6,048,729 Southwest Land Border Encounters in the twenty-nine months since Biden took office. So, why would Biden willingly establish a policy of open borders?

Democrats seem to be committed to diminishing the relevance of citizenship. Jurisdictions across the US have allowed illegal immigrants to obtain driver's licenses and vote in local elections and have eagerly provided them with health care, in-state college tuition rates, and even housing and meals, all at the taxpayers' expense.

Today there is also a growing push for illegal immigrants to receive work permits so they can legally earn a living. This would reverse long-standing policies preventing illegal immigrants from working in order to discourage illegal migration.

Biden's decision to open the border to millions of migrants from around the world is designed to create such a daunting crisis in the US that officials from both parties would feel enormous pressure to endorse a policy of amnesty. It is Biden's hope that these new citizens would then owe their loyalty to the Democrat Party and show their appreciation through votes, which would solidify a Democrat majority throughout the country for the foreseeable future.

It's worth noting that during his second campaign for the presidency, Joe Biden said the following on August 12, 2007: "No great nation can be in a position where they can't control their border." One can only wonder exactly when Joe stopped wanting America to be a great nation.

"It's time to end mass incarceration. This includes legalizing marijuana, sentencing reforms, and abolishing private prisons. With the addition of job training and education, these actions will reduce crime and help build healthy communities."

–Kamala Harris, September 9, 2019

Echoing the sentiments expressed by Harris, in 2020 mayors and city councils across the country passed budgets that cut more than $840 million from US police departments and increased funding for community services by more than $160 million.

According to a Gallup poll in April 2022, 53% of Americans said they were worried a great deal about crime and that those concerns about crime were at their highest level since 2016. Apparently, that didn't matter to Democrat Louisiana Governor John Bel Edwards. Beginning in October 2023, Edwards spent the last four months of his term issuing pardons to forty convicted murderers. That should make us all safer!

"Nobody should be in jail for a nonviolent crime."

–Joe Biden, September 12, 2019

Statements like this have become popular with political candidates in recent years, but they are ridiculous. One only needs to ask the victims of Bernie Madoff if he deserved to be put in prison. Madoff organized the largest Ponzi scheme in history, defrauding approximately 40,000 victims out of billions of dollars, with many victims losing their entire life savings.

By the way, following Donald Trump's conviction for falsifying business records (a nonviolent crime) on May 30, 2024, I've yet to hear Joe Biden state for the record that Trump should not face jail time. What I have heard numerous times are Democrat politicians referring to Donald Trump as a convicted felon. I guess the phrase "justice-involved person," one of the politically correct terms the Left has tried to push on us in recent years doesn't apply to him. That's odd.

"Hell, yes, we're going to take your AR-15, your AK-47."

–Beto O'Rourke, September 12, 2019

O'Rourke, a former Congressman from Texas and presidential candidate, made this comment during a Democrat presidential debate. In 2018, O'Rourke lost his bid for the US Senate to Ted Cruz but was now trying to win the Democrat nomination for president. On November 1, 2019, he announced the end of his presidential campaign before a single state primary had been held. Undaunted, O'Rourke ran for Governor of Texas in 2022 but lost handily to incumbent Greg Abbott, making him a three-time political loser in just four years.

"President Trump withheld Congressionally appropriated aid to Ukraine…This is no joke. Trump continues to put his own personal, political interests ahead of the national interests. He must be impeached."

–Joe Biden, October 18, 2019, in a tweet

Five years after making this tweet, President Joe Biden announced on May 8, 2024, that he would be withholding Congressionally appropriated weapons and ammunition to aid Israel. Given his prior feelings on this subject, Biden should not be surprised to learn that Congressman Cory Mills formally filed articles of impeachment against him shortly after Biden's announcement. For some reason, I suspect Biden's views toward impeachment are different now.

"No man has a right to raise a hand to a woman in anger other than in self-defense, and that rarely ever occurs. And so, we have to just change the culture period. And keep punching at it and punching at it and punching at it. No, I really mean it."

–Joe Biden, November 20, 2019

Biden was asked during a Democrat presidential debate what he would do as president to address sexual violence and harassment against women in America.

"You're a damn liar… Look, the reason I'm running is because I've been around a long time and I know more than most people know and I can get things done. That's why I'm running. And you want to check my shape, man, let's do push-ups together here, man, let's run, let's do whatever you want to do. Let's take an IQ test."

–Joe Biden, December 5, 2019

This comment was a response to a voter during a town hall event in New London, New Hampshire, who questioned Biden about his son Hunter's judgment to work for Burisma, a Ukrainian energy company, and whether Biden was too old to serve as president.

The above comment reminded many of a similar response Biden gave to a questioner at a campaign coffee gathering in Claremont, New Hampshire, on April 3, 1987, during his first campaign for president. He said, "I think I probably have a much higher IQ than you do, I suspect…and I'd be delighted to sit down and compare my IQ to yours if you'd like, Frank."

Several individuals close to Biden have long suggested that Biden is particularly insecure about his intellect, which probably accounts for his bizarre and sometimes unwarranted attempts to defend his intelligence. On May 27, 2019, President Trump said during a press conference in Tokyo that he agreed with North Korea when it called Mr. Biden a low-IQ individual. In response, the Biden campaign noted that Trump's comments were "beneath the dignity of the office."

"You only arrest for the purpose of dealing with a felony that's committed, and I don't count drunk driving as a felony."

–Joe Biden, January 20, 2020

Presidential candidate Joe Biden made this comment after he was asked, "What exact changes would you bring to ICE as an agency?" Biden acknowledged his plans to reduce the deportation of illegal immigrants if he were to be elected.

For some bizarre reason, Biden thinks illegal immigrants convicted of felony drunk driving should be allowed to stay in the US. This is particularly odd when one remembers that in 2007, Biden implied that his own family was tragically involved in an accident caused by a drunk driver in 1972. Biden said at the time, "A tractor-trailer, a guy who allegedly, and I never pursued it, drank his lunch instead of eating his lunch, broadsided my family and killed my wife instantly and killed my daughter instantly and hospitalized my two sons." Although there has never been any evidence to support Biden's claim that the truck driver in this accident had been drinking, one might wonder why, if Biden believed this to be true, he would take such a lax stance against drunk drivers. Each year, nearly 1.5 million people in America are arrested for driving while under the influence of drugs or alcohol. In 2021, 13,384 people were killed in the US by drunk drivers.

"No one has said that. Who said that?"

–Joe Biden, February 3, 2020

Biden was asked on NBC's *Today Show* whether he thought it was wrong for his son Hunter to take his position on the board of Ukrainian energy company Burisma knowing that "… the company wanted access to you." His response, "No one has said that," is something he would end up repeating many times in the coming months whenever he was asked about Hunter and corruption. After being questioned dozens of times about the same issue, Joe eventually learned that actually, a lot of people are saying that.

"You got more questions. Well, I tell you what, if you have a problem figuring out whether you're for me or Trump, then you ain't Black."

–Joe Biden, May 22, 2020

Biden made this comment while speaking with a Black radio show host during his campaign for president. In addition to its arrogance, this comment was also offensive because it implied that Black people who planned to vote for Trump were traitors to their race and somehow weren't real Blacks. This is a typical sentiment among Democrats. They are quick to vilify Blacks anytime they dare to break from conventional wisdom and vote against the Democrat Party.

Over the years, Democrats have dared to call Supreme Court Justice Clarence Thomas an Uncle Tom, and they even described California Gubernatorial Candidate Larry Elder as "A Black face on White supremacy."

Biden's assumption that all Blacks should vote for him is ironic given his history on race relations. As a senator, Biden expressed his concerns over school busing and desegregation in 1977. According to *The New York Times,* Biden said during a Congressional hearing, "Unless we do something about this, my children are going to grow up in a jungle, the jungle being a racial jungle."

Biden was even called out on his record by none other than his future running mate, Kamala Harris. During a Democrat presidential primary debate on June 27, 2019, Harris looked at Biden and said, "There was a little girl in California who was part of the second class to integrate her public schools, and she was bused to school every day. That little girl was me. So, I will tell you that on this subject it cannot be an intellectual debate among Democrats."

Biden started his presidency with an 87% approval rating among Black Americans, higher than any other racial group. By January 2024, his support among Black Americans had fallen to 63%, according to a *USA Today*/Suffolk University poll. I guess a lot of Biden's previous supporters "ain't Black" anymore.

> *"For far too long, the status quo thinking has been to believe that by putting more police on the street, you're going to have more safety. And that's just wrong, that's not how it works."*
>
> –Kamala Harris, June 10, 2020

This comment was made following the death of George Floyd, a Black man who died while being taken into police custody in Minneapolis on May 25, 2020. Floyd's death led to nationwide protests and the onset of a "defund the police" movement in cities across the US. According to 2020 data from the FBI's Uniform Crime Reporting Program released on August 30, 2021, aggravated assaults in America rose by an estimated 12.4% while the murder rate increased by 29.4%, the single largest year-over-year increase on record.

> *"No, I haven't taken a test. Why the hell would I take a test? C'mon, man. That's like saying to you before you got on this pro-gram did you take a test whether you're taking cocaine or not.*

What do you think, huh? Are you a junkie?"

–Joe Biden, August 5, 2020

Presidential candidate Joe Biden was asked by CBS News reporter Errol Barnett, an African-American, if he had taken a cognitive test. Barnett's interview with Biden was part of a virtual convention of the National Association of Black Journalists and the National Association of Hispanic Journalists.

"Here's my promise to you: if I'm elected president…I'll take responsibility instead of blaming others."

–Joe Biden, August 16, 2020, in a tweet

Since taking office, President Joe Biden has blamed the Trump administration for America's chaotic withdrawal from Afghanistan. He also blamed oil company profits for record high gas prices and blamed Russian President Vladimir Putin's invasion of Ukraine for inflation in the US, describing it as "Putin's price hike." He also blamed Republicans after the US Supreme Court ruled against his plan to cancel student loan debt and blamed Republicans for the crisis at the Southern Border. Some promise, Joe!

"Look at how [Trump] steps and look at how I step. Watch how I run up ramps and he stumbles down ramps, OK."

–Joe Biden, September 7, 2020

Seventy-seven-year-old presidential candidate Joe Biden was mocking his opponent, seventy-four-year-old Donald Trump, after Trump was seen cautiously walking down a wet ramp at West Point.

Biden frequently engages in a slow jog when approaching a podium in a contrived and awkward attempt to demonstrate his vigor.

After assuming office, however, Biden's own physical and mental fitness for the job were routinely called into question. On March 19, 2021, he repeatedly fell while climbing the stairs to Air Force One. On June 18, 2022, he fell while trying to stop his bicycle in Rehoboth Beach, Delaware. On February 22, 2023, he fell on stairs in Warsaw, Poland. On May 19, 2023, he fell down stairs at the G7 Summit in Hiroshima, Japan. On June 1, 2023, he fell on stage at the Air Force Academy commencement. In June 2023, Biden also began to forego the tall stairs leading to Air Force One and has instead routinely opted for a much smaller set of stairs to enter the plane. In March 2024, Biden started wearing stability-enhancing sneakers regularly. In April 2024, Biden stopped walking to Marine One by himself and is now flanked by a group of staffers who walk between the president and the nearby press corps in an attempt to obscure footage of his increasingly awkward and shuffling gait.

"You're the worst president that America has ever had."

–Joe Biden, September 29, 2020

Biden said this to Donald Trump during their first presidential debate in 2020. I only wish Trump had used one of Biden's lines in response and called him a "lying dog-faced pony soldier."

"My mother tells the story about how I'm fussing, and she's like, 'Baby, what do you want? What do you need?' And I just looked at her and I said, 'Fweedom.'"

–Kamala Harris, October 6, 2020

This quote appeared in *Elle Magazine's* November 2020 cover story featuring Kamala Harris. According to Harris, she and her parents were attending a civil rights march in Oakland, California, when Kamala supposedly made this comment to her mother after falling out of her stroller. Critics point out that Harris' story is strikingly similar to one told by Martin Luther King Jr. in January 1965. While it may be impossible to know definitively whether Harris' story was plagiarized, she has certainly told it more than once. It seems as though Harris is trying to establish a narrative that even as a young child, she was principled and virtuous in a manner comparable to that of George Washington and his famous cherry tree. (By the way, the cherry tree story is a myth.)

"You'll know my opinion on court-packing the minute the election is over."

–Joe Biden, October 8, 2020

On September 26, 2020, less than six weeks before the 2020 presidential election, President Donald Trump nominated Judge Amy Coney Barrett to the US Supreme Court as an Associate Justice. Exactly one month later and one week before the election, Barrett was confirmed and sworn in as a member of the Supreme Court. Barrett was filling a vacancy on the court created by the death of longtime Justice Ruth Bader Ginsburg.

Democrats were outraged that Donald Trump was able to fill the seat once held by Ginsburg, who was seen as a hero to liberals. This development led many Democrats in Congress to support the idea of increasing the number of justices on the court, a concept commonly known as court packing.

Presidential candidate Joe Biden was repeatedly asked for his opinion about possibly packing the court if elected. He responded with the comment above. On April 15, 2021, Senator Edward Markey and Congressmen Jerrold Nadler, Hank Johnson, and Mondaire Jones introduced the Judiciary Act of 2021, which called for an expansion of the US Supreme Court by adding four seats, creating a thirteen-justice Supreme Court.

That same week, the White House issued a press release, noting, "President Biden will today issue an executive order forming the Presidential Commission on the Supreme Court of the United States…The Commission's purpose is to provide an analysis of the principal arguments in the contemporary public debate for and against Supreme Court reform, including…the membership and size of the Court."

Republican Senators responded to Democrat threats to pack the court by proposing a Constitutional amendment to permanently keep the number of US Supreme Court justices at nine. One of the amendment's sponsors, Ted Cruz, noted, "Don't be fooled by Democrat's hyperbolic rhetoric. Packing the Court means one very specific thing: expanding the number of justices to achieve a political outcome. It is wrong. It is an abuse of power."

In the end, neither the Democrat-led Judiciary Act of 2021 nor the Republican-led proposed Constitutional amendment were passed. Based on his decision to establish a commission to study the idea of packing the court, it appears that Joe Biden forgot all about a comment he made during a Senate hearing on July 13, 1983. Biden stated at the time, "President Roosevelt clearly had the right to send to the United States Senate and the United States Congress a proposal to pack the court…but it was a bonehead idea. It was a terrible, terrible mistake to make and it put in question, for an entire decade, the independence of the most significant body…in this country, the Supreme Court of the

United States of America." Today's Joe Biden could learn a thing or two from yesterday's Joe Biden.

> *"Instead of anybody coming at you and the first thing you do is shoot to kill, you shoot them in the leg."*

–Joe Biden, October 15, 2020

Presidential candidate Joe Biden made this comment during an ABC News town hall event. He was referring to changes he wanted to see in police tactics. Biden's comment was widely condemned by the law enforcement community. Observers were quick to point out that officers only use their firearms as a last resort and that they are trained to stop a threat by aiming at the center mass for good reason. A moving target is incredibly hard to hit, and aiming at the center mass reduces the risk that a bullet might miss and hit an unintended target. One can only imagine the guilt an officer would feel if he accidentally shot an innocent bystander, and it is safe to assume that Biden and other Democrats would be unlikely to come to his defense if he did.

Some observers also pointed out that a gunshot to the leg could also sever the femoral artery, potentially causing a fatal injury. Biden's ignorance on the subject and his assumption that he knows better than officers what they should do in an emergency is shameful. Then again, what can you expect from a man who told his wife, "If there's ever a problem, just walk out on the balcony here, walk out and put that double-barrel shotgun and fire two blasts outside the house." Not only would this act be unlawful in Biden's home state of Delaware, but it can be dangerous. Biden seems to forget that what goes up must come down. Biden also stated, "You want to keep someone away from your house, just fire the shotgun through the door." Apparently, Joe's recommendation to cops is for them to aim at a suspect's leg, but his wife should blindly fire a shotgun through doors and in the air whenever she feels threatened. I'm sure in Joe's mind that makes sense.

"I represent all of you, whether you voted for me or against me. And I'm going to make sure you're represented."

–Joe Biden, October 22, 2020

On March 20, 2020, a Detroit auto plant worker named Jerry Wayne told Biden, "You're working for me, man," to which Biden replied, "I'm not working for you."

"I'm going to take responsibility. When I make a mistake, I'll admit it."

–Joe Biden, November 3, 2020

Biden made this pledge on election day 2020. One might wonder, however, how well he kept his promise after becoming president.

On January 19, 2022, Biden said, referring to the disastrous American withdrawal from Afghanistan, "I make no apologies for what I did."

On March 28, 2022, Biden said, "I make no apologies for it," referring to a previous statement of his when he said about Russian President Vladimir Putin, "For God's sake, this man cannot remain in power." White House staff quickly downplayed the remark, and Biden himself later clarified that he was not calling for a policy change.

On January 19, 2023, Biden said, "I have no regrets" when referring to mishandled classified documents that were found inside the Penn Biden Center and the garage at his Delaware home.

On February 16, 2023, Biden said, "I make no apologies" when referring to his decision to shoot down a Chinese spy balloon only after it had traversed the continental United States. So much for admitting mistakes.

"I sought this office to restore the soul of America…and to make America respected around the world again."

–President-elect Joe Biden, November 7, 2020

On September 19, 2023, President Joe Biden delivered a keynote address to the seventy-eighth session of the United Nations General Assembly. Of the five permanent members of the UN Security Council (United States, China, Russia, United Kingdom, and France), the only leader to attend Biden's speech was Biden himself. The other four leaders were all conspicuously absent. That doesn't sound like respect to me.

No, I don't think it should be mandatory. I wouldn't demand it to be mandatory."

–President-elect Joe Biden, December 4, 2020

Biden was responding to a question about whether COVID-19 vaccines should be made mandatory. However, during a speech on September 9, 2021, Biden said, "We must increase vaccinations among the unvaccinated with new vaccination requirements…This is not about freedom or personal choice. It's about protecting yourself and those around you." He then provided an ominous warning when he referred to unvaccinated Americans, saying, "We've been patient, but our patience is wearing thin." It's comments like these that cause many Americans to fear that if Americans are to lose basic liberties in the future, it will begin in the name of public health.

"I do believe it is absolutely necessary for corporations to show their goodwill. They have to publicly denounce these bills, they have to support and invest in voting rights expansion, and they need to support the federal voting rights standards."

–Stacey Abrams, April 9, 2021

Former Georgia gubernatorial candidate Stacey Abrams made this comment during an interview with the Associated Press (AP). She was asked, "Do you support consumer boycotts and corporate responses like Major League Baseball moving the All-Star Game from metro Atlanta?"

The interview occurred two weeks after the passage of Georgia's Election Integrity Act of 2021. This new law prohibited unsolicited absentee ballots from being sent to voters and introduced new voter ID requirements. Abrams was a prominent critic of the new law, calling it "a redux of Jim Crow in a suit and tie."

In response to criticism of the Election Integrity Act by Abrams and others, Major League Baseball Commissioner Rob Manfred said in a statement, "I have decided that the best way to demonstrate our values as a sport is by relocating this year's All-Star Game and MLB Draft. Major League Baseball fundamentally supports voting rights for all Americans and opposes restrictions to the ballot box." It has been estimated that Georgians lost $100 million when the All-Star Game moved from Atlanta to Denver.

"I am tired of hearing about being the best state in the country to do business when we are the worst state in the country to live."

–Stacey Abrams, May 21, 2022

Abrams, a candidate for governor of Georgia, made this comment during a fundraising dinner. It amazes me how people who have such disdain for their own community and neighbors feel that they are the best people to lead them forward.

> *"My sister-in-law, she is Latino, and her family. I love hanging out with them and practicing my español, un piquito. So, but yeah, I've learned so much from her family."*
>
> –Katie Hobbs, October 3, 2022

Hobbs, who was serving as Arizona's Secretary of State, made this comment at a Hispanic Chamber of Commerce Forum during her campaign for governor. She was asked by a town hall moderator what she had learned from the Latino community in Arizona. Surprised by her weak answer, the moderator then said to Hobbs, "So there is not one specific lesson you can share, other than the español? It's one-third of the state."

Chapter 2

Presidents

"It has been said that politics is the second oldest profession. I have learned that it bears a striking resemblance to the first."

–Ronald Reagan

"I don't know, not having been there and not seeing all the facts, what role race played in that, but I think it's fair to say, number one, any of us would be pretty angry; number two, that the Cambridge police acted stupidly."

–President Barack Obama, July 22, 2009

During a news conference at the White House, Obama was responding to a question about an incident in which Harvard professor Henry Louis Gates Jr., who Obama identified as a personal friend, was arrested by Cambridge police one week earlier. A witness observed Gates forcing open the front door of his own home and mistook him for a burglar. Cambridge Police Sergeant James Crowley responded to the 911 call. Crowley stated that Gates shouted at him and insulted him, repeatedly accusing him of racial bias. After warning Gates multiple times that he was becoming disorderly, Crowley arrested Gates after he followed the officer outside, continuing his tirade. Crowley later stated that he was dismayed by President Obama's comments and insisted that he had done nothing wrong.

Fellow officers and state politicians publicly vouched for Sergeant Crowley, saying they strongly doubted that race played a role in his actions. In addition, the Cambridge Police Chief said Crowley's actions were consistent with his training and were without bias.

Meanwhile, in a television interview, Professor Gates complained about how vulnerable all Black men are to rogue policemen. Referring specifically to Sergeant Crowley, who happens to be a racial profiling awareness instructor with the Cambridge Police Department, Gates said, "This man clearly was a rogue policeman."

Ultimately, prosecutors decided not to pursue the disorderly conduct charge against Gates. However, the arrest of Gates sparked a sometimes heated national conversation about race. Many have since referenced the controversy surrounding the arrest of Professor Gates and President Obama's statement publicly criticizing the Cambridge police as a significant event that helped reignite racial conflict in America.

In the years that followed, several other controversial and highly publicized encounters between police officers and Black suspects further increased racial divisiveness in the country. Two weeks after the arrest of Professor Gates, in an apparent attempt to diffuse the tensions between those who expressed support for Professor Gates and those who expressed support for Sergeant Crowley, President Obama hosted a "beer summit" in the Rose Garden of the White House, which was attended by Obama, Vice President Biden, Professor Gates, and Sergeant Crowley. However, Obama never publicly apologized for his inflammatory statement nor accepted any responsibility for the harmful impact it had on the nation.

"Shovel-ready was not as shovel-ready as we expected."

–President Barack Obama, June 13, 2011

Soon after taking office, Obama and his Democrat colleagues in Congress pushed hard for a stimulus bill to revitalize the economy. To promote this bill, Obama and his allies frequently referenced the impact it would have on "shovel-ready jobs." On February 17, 2009, the $831 billion American Recovery and Reinvestment Act was signed into law. In 2011, the US unemployment rate was still 8.9%, prompting Obama to make the comment above.

"Look, if you've been successful, you didn't get there on your own. You didn't get there on your own. I'm always struck by people who think, well, it must be because I was just so smart... If you've got a business, you didn't build that. Somebody else made that happen."

–President Barack Obama, July 13, 2012

President Obama made this statement at a campaign event in Roanoke, Virginia. In a television interview on July 23, 2012, Republican presidential nominee Mitt Romney responded to Obama's comment, saying "This is an ideology which says 'Hey, we're all the same here, we ought to take from all and give to one another and that achievement, individual initiative and risk-taking and success are not to be rewarded as they have in the past.' It's a very strange and is some respects foreign to the American experience type of philosophy...So his whole philosophy is an upside-down philosophy that does not comport with the American experience."

"We have been very clear to the Assad regime, but also to other players on the ground, that a red line for us is we start seeing a whole bunch of chemical weapons moving around or being utilized. That would change my calculus. That would change my equation."

–President Barack Obama, August 20, 2012

Obama made this comment after he was asked what would lead him to use military force in Syria. On December 23, 2012, the first allegations of chemical weapons use were reported in Syria. Over the next several months more chemical attacks were reported.

On June 13, 2013, Deputy National Security Advisor for Strategic Communications Ben Rhodes wrote in a statement, "Following a deliberative review, our intelligence community assesses that the Assad regime has used chemical weapons, including the nerve agent sarin, on a small scale against the opposition multiple times in the last year. Our intelligence community has high confidence in that assessment given multiple, independent streams of information. The intelligence community estimates that 100 to 150 people have died from detected chemical weapons attacks in Syria to date; however, casualty data is likely incomplete. While the lethality of these attacks make up only a small portion of the catastrophic loss of life in Syria, which now stands at more than 90,000 deaths, the use of chemical weapons violates international norms and crosses clear red lines that have existed within the international community for decades."

Despite Rhodes' confirmation that Syria had violated President Obama's "red line," the US government still took no military action against Syria. More than two months later, on August 31, 2013, President Obama delivered remarks in which he finally acknowledged

Syria's use of chemical weapons, stating "All told, well over 1,000 people were murdered." He went on to say, "This attack is an assault on human dignity. It also presents a serious danger to our national security. It risks making a mockery of the global prohibition on the use of chemical weapons… In a world with many dangers, this menace must be confronted."

On September 9, 2013, Secretary of State John Kerry was asked whether there was anything that Syrian President Bashar al-Assad could still do to avoid a US military attack. Kerry responded with a seemingly off-handed comment: "Sure, he could turn over every bit of his weapons to the international community within the next week without delay, but he isn't about to."

Officials at the State Department were quick to clarify Kerry's comment by saying it was merely a rhetorical argument and not an actual proposal because Assad "cannot be trusted." Nevertheless, that same day Syria agreed to Kerry's suggestion, saying they would place their chemical weapons under international control so they could later be destroyed.

President Obama's inaction against Syria and his failure to enforce his own "red line" clearly damaged and weakened US influence around the world. Five years later, on September 2, 2018, former Secretary of State John Kerry told CBS News' *Face the Nation,* "We paid a price for the way it played out without the red line being enforced by the bombing…We paid a price for that. There's no question about that. We paid a price. And all the explanations and everything else doesn't change the perception, and perceptions sometimes are very telling in diplomacy and politics."

It sure seems ironic that Kerry's critique of the price America paid for its clumsy response to chemical weapons use in Syria was partly the result of his own words.

"The 1980s are now calling to ask for their foreign policy back."

–President Barack Obama, October 22, 2012

President Obama said this to Mitt Romney during their third presidential debate. Obama was criticizing his opponent after Romney had previously identified Russia as the biggest geopolitical threat facing America. Events over the next ten years, however, caused many to believe that Romney's assessment was quite accurate.

For example, on February 20, 2014, Russian military forces invaded Crimea, marking the beginning of the Russo-Ukrainian War. In 2019, Special Counsel Robert Mueller wrote in his *Report on the Investigation into Russian Interference in the 2016 Presidential Election* that "The Russian government interfered in the 2016 presidential election in sweeping and systematic fashion."

Then, on February 24, 2022, Russia commenced a large-scale invasion of Ukraine, leading to the death of tens of thousands and Europe's largest refugee crisis since World War II. During the first year of the war, the United States Congress allocated more than $75 billion in humanitarian and military support to Ukraine. It's funny: no one seems to be making many jokes about the geopolitical threat posed by Russia anymore.

Moreover, Mitt Romney never received much credit for his outlook, and Obama never received much criticism for his short-sightedness. Given that the President of the United States is probably the most informed individual in the nation, their judgment is critical. They need to see the threats that are coming down the road.

Unfortunately, Obama was repeatedly wrong in his analysis, such as the time when during an interview with *The New Yorker* in 2014 he made an analogy between ISIS and a Junior Varsity Team.

Unfortunately, Joe Biden has perhaps even less talent for anticipating threats. On May 1, 2019, Biden said, "China is going to eat our lunch? Come on, man...I mean, you know, they're not bad folks, folks. But guess what, they're not competition for us."

On July 8, 2021, Biden was asked whether a Taliban takeover of Afghanistan was inevitable. Biden's response was "No, it is not."

Another example was on July 19, 2021, when Biden said, "Some folks have raised worries that this could be a sign of persistent inflation. But that is not our view." Biden assured the public that inflation would be "transitory."

Each of these statements by Biden was soon proven false, but that hasn't stopped his supporters like Vice President Kamala Harris from trying to paint a positive image of Biden. Harris once said that Biden "is extraordinarily smart. He has the ability to see around the corner in terms of what might be the challenges we face as a nation or globally."

I believe a more realistic and accurate description of Biden's judgment was provided by Robert Gates, who served as Secretary of Defense under George W. Bush and Barack Obama. Gates wrote in his 2014 memoir, *Duty: Memoirs of a Secretary at War,* that Joe Biden has "...been wrong on nearly every major foreign policy and national security issue over the past four decades."

"There are those who dismiss the Great Society as a failed experiment and an encroachment on liberty; who argue that government has become the true source of all that ails us...I reject such thinking."

–President Barack Obama, April 10, 2014

Lyndon Johnson's Great Society program failed on many levels. It marked the start of a decades-long war on poverty that cost trillions of dollars. Nevertheless, in 2022 nearly 38 million people (11.5%) in the US still lived in poverty. The Great Society also significantly expanded the size and scope of the federal government. It introduced a variety of new entitlement programs and increased government encroachment into the economy.

One of the lasting consequences of L.B.J.'s Great Society was the increased dependence of Americans on the welfare state, which created drastic changes in America. One of those unforeseen consequences is the rise of single-parent families. According to the Annie E. Casey Foundation, nearly 24 million children live in single-parent families in the US today. Nearly 30% of single parents live in poverty, compared to just 6% of married parents. Children in single-parent families are more likely to experience emotional and behavioral health challenges and are more likely to drop out of high school.

This trend toward fatherlessness has been a cause for concern for decades. One example was a comment by Vice President Dan Quayle in May 1992. Quayle observed, "Bearing babies irresponsibly is simply wrong. Failing to support children one has fathered is wrong. We must be unequivocal about this. It doesn't help matters when primetime TV has Murphy Brown, a character who supposedly epitomizes today's intelligent, highly paid professional woman, mocking the importance of fathers by bearing a child alone and calling it just another lifestyle choice."

Yet, when those concerns were raised years ago, they were met with condemnation and ridicule, and single motherhood continued to be celebrated in numerous other television programs that followed. This trend hit the Black community the hardest. In 1950, just 9% of Black children lived without their father. Sadly, today 64% of Black children live in single-parent families. Tommy Sotomayor directed a powerful documentary film about this problem called *A Fatherless America*. In the film, which I highly recommend, he explores this disturbing trend and the crushing impact it has had on the Black community.

Economist Thomas Sowell put it this way. "The Black family, which had survived centuries of slavery and discrimination, began rapidly disintegrating in the liberal welfare state that subsidized unwed pregnancy and changed welfare from an emergency rescue to a way of life." Sotomayor points out in his film that in America today, there is a virtual war on masculinity and fatherhood. We all understand that it takes a man and a woman to create a child but there is a prevailing belief today that it doesn't take a man and a woman to properly raise a child. No one ever said that parenthood is easy, but raising a child is the most important job a person can have, and a healthy nuclear family is the best gift parents can give a child.

When my own marriage fell apart, I was sad that my relationship with my wife was ending, but I was devastated when it hit me that I was about to become a part-time parent against my wishes. Suddenly I was deprived of the joy of seeing my kids at the breakfast table each morning and the dinner table each night. Nevertheless, I tried to be the best father I could be in the time I had with my two sons. Like every father, I'm not perfect, but what's most important is to be involved. It is simply unacceptable for the plague of fatherlessness to continue. If it does, our society will slowly disintegrate.

"I guess to make a broader point, so often in the past there's been a sharp division between Left and Right, between capitalist and communist or socialist, and especially in the Americas, that's been a big debate…I think your generation, you should be practical and just choose from what works. You don't have to worry about whether it neatly fits into socialist theory or capitalist theory…

and so you don't have to be rigid in saying it's either this or that."

–President Barack Obama, March 23, 2016

President Obama made this statement during a visit to Buenos Aires, Argentina, at a town hall event for the Young Leaders of the Americas Initiative. His nonchalant remarks about communism and socialism stand in stark contrast to those of other US presidents.

In an address to the United Nations on September 24, 2019, President Trump said, "Events in Venezuela remind us all that socialism and communism are not about justice, they are not about equality, they are not about lifting up the poor and they are certainly not about the good of the nation. Socialism and communism are about only one thing: power for the ruling class. Today I repeat a message to the world that I have delivered at home: America will never be a socialist country."

"And demagogues promise simple fixes to complex problems. They promise to fight for the little guy even as they cater to the wealthiest and the most powerful. They promise to clean up corruption and then plunder away. They start undermining norms that ensure accountability, try to change the rules to entrench their power further...It's not conservative. It sure isn't normal. It's radical. It's a vision that says the protection of our power and those who back us is all that matters, even when it hurts the country."

–Former President Barack Obama,
September 7, 2018

Democrats introduced HR51, the Washington D.C. Admission Act, on January 3, 2019, and reintroduced the bill on January 4, 2021. This bill would admit the nation's capital as the union's fifty-first state. 76% of registered voters in Washington, D.C. are Democrats.

Democrats introduced HR1, the For the People Act, on January 4, 2021. Republicans described the bill as an effort to federalize state and local elections. The bill would limit political expression, require states to automatically register eligible voters, authorize same-day voter registration, restrict states from purging eligible voters from registration rolls, and restore voting rights for felons. As the Senate prepared to vote on HR1, Senate Majority Leader Chuck Schumer proposed changing Senate rules to eliminate the filibuster, which would allow the bill to be passed with a 51-vote majority rather than the 60 needed to override a filibuster. The proposed rule change and the bill failed to pass the Senate on January 20, 2022.

Democrats introduced HJ Resolution 14 on January 11, 2021. This proposal to amend the US Constitution would eliminate the electoral college and provide for the direct election of the President and Vice-President. Democrat support for this proposal was influenced by the 2016 presidential election, in which Hillary Clinton won the popular vote by approximately 2.9 million votes.

On April 14, 2021, Democrats introduced HR 2584, the Judiciary Act of 2021. This bill would "pack the court" by expanding the United States Supreme Court to thirteen justices. The bill was intended to enable President Biden to appoint four new justices, shifting the court's balance.

Democrats introduced HJ Resolution 23 on February 3, 2021. This proposal to amend the US Constitution would replace the 26th Amendment and lower the voting age in America to 16 years old. Democrat support for this proposal was influenced by the 2020 presidential election, in which Joe Biden received approximately 60% of the votes from 18-to-29-year-olds.

Despite Barack Obama's critique of Republicans, it sure seems like Democrats believe that protecting power is all that matters.

"I think a full investigation would show that Trump didn't actually win the election in 2016. He lost the election, and he was put into office because the Russians interfered on his behalf."

–Former President Jimmy Carter, June 27, 2019

Carter apparently felt compelled to join a chorus of other Democrats who argued that Trump lost the 2016 presidential election. Among them, of course, was Hillary Clinton, whom Trump defeated in 2016, and who also refused to accept the results. On September 29, 2019, she said, "He knows he's an illegitimate president."

Like Clinton and others, Carter believed that Trump colluded with Russia to alter the results of the election. One hopes that Carter later recognized his mistake and regretted his decision to believe what turned out to be propaganda based primarily on a fallacious dossier paid for by the Clinton campaign.

Many people from my generation have long considered Jimmy Carter to be the worst president of our lifetime. However, Carter may be relieved to learn that this title has now passed to Joe Biden. Carter and Biden were both incompetent leaders whose policies damaged America's international standing, created high energy prices and high inflation, and led to a significant decline in American unity.

Carter was so concerned about this last point that he delivered a famous speech on July 15, 1979, which is often described as his Malaise Speech. In it, he said, "I want to talk to you right now about a fundamental threat to American democracy...It is a crisis of confidence...The erosion of our confidence is threatening to destroy the social and the political fabric of America."

Carter went on to say, "For the first time in the history of our country, a majority of our people believe that the next five years will be worse than the past five years…As you know, there is a growing disrespect for government and for churches and for schools, the news media, and other institutions. This is not a message of happiness or reassurance, but it is the truth and it is a warning."

Joe Biden would be well advised to read Carter's speech and heed his warning. Sadly, on October 14, 2023, an Associated Press/NORC Research Center poll reported that 78% of respondents said America is heading in the wrong direction. Only 21% said America is heading in the right direction. Given the remarkable and disturbing similarities between these two administrations, you might ask why I consider Biden to be the lesser of the two. It's simple. Despite all of his faults as a president, Jimmy Carter was by most accounts an honest and decent human being. Joe Biden is not only an incompetent leader, but I believe history will find him to be the most corrupt president in US history.

"But what I never lost sight of, and what I think has been our tradition, is the recognition that the Fourth Estate is vital to a functioning democracy. The notion that you would threaten them, or call them an enemy of the state, or try to delegitimize the press that does the job of fact-checking and expecting evidence when you float accusations, that kind of bullying behavior we haven't seen to the extent that we've seen it recently."

–Former President Barack Obama,
December 10, 2020

Obama was criticizing the Trump administration in the comment above. However, he seems to have forgotten about a serious event that occurred during his own presidency. On June 11, 2009, Fox News Chief Washington Correspondent James Rosen reported a story about North Korea's potential to conduct a nuclear test in response to tighter United Nations sanctions. In his report, Rosen cited Central Intelligence Agency sources.

The Obama Administration was angry about the leak of this intelligence and was committed to finding its source. An investigation was launched, and it narrowed in on a State Department arms expert named Stephen Jin-Woo Kim as the possible leaker. Under the personal direction of Attorney General Eric Holder, James Rosen's telephone and email records were collected, and his State Department key card was monitored. To secure their search warrant for Rosen's records, the FBI claimed that Rosen broke the law and described him as a co-conspirator in court records.

When news broke about the Justice Department's secret investigation into Rosen, multiple news agencies expressed their indignation. Fox News Executive Vice President of News Michael Clemente said his organization was "outraged to learn today that James Rosen was named a criminal co-conspirator for simply doing his job as a reporter." The *New York Times* editorial board added, "With the decision to label a Fox News television reporter as a possible 'co-conspirator' in a criminal investigation of a news leak, the Obama administration has moved beyond protecting government secrets to threatening fundamental freedoms of the press to gather news."

"This is our historic moment of crisis and challenge, and unity is the path forward."

–President Joe Biden, January 20, 2021

In stark contrast to the comment above, which Biden made during his inaugural address, in a speech on August 25, 2022, Biden said, "The MAGA Republicans don't just threaten our personal rights and economic security, they're a threat to our very democracy. They embrace, embrace, political violence. They don't believe in democracy...It's not just Trump, it's the entire philosophy that underpins the, I'm going to say something, it's like semi-fascism...I don't respect these MAGA Republicans."

Many Americans feel that our country is more divided today than it has been in decades. What's sad is that Biden's plea for unity during his inaugural address is actually an important cause. The problem is, he doesn't seem to believe or practice what he says. As Andrew Jackson once said, "Without union, our independence and liberty would never have been achieved; without union, they never can be maintained."

"I want the world to hear today: America is back. America is back. Diplomacy is back at the center of our foreign policy...We will compete from a position of strength by building back better at home, working with our allies and partners, renewing our role in international institutions, and reclaiming our credibility and moral authority, much of which has been lost."

–President Joe Biden, February 4, 2021

During the hectic US withdrawal from Afghanistan, US State Department spokesperson Ned Price told reporters on August 12, 2021, "The embassy remains open...This is not an abandonment. This is not an evacuation. This is not a wholesale withdrawal. What this is is a reduction in the size of our civilian footprint."

Three days later, the US flag was taken down at our embassy in

Kabul and the US officially withdrew from Afghanistan on August 31, 2021. Many observers have criticized the Biden Administration for the way it handled the US departure from Afghanistan, including former President Donald Trump, who described it as "The most embarrassing, incompetent, and humiliating event in the history of the United States."

Unfortunately, this was just the beginning. Since then, the Biden Administration has closed three more US embassies in Ukraine, Belarus, and Sudan, marking a sad chapter in US foreign relations and giving a global perception that US influence around the world is weakening. Making matters even worse is a promise by Joe Biden to shutter the US embassy in Jerusalem and replace it once again with a consulate to be used to strengthen diplomatic ties with the Palestinians.

In 1995, Congress passed the Jerusalem Embassy Act, which called for the relocation of the US embassy from Tel Aviv to Jerusalem in recognition of that city as Israel's capital. After decades of inaction, the US embassy was finally moved to Jerusalem during the Trump Administration in 2018. Biden's promise to move the embassy back to Tel Aviv has damaged our relations with Israel.

In the wake of these setbacks in the Biden Administration's foreign policy, many observers believe that our adversaries, including Russia and China, have become emboldened. Some insist that our chaotic withdrawal from Afghanistan prompted Russia to invade Ukraine, and others think it has only increased the odds of a Chinese invasion of Taiwan.

Navy veteran and Republican candidate for US Senate from Virginia Hung Cao said it well: "When there is a leadership void in the world, there is a long line of countries waiting to fill that void. In less than three years, we have left a huge crater in the world diplomatic forum."

"Corruption attacks the foundations of democratic institutions, drives and intensifies extremism, and makes it easier for authoritarian regimes to corrode democratic governance. Corruption is a risk to our national security, and we must recognize it as such."

–President Joe Biden, June 3, 2021

Anyone who has followed the Biden influence-peddling scandal knows how outrageous this comment is. The scandal is complicated because the president's son, Hunter Biden, took great effort to hide the details of his business ventures in part to avoid paying required taxes and in part to protect his father's role while he was vice president.

Financial records reveal that Hunter created dozens of limited liability corporations (also known as shell companies) and bank accounts that were reportedly used to funnel tens of millions of dollars from several countries.

One of these LLCs was called Oneida Holdings, and it was formed by Hunter Biden, Jim Biden (the president's brother), Tony Bobulinski, James Gilliar, and Rob Walker. On May 13, 2017, Gilliar sent an email to Tony Bobulinski, Hunter Biden, and Rob Walker documenting that each of them would receive a 20% share in the business with 10% going to Jim Biden and the remaining 10% "held by H for the big guy." Bobulinski later revealed to the media that "the big guy" referred to Joe Biden. Bobulinski also shared a text message he received from James Gilliar on May 20, 2017, which read, "Don't mention Joe being involved, it's only when u are face to face, I know u know that but they are paranoid."

Oneida Holdings soon entered into a joint venture with another company called Hudson West IV, in which Oneida Holdings provided Hudson with consulting services for projects in China. On July 30,

DID I HEAR YOU RIGHT?

2017, Hunter wrote to one of his business partners, a Communist party official named Henry Zhao, telling him, "I am sitting here with my father and we would like to understand why the commitment made has not been fulfilled. Tell the director that I would like to resolve this now before it gets out of hand, and now means tonight. And Z, if I get a call or text from anyone involved in this other than you, Zhang, or the chairman, I will make certain that between the man sitting next to me and every person he knows and my ability to forever hold a grudge that you will regret not following my direction. I am sitting here waiting for the call with my father." When he was later asked whether he was sitting with Hunter when the message was sent Joe Biden later said, "No. I wasn't."

The president of Hudson West IV was Gongwen "Kevin" Dong, a reported associate of Ye Jianming, who at the time was chairman of China's largest private energy company, CEFC. According to a December 2018 article in *The New York Times*, Hunter met privately with Ye at a hotel in Miami in May 2017, when Mr. Ye proposed a partnership to invest in American infrastructure and energy deals. After reading this online article, Joe Biden left a voicemail for his son Hunter saying, "Hey pal, it's Dad. It's 8:15 on Wednesday night. If you have a chance, give me a call. Nothing urgent, I just wanted to talk with you. I thought the article released online—it's going to be printed tomorrow in the *Times*—was good. I think you're clear."

On August 3, 2017, Hunter used the encrypted WhatsApp messaging service to contact Kevin Dong. The message read, "K- Very simple: 10M per annum budget to use to further the interest of the JV [Joint Venture]. This move to 5M is completely new to me and is not acceptable obviously…if the Chairman doesn't value this relationship is being worth at least 5M, then I'm just baffled." Hunter also added "I'm tired of this Kevin…The Biden's [sic] are the best at doing exactly what Chairman wants from this partnership. Please let's not quibble over peanuts."

Five days after the messages were sent, CEFC moved roughly $5 million to a Hudson West III bank account. Hunter Biden and Kevin Dong had opened a line of credit under that business name. According to a report by the Senate Homeland Security Committee and Senate Finance Committee, the president's brother Jim and his wife Sara used credit cards associated with this account.

In the presidential debate on October 22, 2020, Joe Biden was asked, "Vice President Biden, there have been questions about the work your son has done in China and for a Ukrainian energy company when you were vice president; in retrospect, was anything about those relationships inappropriate or unethical?" Biden responded, saying "Nothing was unethical….My son has not made money in terms of this thing about, what are you talking about, China."

Biden has also repeatedly denied any connection or involvement with Hunter's businesses. While campaigning for president on August 28, 2019, Joe Biden said, "I have never discussed, with my son or my brother or with anyone else, anything having to do with their businesses. Period. And what I will do is the same thing we did in our [the Obama] administration. There will be an absolute wall between personal and private [business interests] and the government."

He repeated this assertion on September 21, 2019, saying, "I have never spoken to my son about his overseas business dealings." However, as more and more evidence came to light, the Biden defense narrative changed somewhat when White House Press Secretary Karine Jean-Pierre said on July 24, 2023, "I've been asked this question a million times. The answer is not going to change. The answer remains the same. The president was never in business with his son."

The story took yet another turn on December 13, 2023, when Hunter

Biden announced publicly, "My father was not financially involved in my business."

Congressman James Comer, Chairman of the House Committee on Oversight and Accountability, provided an alternative view of the Biden scandal when he explained, "Joe Biden lied to the American people when he said he had no knowledge about his son's business dealings and was not involved. Joe Biden was the brand that his son sold around the world to enrich the Biden family."

It's worth noting that the examples of corruption mentioned here barely scratch the surface of Biden, Inc. Joe would do well to remember a line he wrote in his 2008 memoir, *Promises to Keep*: "The greatest sins on this earth are committed by people of standing and means who abuse their power."

> *"The Second Amendment, from the day it was passed, limited the type of people who could own a gun and what type of weapon you could own. You couldn't buy a cannon...The point is that there has always been the ability to limit, rationally limit, the type of weapon that can be owned and who could own it."*
>
> –President Joe Biden, June 23, 2021

In his remarks about gun crime prevention, Biden repeated a familiar claim. Unfortunately, the claim is totally false. When the Second Amendment to the US Constitution was ratified, there were no limitations in place on who could own a gun or what type of weapon they could own. Federal gun regulation was first passed in 1934.

As for Biden's frequent reference that owning a cannon has always been against the law, he might be surprised to learn that many collectors across the United States legally own cannons to this day. Nonetheless,

Biden, who frequently describes himself as a "Second Amendment guy," continues to use this example regularly. It would be reasonable to conclude that he is either woefully misinformed by his staff or it just doesn't bother him to repeatedly lie to the American public as long as the lie helps to strengthen his argument.

"The Afghan troops have 300,000 well-equipped, as well-equipped as any army in the world, and an air force against something like 75,000 Taliban. It is not inevitable…The likelihood there's going to be the Taliban overrunning everything and owning the whole country is highly unlikely."

–President Joe Biden, July 8, 2021

President Biden was responding to a reporter who asked him, "Is a Taliban takeover of Afghanistan now inevitable?" In spite of Biden's confidence that Afghanistan would be in good hands with the Afghan army, the Taliban seized control of the country in just ten days following the US military's hasty withdrawal. Sadly, thirteen US service members were killed by a suicide bomber during the chaotic departure. Adding insult to injury, the Afghan troops, who Biden noted were "as well-equipped as any army in the world," quickly forfeited to the Taliban approximately $7 billion in US military hardware, including Black Hawk helicopters, A-29 Super Tucano light attack planes, armored vehicles, and approximately 316,000 small arms.

"There's going to be no circumstance where you see people being lifted off the roof of a embassy of the United States from Afghanistan. It is not at all comparable."

–President Joe Biden, July 8, 2021

President Biden was responding to a reporter during a press conference who asked him, "Do you see any parallels between this withdrawal and what happened in Vietnam?" In spite of Biden's assurances, on August 15, 2021, US Chinook helicopters were seen landing at the US embassy in Kabul, Afghanistan, for an emergency evacuation of diplomatic personnel. Ironically, Chinook helicopters were also used during the hasty evacuation of US embassy staff in Saigon, Vietnam, in 1975. Photos comparing the two events were quickly posted online with many describing the current situation as Biden's "Saigon moment."

In an apparent attempt to differentiate the two events, *The New York Times* noted that the Chinook helicopters being used at the embassy in Kabul were landing on a pad next to the embassy rather than the roof. For what it's worth, during the 1975 embassy evacuation in Saigon, helicopters landed on both the embassy roof as well its parking lot after US Marines cut down trees to create an emergency landing zone.

One person who publicly expressed his disgust for the way the Biden Administration handled the withdrawal from Afghanistan was Marine Corps Lieutenant Colonel Stuart Scheller. Scheller posted videos to Facebook and LinkedIn which demanded those responsible for the chaotic withdrawal and the death of thirteen service members at Kabul Airport be held accountable.

In response to his actions, Scheller was relieved of his command and spent one week in a military brig. He was eventually found guilty in a court martial of six misdemeanor charges, including conduct unbecoming an officer and a gentleman. He was fined $5,000 and discharged from the Marine Corps. It's sad to know that the only person who lost his job following our failed exit from Afghanistan was a Marine who simply told the truth.

"I used to drive an eighteen-wheeler, man."

–President Joe Biden, July 28, 2021

Biden made this statement during a visit to a Mack truck factory in Lower Macungie Township, Pennsylvania. It caused many who heard it to question its truthfulness. Nevertheless, Biden seemed to double down on his assertion when he visited Dakota County Technical College in Rosemount, Minnesota, on November 30, 2021, when he said, "I used to drive a tractor-trailer." After reporters asked for information to verify the president's claim, the White House responded by clarifying that Biden once drove a school bus during a summer job. Does that response really count as authentication in today's America?

"The commitment holds to get everyone out that, in fact, we can get out and everyone that should come out."

–President Joe Biden, August 19, 2021

Biden was responding to a question during an interview on ABC News that asked whether US troops would stay in Afghanistan until all of our Afghan allies were safely out of the country. During the interview, Biden estimated the number of our Afghan allies to be evacuated at 50,000 to 65,000. The US State Department is authorized to provide Special Immigrant Visas to those who worked with the US Armed Forces as an interpreter or translator as well as those who were employed by or on behalf of the US government in Afghanistan.

In March 2022, the US Department of State released an After Action Review on Afghanistan. This report from the Biden administration attempted to shift much of the blame for the chaotic US withdrawal from Afghanistan on the Trump administration, which had left office seven months earlier. One section of the report noted "the AAR (After Action Review) team was struck by the differences in style and decision making, most notably the relative lack of an interagency process in the Trump administration and the intense interagency process that characterized the initial period of the Biden administration. This included a particular focus very early in the Biden administration on the fate of those eligible for SIVs (Special Immigrant Visas) as well as larger numbers of other at-risk Afghans who might need assistance in the event of a Taliban victory."

According to the State Department's Afghan Special Immigrant Visa Quarterly Report to Congress, as of March 31, 2023, there were still more than 152,000 Afghan SIV applications pending.

"We will maintain the fight against terrorism in Afghanistan and other countries. We just don't need to fight a ground war to do it. We have what's called over-the-horizon capabilities, which means we can strike terrorists and targets without American boots on the ground...We've shown that capacity just in the last week. We struck ISIS-K remotely days after they murdered thirteen of our service members and dozens of innocent Afghans."

–President Joe Biden, August 31, 2021

Biden made this comment one day after completing the withdrawal of American forces from Afghanistan. After he had announced his intentions in April 2021 to remove all troops, many experts argued that it would be prudent to maintain a small American military presence in the country. Biden rejected the need for such a force by repeatedly touting the US military's ability to rely on over-the-horizon capabilities moving forward.

To support his decision, his above comment references a drone attack launched by the US military against ISIS-K on August 29, 2021. Unfortunately, on September 17, 2021, the Pentagon acknowledged that the drone strike in question did not kill ISIS-K terrorists as originally claimed. Sadly, the strike tragically killed ten Afghan civilians, including seven children.

"I used to think that hate could be defeated, it could be wiped out. But I learned a long time ago, it can't. It only hides...and it's been given too much oxygen in the last four, five, seven, ten years, and it has seen itself, whether it was, I remember spending time at the, you know, going to the, you know, the Tree of Life Synagogue, speaking with the, just, it just is amazing these things are happening, happening in America."

–President Joe Biden, September 2, 2021

Biden made these remarks during a speech to Jewish leaders in advance of the high holidays. On October 27, 2018, a gunman shot and killed eleven worshippers and wounded six others at the Tree of Life Synagogue in Pittsburgh, including four police officers, in the deadliest antisemitic attack in US history. In response to Biden's claim that he visited the synagogue, the synagogue's Executive Director, Barb Feige, advised the *New York Post* that Biden did not actually visit but did speak to the Rabbi, Jeffrey Meyers, by phone in 2019.

"It was horrible what, to see as you saw, to see people treated like they did: horses nearly running them over and people being strapped. It's outrageous. I promise you, those people will pay."

–President Joe Biden, September 24, 2021

61

Biden was referencing a highly publicized video of US Customs and Border Protection agents on horseback who were trying to prevent illegal immigrants from entering the US. Some of those who saw the footage, including Biden, believed that agents were using their reins to whip, or strap, unarmed Haitian migrants.

Vice President Kamala Harris also couldn't resist the urge to comment on the story, saying it reminded her of tactics "used against African Americans during times of slavery."

The White House quickly announced the launch of an investigation and confirmed that horses would no longer be used by Border Patrol agents in Del Rio, Texas. During the investigation, it was made clear that the footage was deceiving. The agents on horseback were simply using their reins to control their horses and never used them to strike any of the migrants. Even the photographer who captured the images stated that they had been misconstrued. The four agents in question were cleared of any criminal charges but, in what appeared to many to be political retribution so Joe Biden could save face, the agents were relieved from their normal duties and charged with administrative violations by the Department of Homeland Security. Border Patrol union chief Brandon Judd summed up the whole debacle this way: "Unfortunately, the president made this the spectacle it's become. If he would have just kept his mouth shut and let the process play out like it should have instead of passing judgment before the facts were in, we wouldn't be discussing this right now."

"The violent, deadly insurrection on the Capitol nine months ago, it was about White supremacy, in my view."

–President Joe Biden, October 21, 2021

The riot at the US Capitol on January 6, 2021, has been described as an armed insurrection. This description reminds me of a famous quip by Voltaire when he wrote, "The Holy Roman Empire was neither Holy, nor Roman, nor an Empire." Likewise, the Capitol riot was neither armed nor an insurrection.

On January 5, 2022, Attorney General Merrick Garland said, "In the aftermath of the attack, the Justice Department began its work on what has become one of the largest, most complex, and most resource-intensive investigations in our history... Led by the US Attorney's Office for the District of Columbia and the FBI's Washington field office, DOJ personnel across the department in nearly all fifty-six field offices, in nearly all ninety-four United States Attorney's offices, and in many main justice components have worked countless hours to investigate the attack. Approximately seventy prosecutors from the District of Columbia and another seventy from other US Attorney's offices and DOJ divisions have participated in this investigation. So far, we have issued over 5,000 subpoenas and search warrants, seized approximately 2,000 devices, poured through over 20,000 hours of video footage, and searched through an estimated fifteen terabytes of data."

After all this work, there is still zero evidence that rioters on January 6 used a single knife or gun. The riot has also been described as deadly. This description is accurate, but not for the reasons Democrats would have us believe.

There was one fatality at the Capitol on January 6: an unarmed protestor by the name of Ashli Babbit who was shot unnecessarily by a Capitol police officer. Nevertheless, the officer in question was never criminally charged or even terminated for his actions.

Democrats claim that as many as five officers died during the attack. The truth is, all five officers died in the days and weeks after the riot, and none of them died from physical injuries sustained on January

6. The riot on January 6 was violent, ugly, and wrong, but it is still best described as a protest that turned into a riot. It was in no way an "armed and deadly insurrection." Nevertheless, Democrats have used this description so often that it has become widely accepted as true.

The Democrat-run January 6 Congressional committee tried to ensure that the event would be forever recognized as an insurrection. It is disgusting that Democrats continue to make political hay out of this event. The White House and the Justice Department frequently cite the January 6 riot as evidence linking Trump supporters with domestic terrorists, claiming that both groups pose a grave threat to the country and seek to destroy American democracy.

Joe Biden has repeatedly described January 6 as the worst attack on American democracy since the Civil War, and in the comment above he inexplicably tries to link the January 6 riot with White supremacy. Since January 6, 2021, the Biden administration has used the Justice Department to investigate, intimidate, arrest, and prosecute approximately 1,100 people. The majority of these individuals were not engaged in any violence on January 6. Their prosecution underscores Joe Biden's message to the American people that political dissent will not be tolerated.

"Yes, we have a commitment to do that."

–President Joe Biden, October 21, 2021

Biden made this comment during a town hall discussion in Baltimore when he was asked whether the US would come to Taiwan's defense if China attacked. This wouldn't be the only time Biden would make such an assertion. At a press conference in Tokyo on May 23,

2022, Biden was asked if the US would intervene militarily to defend Taiwan. He responded by saying, "That's the commitment we made." Again, on September 18, 2022, Biden said "Yes" when he was asked during a *60 Minutes* interview whether US forces would defend Taiwan if it was invaded.

Biden's repeated guarantees of US military support for Taiwan if attacked represent a major change in US policy. Following the end of World War II, a deadly civil war between the Chinese Communist Party and the Nationalist Party that originated in the 1920s once again resumed. On October 1, 1949, Chinese Communist leader Mao Zedong declared victory and announced the creation of the People's Republic of China (PRC). Nationalist forces under their leader, Chiang Kai-shek, fled to Taiwan, roughly 100 miles across the Taiwan Strait. Taiwan, which is officially known as the Republic of China (ROC), has been governed independently ever since.

The PRC continues to see Taiwan as a renegade province and has vowed to "unify" Taiwan with mainland China. Officially, the United States has had a longstanding One China Policy. According to the US Department of State's website, "The United States approach to Taiwan has remained consistent across decades and administrations…We do not support Taiwan independence."

Unofficially, the United States has long practiced a policy of strategic ambiguity. Simply put, this means the US has created deliberate uncertainty as to whether it would intervene in a war between the PRC and the ROC. This strategy seeks to create a dual deterrence. First, it hopes to prevent the PRC from invading Taiwan. Second, it hopes to prevent Taiwan from declaring independence from China, which would likely prompt the use of force by China against Taiwan. Through his offhanded comments, Joe Biden has thrown both official and unofficial US policy out the window, causing widespread anger and instability.

On September 20, 2022, US National Security Advisor Jake Sullivan tried to downplay and clarify the president's remarks, telling reporters, "The President is a direct and straightforward person. He answered a hypothetical. He's answered it before in a similar way. And he has also been clear that he has not changed US policy towards Taiwan."

With such mixed messages, one can only wonder whether Joe Biden intended to announce a change in US policy toward Taiwan, or, despite his long tenure on the Senate Foreign Relations Committee, he doesn't even know what the existing policy is.

"Let's go, Brandon. I agree."

–President Joe Biden, December 24, 2021

Joe and Jill Biden were answering calls to the North American Aerospace Defense Command's (NORAD) Santa tracking hotline on Christmas Eve at the White House. One caller spoke politely with the First Couple for a short while but ended his call by saying "I hope you guys have a wonderful Christmas as well. Merry Christmas, and let's go Brandon."

Little did Joe Biden realize at the time that the phrase "Let's go Brandon" was actually a pejorative, which is why he responded the way he did. The phrase originated on October 2, 2021, at a NASCAR race at Talladega Superspeedway in Alabama. An NBC sports reporter was interviewing the winner of the day's race, a driver named Brandon Brown, when she heard a chant in the crowd. She misunderstood the chant and believed the fans were yelling, "Let's go, Brandon." In reality, the crowd was chanting, "F*** Joe Biden."

"It seems like yesterday, the first time I got arrested."

–President Joe Biden, January 11, 2022

While delivering remarks on voting rights to an audience at Clark Atlanta University, Biden appeared to refer to an alleged incident that happened when he was a teenager. On multiple occasions, he claimed that after a real estate agent sold a home to a Black couple in a neighboring town in Delaware, protests erupted, and he went to the home of the Black couple and stood with them on their front porch, leading to his arrest by police.

Biden has also stated that he was arrested trying to see Nelson Mandela in South Africa. In addition, he said he was arrested for trying to enter an all-female dorm room at Ohio University during the 1960s. Biden also claimed that he was arrested for wandering onto the Senate floor as a star-struck kid. The *Washington Post* reported on January 13, 2022, that "There's no evidence we can find that Biden was ever arrested." In spite of his well-deserved reputation for telling tall tales that either blur the facts or include outright lies, Biden is fiercely defended by his staff. As Deputy White House Press Secretary Andrew Bates put it, "Like he promised, he gives the American people the truth right from the shoulder and takes pride in being straight with the country about his agenda and his values, including by sharing life experiences that have shaped his outlook and that hard-working people relate to."

"Hi, Kamala. I love you. You always have my back. You're really amazing. You're the best partner I could imagine."

–President Joe Biden, January 20, 2022

Biden said this during his opening remarks at a Democrat National Committee Grassroots Event, to which Harris replied, "I do." As odd as many people found this exchange, it paled in comparison to another awkward moment that took place just over one year later on February 7, 2023, when First Lady Jill Biden entered the House Gallery for the State of the Union Address and was greeted by Second Gentleman Douglas Emhoff with a kiss on the lips.

When asked about the encounter, Kamala Harris said she did not see the video of the kiss. Meanwhile, Vice President Harris has also not been shy about identifying some of the things she loves most. On October 22, 2022, during a discussion about abortion at Metropolitan State University in St. Paul, Minnesota, Harris said, "So, among the many things that I like, I love Venn diagrams. You know, the three circles? I love Venn diagrams. I just like, just throw it into a Venn diagram. It'll tell you everything you need to know about any issue, especially where there is, you know, you're trying to understand the intersection and the connections, right?"

Harris reaffirmed this affection on January 12, 2023, during a discussion at the University of Michigan, when she said "I love Venn diagrams. I do. I love Venn diagrams. So, the three circles and you can do more. Nobody says a Venn diagram has to only be three circles, right?"

Again, on July 28, 2023, Harris mentioned Venn diagrams during a moderated conversation about reproduction. "You know, I asked my team—I'm so in love with Venn diagrams. I really do. The three circles, you know, and then they overlap. And so, Venn diagrams can help you sort through."

In addition to this obvious love, Harris has made it clear that other things also tickle her fancy. During the January 2023 discussion at the University of Michigan, Harris also said "I, you know, what also excites me, when I, among the many things? I'm excited about electric school buses. I love electric school buses. I just love them for so many reasons. Maybe because I went to school on a school bus. Hey, raise your hand if you went to school on a school bus, right?"

On October 26, 2022, in Seattle she said, "So here's the thing, who doesn't love a yellow school bus, right? Can you raise your hand if you love a yellow school bus, right?" I'm sure the American public finds great comfort in learning about the things our leaders love the most.

"I've been in and out of Iraq and Afghanistan over forty times."

–President Joe Biden, March 1, 2022
(First State of the Union address)

In 2019, following a *Washington Post* article that pointed out a separate false claim Biden had made about a previous trip he had taken to Afghanistan, Biden's presidential campaign set the record straight by acknowledging that his total number of trips to Iraq and Afghanistan was actually twenty-one. Undeterred and in typical Joe-Biden style, he later told a group of veterans at a town hall event on December 16, 2022, "I've been in and out, not as obviously a combatant, but in and out of Afghanistan, Iraq, and those areas thirty-eight, thirty-nine times."

Ironically, most Americans would probably be impressed that over the course of his long political career, Biden has visited Iraq and Afghanistan twenty-one times. Yet, for some inexplicable reason, Biden seems to have a compulsive need to exaggerate whenever he shares a personal anecdote. His chronic pension for hyperbole has led many to question his honesty and integrity.

"Let me close what I've long said. America is a nation that can be defined in a single word. I was in the footin [sic], ah, foot, excuse me, foothills of the Himalayas with Xi Jinping traveling with him, travelled 17,000 miles when I was vice-president. I don't know that for a fact."

–President Joe Biden, April 8, 2022

This is how Biden concluded his remarks at the White House congratulating Katanji Brown Jackson on her confirmation by the US Senate as Associate Justice of the US Supreme Court. The single word that defines America must have been lost by Biden somewhere on his long journey in the Himalayas with the Chinese President.

"I was appointed to the Academy in 1965 by a senator who I was running against in 1972…He was a fine man, and his name was J. Caleb Boggs."

–President Joe Biden, May 27, 2022

Biden's remarks were made at the United States Naval Academy's class of 2022 graduation and commissioning ceremony. Curators at the Delaware Historical Association searched Senator Boggs' archives but failed to find evidence to support Biden's claim. Chief Curator Leigh Rifenburg told *The New York Post*, "To be safe, we searched the full range of dates from 1960 to 1965."

Biden's claim that he was appointed in 1965 also raised questions because Biden graduated from the University of Delaware in 1965, and the Naval Academy does not grant graduate degrees. The Naval Academy explained that it does not maintain records of preliminary applications and therefore has no relevant records.

This claim was by no means the first time Biden was found to be exaggerating his academic record. On April 3, 1987, during his first presidential campaign, Biden said, "I went to law school on a full academic scholarship, the only one in my class who had a full academic scholarship...and, in fact, ended up in the top half of my class."

In the same speech, Biden also claimed that he had been named the outstanding student in the political science department as an undergraduate at the University of Delaware and that he graduated from Delaware with three undergraduate degrees. On September 21, 1987, Biden admitted these claims were inaccurate. According to the *Washington Post*, Biden attended law school on a half-time scholarship based on financial need and graduated seventy-sixth out of a law school class of eighty-five.

The Post also reported that Biden received only one undergraduate degree with a dual major in history and political science. In his clarifying remarks, Biden also noted, "With regard to my being the outstanding student in the political science department, my name was put up for that award by Professor David Ingersoll." Biden's tendency to embellish his record is legendary. He has been caught lying many times during his career. During his first campaign for president, it was revealed that he had plagiarized a speech by a United Kingdom member of Parliament during a campaign event at the Iowa State Fair on August 23, 1987. Then on September 18, 1987, the *New York Times* reported that Biden had also been caught plagiarizing during law school and asked school administrators not to be expelled. Five days later, Biden suspended his presidential campaign.

"Today, we received news that our economy had zero percent inflation in the month of July."

–President Joe Biden, August 10, 2022

The inflation rate at the time this comment was made was 8.5%. Perhaps Joe needs to be reminded of what he said in his inaugural address: "We must reject a culture in which facts themselves are manipulated and even manufactured."

"How that could possibly happen? How anyone could be that irresponsible…just totally irresponsible."

–President Joe Biden, September 18, 2022

Biden was referencing the FBI's seizure of classified documents at former President Trump's home. He was asked what he thought when he heard the news. Incidentally, Trump's home, Mar-a-Lago, is a property that is guarded twenty-four hours a day by the US Secret Service.

At the time of the FBI raid, Trump's office was discussing with the National Archives and Records Administration how the documents could either be returned to the National Archives or securely maintained on his premises. Following a recommendation by the National Archives, Trump's team had recently upgraded the locks on the space where the documents were kept.

Meanwhile, on November 2, 2022, an attorney working for Joe Biden discovered previously unknown classified documents at Biden's private office at the Penn Biden Center for Diplomacy and Global Engagement, a Washington D.C. thinktank where Biden worked after leaving the vice presidency. Ironically, this discovery did not result in a raid by the FBI.

The documents were discovered six days before the midterm election, but their existence was not made public until January 2023. Unlike the president, the vice president does not have the legal authority to declassify documents and is not allowed to privately maintain classified documents.

On January 12, 2023, it was announced that additional classified documents were discovered at Biden's Wilmington, Delaware home, including some found in his garage near his Corvette. In a weak attempt to defend his actions, Biden told the White House press corps, "By the way, my Corvette's in a locked garage, OK. So, it's not like they're sitting out on the street."

Biden's allies in Congress quickly came to his defense. Congressman Hank Johnson even suggested Biden was being framed, saying, "Things can be planted in places and then discovered conveniently. That may be what has occurred here."

Even after a Special Counsel was appointed by Attorney General Merrick Garland on January 12, 2023, to investigate the matter, Biden's personal attorneys, who did not possess security clearances, were allowed to continue searching for additional classified documents in Biden's residence. Inexplicably, the Department of Justice decided it wasn't necessary to have the FBI supervise the search.

Days later, it was announced that even more classified documents were found there, some of which dated back to Biden's tenure in the Senate. It wasn't until February 1, 2023, that the FBI finally decided to search Biden's vacation home in Rehoboth Beach, Delaware.

It's worth remembering that by possessing classified documents in these places, Biden committed a crime. With that in mind, what took the FBI so long to search Biden's Rehoboth Beach home, and why did the FBI treat Joe Biden so differently than they did Donald Trump?

Interestingly, in the intervening time, Biden spent the weekend at the Rehoboth Beach home. The FBI's search of the home found no classified documents present. With all of this happening, why would the FBI wait until after Biden spent the weekend at this home before conducting a search there? I do not suggest that Biden destroyed any classified documents during his visit to the home, but the fact that he could have done so if he were so inclined is unacceptable. Would an average American under such scrutiny be allowed access to a location like this if the FBI had reason to believe that classified information might be found there? Can you say "double standard"?

"I want to thank all of you here, including bipartisan elected officials like Representative McGovern, Senator Braun, Senator Booker, Representative Jackie are you here? Where's Jackie? I didn't think she was, she was supposed to be here, to help make this a reality."

–President Joe Biden, September 28, 2022

Representative Jakie Walorski died in a car crash in Northern Indiana on August 3, 2022. That day, the White House issued a statement from President Biden which read, "Jill and I are shocked and saddened by the death of Congresswoman Jackie Walorski of Indiana along with two members of her staff in a car accident today in Indiana." In an attempt to excuse Biden's incredible mistake, White House Press Secretary Karine Jean-Pierre simply stated, "She was on top of mind." Apparently, Representative Walorski was so top of mind that Biden forgot she had died one month earlier.

"I told him how proud of him I was and thanked him for all the

work he and his Coasties are doing to save lives."

–President Joe Biden, September 30, 2022

Biden was referring to a phone call he had with US Coast Guard Aviation Survival Technician Second Class Zach Loesch. The day before the call, Loesch and his colleagues rescued over 100 people from the Southwest Florida coast following Hurricane Ian. After his call with the president, Loesch told Breitbart News that he was scheduled to be discharged from the Coast Guard within thirty to sixty days for refusing to take the COVID-19 vaccine.

In August 2021, Secretary of Defense Llyod Austin mandated the COVID-19 vaccine for all service members. This decision to discharge unvaccinated service members was not only unnecessary but unfair. As Loesch stated, "If I had asked any of the people I saved yesterday if they wanted to come with me even though I am unvaccinated, every single one of them would have said yes."

In total, approximately 8,400 service members were discharged from the military for refusing the COVID-19 vaccine. Critics of the policy soon pointed out that the mandate was hurting recruiting and retention efforts. Eventually, in January 2023 Biden signed the National Defense Authorization Act, rescinding the vaccine mandate in the military. Nevertheless, ten months later, only forty-three service members who had been discharged had sought to be reinstated in the military. The Department of Defense reported that it missed its fiscal year 2023 recruitment goals by 41,000; the Army, Navy, and Air Force all missed their targets.

"We have a very, in relative terms, a large Puerto Rican population in Delaware relative to our population…I was sort of raised

in the Puerto Rican community at home, politically."

–President Joe Biden, October 3, 2022

The 1970 US Census indicates that in the entire state of Delaware, 2,154 people were either born in Puerto Rico or descended from Puerto Rican parents, constituting .39% of the state's population at the time. A cynic might imply that Joe Biden likes to try to be all things to all people, but I'm sure that's not true.

However, on July 15, 2022, in his remarks at an East Jerusalem Hospital Network event, Biden noted, "My background and the background of my family is Irish-American." For good measure, on December 16, 2022, he told a group of veterans in Delaware, "I may be Irish, but I'm not stupid." At the same event he also added, "I married Dominic Giacoppa's daughter, so you know, I got a little Italian in me now, you know?"

Then, during a visit to Poland on February 21, 2023, Biden said "As a young man...we moved down to Delaware, to a town called Claymont, Delaware, which was a working-class town, and everyone in town was either Polish or Italian."

To spice things up further, on January 15, 2023, Biden spoke at the Ebenezer Baptist Church in Atlanta, where he told the congregation, "I may be a practicing Catholic, but I used to go to 7:30 Mass every morning in high school and then in college before I went to the Black church. Not a joke."

Just in case that didn't settle the question as to who Joe Biden really is, on September 14, 2023, Biden had a call with Jewish faith leaders for the high holidays in which he said "I, you might say was raised in the synagogues in my state. You think I'm kidding. I'm not." Biden appears to have taken the advice of his mother literally as he later told an audience, "My Mother would say 'You gotta be who you say you are.'"

"Just imagine, I mean it sincerely, I say this as a father of a man who won the Bronze Star, the conspicuous service medal, and lost his life in Iraq."

–President Joe Biden, October 12, 2022

Biden made this comment during a service to designate Camp Hale in Colorado as a new national monument. According to the White House press release, "This monument preserves and protects the mountains and valleys where the US Army's 10th Mountain Division prepared for their brave service that ultimately brought WWII to a close."

When Biden addresses the military community, he often refers to the service of his son, Beau. A cynic might say he borrows his son's valor in order to bolster his own credentials. Whatever the reason, he has frequently lied about his son's death over the years by saying Beau died in Iraq. Beau Biden was an officer in the Delaware Army National Guard who served as an attorney with the Judge Advocate General's Corps and was stationed in Iraq in 2009. In 2010, according to his father's office at the time, Beau suffered a mild stroke. In 2013, he was diagnosed with brain cancer, and he died in 2015 at the age of 46. While Beau Biden's passing at such an early age is tragic, it should be noted that his death occurred at the Walter Reed Medical Center in Bethesda, Maryland six years after his service in Iraq. This is why it is disturbing to hear Joe Biden repeatedly tell audiences that his son died in Iraq.

Joe has placed potential blame for his son's death on toxic burn pits used by the US military in Iraq. He has also acknowledged that he has no direct scientific evidence linking burn pits to Beau's cancer. With that in mind, one might think Joe would tread carefully around this topic whenever he speaks with the relatives of service members who have been killed in Iraq and Afghanistan. Not so. Following the tragic death of thirteen service members at Kabul Airport during the chaotic withdrawal of American forces from Afghanistan, Biden met the families of those killed when the remains of their loved ones arrived at Dover Air Force Base. Facing these distraught families, many of whom placed the blame for the tragedy at Kabul Airport at the feet of the president, Biden would have been well-advised to simply offer his condolences and listen.

Instead, Joe did what he frequently does when addressing victims of tragedy: he tried to relate to their loss by referencing his own hardships. In other words, he shifted the focus from them to him. According to Cheryl Rex, one of the Gold Star mothers in attendance, "When [Biden] approached me, his words to me were, 'My wife, Jill & I, know how you feel. We also lost our son and brought him home in a flag-draped coffin.' " Rex went on to say, "My heart started beating faster and I started shaking, knowing that their son died from cancer and they were able to be by his side. How could someone be so heartless to say he knew how I felt a little over twenty-four hours after learning of my son's death?"

As if this wasn't bad enough, Biden received widespread criticism for repeatedly looking at his watch during the dignified transfer ceremony at Dover Air Base. According to Darin Hoover, one of the Gold Star fathers in attendance, "They would release the salute and he looked down at his watch on every last one. All thirteen, he looked down at his watch." Hoover went on to say, "I found it to be the most disrespectful thing I've ever seen."

"Fighting this battle every day is a key reason why I ran for President of the United States."

–President Joe Biden, October 13, 2022

Biden was referring to inflation, which was 1.4% in January 2021, when Biden took office. By June 2022, it had reached 9.1%, a new forty-year high. Republican Senator Bill Hagerty observed, "If inflation remains zero, he will still hold the record of the century for the most inflation any President has created in America."

"Some airlines, if you want six more inches between you and the seat in front, you pay more money. But you don't know it until you purchase your ticket. Look, folks, these are junk fees. They're unfair and they hit marginalized Americans the hardest, especially low-income folks and people of color."

–President Joe Biden, October 26, 2022

This comment received widespread ridicule from conservatives over Biden's attempt to link expensive airline seats with racism. Whatever the issue, from the pandemic to airline seats, it seems Democrats are always quick to point out that low-income people and people of color are hit hardest. It's gotten to the point that Americans probably wouldn't question Democrats if they claimed that sharks and lightning target low-income and people of color disproportionately.

"And because of the action we've taken, gas prices are declining. We're down $1.25 since the peak this summer, and they've been falling for the last three weeks as well and adding up real savings for families. Today the most common price of gas in America is $3.39, down from over $5.00 when I took office."

–President Joe Biden, October 27, 2022

The average national gas price when Biden took office was $2.42.

"Across the country, some of the folks who tried to undermine our democracy are running for offices that will oversee the next election. And if they win, there's no telling what might happen."

–Former President Barack
Obama, October 28, 2022

This comment was made at a campaign rally in College Park, Georgia. That same day, the husband of the Speaker of the House, Nancy Pelosi, was attacked during a home invasion.

Media outlets quickly blamed the attack on Paul Pelosi on extreme Republicans and their rhetoric. For instance, in its report on the attack, the Associated Press claimed the assault "...carried chilling echoes of the January 6, 2021, insurrection at the Capitol, when rioters chanted menacingly for the Speaker as they rampaged through the halls trying to halt certification of Joe Biden's victory over Donald Trump... The nation's political rhetoric has become increasingly alarming, with ominous threats to lawmakers at an all-time high."

Ironically, the next day, October 29, 2022, while speaking at a campaign rally in Detroit, Michigan, former President Obama's message seemed to change dramatically. "If our rhetoric about each other gets that mean, when we don't just disagree with people, but we start demonizing, making wild, crazy allegations about them, that creates a dangerous climate...We got politicians who work to stir up division, to try to make us angry and afraid of one another for their own advantage."

"Do you know how much it costs to make that insulin drug for diabetes? It was invented by a man who did not patent it because

he wanted it available for everyone. I spoke to him, OK?"

–President Joe Biden, November 1, 2022

Biden was speaking at a Democrat party rally in Hallandale, Florida, where he emphasized the need to lower healthcare costs. According to *The New York Post*, "Dr. Frederick Banting and Professor John James Richard Macleod were awarded the Nobel Prize in medicine in 1923 for their 1921 discovery of insulin. Banting died in 1941 and Macleod in 1935. Biden was born in 1942."

This is hardly the first time Democrat politicians have made false claims about seemingly trivial issues. For example, voters may remember Hillary Clinton claiming during a visit to Nepal in 1995 that she was named after Sir Edmund Hillary, who, along with his Tibetan partner, became the first to reach the summit of Mount Everest. The problem with her claim was that Clinton was born in 1947, and Hillary didn't climb Mount Everest until 1953.

One might ask why Democrats lie so often about trivial things. Sometimes it appears they are pandering to a particular audience; sometimes they appear to be trying to make themselves more likeable; and other times, it seems as though they are trying to create a personal connection to an issue with which they have none.

Whatever the reason, it wouldn't be wrong to conclude that politicians who are willing to lie to the American people about little things are likely to lie to them about serious issues as well. Joe's political partner, Kamala Harris, said it well in her memoir when she noted, "You have to sweat the small stuff because sometimes it turns out that the small stuff is actually the big stuff."

Another relevant quote was made by Hillary Clinton in a speech she gave to Wellesley College graduates in 2017. "You are graduating at a time when there is a full-fledged assault on truth and reason...It matters because if our leaders lie about the problems we face, we'll never solve them. It matters because it undermines confidence in government as a whole, which in turn breeds more cynicism and anger...I believe with all my heart that the future of America, indeed the future of the world, depends on brave, thoughtful people like you insisting on truth and integrity, right now, every day."

"We believe we should leave no one behind because each one of us is a child of God, and every person, every person is sacred. If that's true, then every person's rights must be sacred as well. Individual dignity, individual worth, individual determination, that's America."

–President Joe Biden, November 2, 2022

Who could argue with the sentiment in this statement? Well, apparently Joe Biden himself can. It's ironic that Joe, a Roman Catholic, has such strong feelings about the individual dignity and individual worth of every child of God, yet he has become perhaps the strongest advocate for abortion in the history of the US presidency. Over the years, Biden's views on abortion have significantly changed. Biden rarely uses the word abortion, instead using phrases like women's health care and a woman's right to choose.

In 2006, he told an interviewer he did "...not view abortion as a choice and a right." However, in 2019 he announced, "If I believe health care is a right, as I do, I can no longer support an amendment that makes that right dependent on someone's ZIP code." Biden was referring to the Hyde Amendment, which took effect in 1980. It prohibits the use of federal funds to pay for an abortion.

Biden was a longtime supporter of the Hyde Amendment but suddenly changed his view when he sought the Democrat nomination for president. It's interesting that someone who has been in politics for fifty years and is a Roman Catholic suddenly has an epiphany at the age of seventy-six that abortion is a sacred right. This evolution in values wouldn't have anything to do with politics, would it?

People across the US clearly have strong views about abortion and are passionate about those views. While I strongly denounce abortion as a sin, I understand that others have a different perspective. What I don't have any respect for, however, is a politician who changes his view on such an important topic simply to make himself more electable. As Winston Churchill once said, "Some men change their party for the sake of their principles; others, their principles for the sake of their party."

If that isn't bad enough, on April 24, 2024, Biden outraged Catholics like me when he mocked our faith by jokingly making the Sign of the Cross as he listened to a pro-abortion speech in Florida. For God's sake, Joe, do you have any convictions?

"Nothing!"

–President Joe Biden, November 9, 2022

Biden made this assertion one day after the midterm elections when he was asked what he planned to do differently to improve the economy and the prevailing view among voters that the country was moving in the wrong direction.

"Because there are more important things going on."

–President Joe Biden, December 6, 2022

Biden was visiting Arizona to give a brief speech at a computer chip company when he was asked by a reporter, "Why go to a border state and not visit the border?"

"You know, I, my dad, when I got elected Vice President, he said, 'Joey, Uncle Frank fought in the Battle of the Bulge.' He was not feeling very well now, not because of the Battle of the Bulge. But he said, 'And he won the Purple Heart. And he never received it. He never, he never got it. Do you think you could help him get it? We'll surprise him.' So, we got him the Purple Heart. He had won it in the Battle of the Bulge. And I remember he came over to the house, and I came out, and he said, 'Present it to him, okay?' We had the family there."

–President Joe Biden, December 16, 2022

Biden shared this anecdote during a veterans summit in Delaware. Unfortunately, there are multiple flaws in Biden's story. Biden's father died in 2002, six years before Joe was elected Vice President, and if that isn't problematic enough, his Uncle Frank died in 1999. Yet somehow Joe remembered "He came over to the house" when Joe was Vice President to receive his medal. While it's sad to think that Joe's Uncle Frank may have never received the Purple Heart he earned, it's safe to say that Uncle Frank still fared better than Joe's Uncle Bosie.

According to a speech Joe Biden gave on April 17, 2024, Uncle Bosie "…got shot down in New Guinea, and they never found the body because there used to be, there were a lot of cannibals, for real, in that part of New Guinea."

According to US military records, Biden's Uncle Bosie died in a plane crash in the Pacific Ocean with no reference to cannibalism.

Claims like these should ring loud alarm bells to anyone who hears them. Either Biden is such a chronic liar that he won't hesitate to make up a story if he thinks it might ingratiate himself with his audience, or he is so decrepit that he no longer remembers the actual circumstances involved in his stories. Worse yet is the possibility that both of these explanations may be true; perhaps Biden has repeated so many false stories over the decades that he has come to believe they actually occurred.

> *"So, my hope this Christmas season is that we take a few moments of quiet reflection, find that stillness in the heart of Christmas, it's at the heart of Christmas, and look, really look at each other, not as Democrats or Republicans, not as members of team red or team blue, but as who we really are, fellow Americans, fellow human beings worthy of being treated with dignity and respect. I sincerely hope this holiday season will drain the poison that has infected our politics and set us against one another. I hope this Christmas season marks a fresh start for our nation."*

> —President Joe Biden, December 22, 2022

This statement was thoughtful, hopeful, and appropriate. Unfortunately, it was also extremely hypocritical. While Biden's tone in this statement sounds genuine and sincere, it is worth remembering that in the preceding months, Biden repeatedly delivered public comments that were arguably some of the most divisive words ever spoken by a US President.

On September 1, 2022, in Philadelphia, President Biden stated, "Donald Trump and the MAGA Republicans represent an extremism that threatens the very foundations of our republic…They promote authoritarian leaders and they fan the flames of political violence that are a threat to our personal rights, to the pursuit of justice, to the rule of law, to the very soul of this country."

On August 25, 2022, in Rockville, Maryland, Biden said, "Trump and the extreme MAGA Republicans have made their choice to go backwards, full of anger, violence, hate, and division."

On January 11, 2022, in Atlanta, President Biden shouted, "Do you want to be on the side of Dr. King or George Wallace? Do you want to be on the side of John Lewis or Bull Connor? Do you want to be on the side of Abraham Lincoln or Jefferson Davis?"

As I'm not a medical professional, I will not speculate as to whether Joe Biden may suffer from some type of split personality. However, at the very least he seems to think he can have things both ways. At one moment he seems perfectly comfortable viciously attacking his political opponents, and then on another occasion Americans find themselves listening to a sermon on peace and unity by Reverend Joe. At the very least, one could reasonably conclude that Joe Biden suffers from an amazing lack of self-awareness.

> *"There can no longer be any question, none: in today's inter-connected world, we cannot wall ourselves off from shared problems."*
>
> –President Joe Biden, January 10, 2023

Meanwhile, that very week at Biden's vacation home in Rehoboth Beach, Delaware construction began on a security wall at a cost of $490,324 to American taxpayers. Really, Joe?

"They said, that Biden really is stupid. Where's Doug?"

–President Joe Biden, January 26, 2023

Biden said this while delivering a speech about the economy to Local Steamfitters Union 602. Biden began his address by sharing a self-deprecating story about a time when he asked his audience to take a seat during his 2020 presidential campaign only to realize that "There wasn't a single chair in the place. They said, that Biden really is stupid," he added.

Then, incredibly and without skipping a beat, he asked "Where's Doug? Congressman?" as he scanned the crowd before him. "Oh, there you are. Doug, thanks for the passport into town." He went on to reference Doug several more times. Then, after speaking about Congressional Republicans and the economy for a few minutes he suddenly appeared to realize that his friend "Doug" was actually Congressman Don Beyer.

"I've been saying that during this last campaign, in the off-year campaign, Doug knows this—Don—look, here's the deal, they want to cut your Social Security and Medicare," he continued. Later in the same speech, Biden made another mistake as he criticized former President Trump's impact on the economy, saying, "The deficit went up four years in a row, accounting for 40% of the entire 200 years of debt. You hear me?"

He then corrected himself for having significantly overstated the percentage of national debt accrued during the Trump years. However, he also made another peculiar remark while referring to Trump when he said, "No president added more to the debt in four years than my president." One can only assume he meant to say, "my predecessor."

Further demonstrating his remarkable inability to remember details, Biden also said during the same speech that his administration had "…funded 700,000 major construction projects, 700,000 all across America." Later in the speech, while referring to federal individual income taxes, he claimed that billionaires "…pay virtually only 3% of their income now, 3% they pay." The White House revised the official transcript of Biden's speech to note that the actual number of construction projects Biden referenced was 7,000, and the 3% federal individual income tax figure he referenced for billionaires was actually 8%.

It's an interesting coincidence that every time Biden makes a mistake when citing data, the error always works in his favor. Whatever the reason may be for Biden's inability to be clear and accurate when he speaks extemporaneously, it's probably safe to assume that his staff in the White House Communications Department probably cringe every time he's handed a microphone because they know it will fall to them to clean up the mess that will inevitably follow.

A few days before Biden delivered this speech, the White House advised that the 80-year-old president would be announcing his decision whether he would be seeking a second term as president in the coming weeks. Biden has long been associated with embarrassing gaffs but as he began the third year of his presidency, multiple misstatements in his public addresses led to increased speculation about his mental fortitude. One thing his advisors might suggest to him moving forward is that if you plan to start your speech by making fun of the fact that many Americans think you're stupid, try extra hard not to strew the rest of the speech with embarrassing mistakes and false claims.

"Only 3.5 million people even had their first vaccination because the other guy and the other team didn't think it mattered a whole lot."

–President Joe Biden, January 26, 2023

Biden said this during a speech about the economy in Springfield, Virginia. He was referencing the COVID-19 pandemic and President Trump's response to it prior to Biden's inauguration.

What a reckless and shameful claim! Not only does Biden cite a completely inaccurate number here but he has the audacity to suggest that public access to the vaccines was limited because former President Trump and "the other team didn't think it mattered." Making things even worse was the casual and matter-of-fact way Biden delivered this line.

An accusation like this is highly inflammatory but Biden appeared to make the comment with little forethought. In doing so, one gets the impression that Biden believes his view of Donald Trump as some type of heartless monster is naturally shared by all Americans. It should be noted that during Donald Trump's presidency, $18 billion was allocated for Operation Warp Speed, a public-private partnership launched in May 2020 to develop, manufacture, and distribute COVID-19 vaccines.

Under normal circumstances, development of new vaccines can take ten to fifteen years. With the help of Operation Warp Speed, three COVID-19 vaccines were developed by pharmaceutical companies in roughly one year. With regard to Biden's claim that only 3.5 million people had their first vaccination when he took office, according to data from the Centers for Disease Control and Prevention the actual number was approximately 19 million.

Sadly, this wasn't the first time the Biden Administration attempted to discredit the Trump administration. On May 12, 2022, the White House tweeted, "When President Biden took office, millions were unemployed and there was no vaccine available."

"My word as a Biden: I've never been more optimistic about America's future than I am today."

–President Joe Biden, January 29, 2023, in a tweet

Following this tweet, Biden received widespread criticism for appearing to be out of touch with the American people. On the same day as Biden's tweet, NBC News released disturbing poll results: only 36% of Americans approved of Biden's handling of the economy.

The NBC news poll also reported that "…his lowest marks come on being honest and trustworthy (34%), having the ability to handle a crisis (32%), being competent and effective as president (31%), having the necessary mental and physical health to be president (28%) and uniting the country (23%)."

Perhaps most damaging of all, NBC News went on, "71% of Americans say the nation is on the wrong track. We are in the longest sustained period of a wrong-track number that high in the history of our poll. It's nearly been two and a half years of this sustained pessimism."

One day after Biden's tweet, Gallup reported that Americans identified government and poor leadership as the most important problem facing the country today. Interestingly, this was the top issue for Republicans/Republican-leaning Independents, as well as Democrats/Democrat-leaning Independents.

Only four days before Biden's tweet, Gallup had reported more bad news for President Biden, noting that he averaged a dismal 41% approval rating during his second year in office, one of the lowest second-year presidential approval averages Gallup had encountered.

In spite of clear indications like these from the American people that his presidency was failing them, Biden appeared to keep his head blissfully buried in the sand. Instead of acknowledging the country's obvious quandary, Biden expressed his absolute optimism for America's future. It's intriguing to note that Biden's claim of optimism also appears to be a familiar theme for him.

On May 10, 2009, Vice President Biden delivered a commencement address at Syracuse University where he said, "I am more optimistic today than I have ever been in my life." More than eleven years later, during his own campaign for the presidency, Biden participated in an ABC News town hall event on October 15, 2020, and said once again, "I've never been more optimistic of the prospects for this country than I am today. And I really mean that."

As he settled into his role as president, Biden appeared to express the sentiment with increasing frequency. At the White House Correspondent's Dinner on April 30, 2022, Biden told the audience, "I give you my word as a Biden, I've never been more optimistic about America than I am today. I really mean it."

One month later, in his commencement address at the University of Delaware on May 28, 2022, Biden again said, "I'm optimistic. I've never been more optimistic in my entire life…and I mean this, my word as a Biden. I mean it."

As the 2022 midterm elections approached, Biden told Democrat volunteers at the Service Employees International Union (SEIU) union hall in Portland, Oregon on October 15, 2022, "…the truth of the matter is I've never been more optimistic about America's prospects."

You can judge for yourself if Biden is truly one of those people who, no matter how bad things get, still wakes up every day and says to himself, I'm more optimistic today than I was yesterday or if his repeated claims of optimism—punctuated by his insistence that he's really telling the truth this time by adding phrases like "my word as a Biden" or "I really mean it,"—are just a line that he was told many years ago polls well with the American people…a line, perhaps, that he tends to fall back on whenever he's confronted with bad news.

In a dramatic break from his perpetual optimism, Biden told the Democrat Senatorial Campaign Committee on October 6, 2022, that the threat of nuclear Armageddon was at its highest point in 60 years.

Then on March 13, 2023, he told *The Daily Show*, "If we don't keep the temperatures from going above 1.5 degrees Celsius raised, you know we're in real trouble. That whole generation is damned. I mean, that's not hyperbole."

Oh well, so much for optimism.

"More than half of the women on the, in my administration are women."

–President Joe Biden, February 2, 2023

Although this comment was a simple gaffe by the president, one could also understand how easy it is to be confused about gender; for example, the application for San Francisco's Transgender Guaranteed Income Program (GIFT) features no fewer than 130 gender and sexuality and pronoun options, encouraging applicants to check all that apply. In case Biden's comment above didn't confuse you enough, on August 8, 2019, he also said, "Poor kids are just as bright and just talented as White kids," and on November 19, 2023, he said, "I like kids better than people."

"Do I take any blame for inflation? No…because it was already there when I got here, man. Remember what the economy was like when I got here? Jobs were hemorrhaging, inflation was

rising, we weren't manufacturing a damn thing here. We were in real economic difficulty. That's why I don't."

–President Joe Biden, February 3, 2023

Biden was responding to a reporter's question during a press conference. Once again, his blatantly false claims and absolute refusal to accept any responsibility for the nation's economic crisis during his watch left many Americans stunned.

The rate of inflation was 1.4% when Biden was sworn in as president. However, immediately after taking office, Biden and the Democrat-controlled Congress embarked on a massive spending spree, ignoring repeated warnings by economists that doing so would increase inflation. Not surprisingly, inflation rose dramatically, reaching a peak of 9.1% in June 2022, which was the highest inflation rate since 1981.

In an op-ed for Fox News, on November 7, 2022, Republican Leader of the House Committee on Budget Jason Smith expressed his dismay, writing, "President Biden has set records for the biggest increase in spending and debt in a president's first 20 months in office." Even when Biden made this statement to reporters in February 2023, inflation remained high at 6.5%. In addition, contrary to Biden's assertion that "jobs were hemorrhaging" when he took office, the economy actually added 273,000 jobs in February 2020, and unemployment at the time was 3.5%, nearly equal to the unemployment rate of 3.4% at the time of Biden's comment.

"Some Republicans want Medicare and Social Security to sunset."

–President Joe Biden, February 7, 2023

Biden made this false claim during his State of the Union Address. Without identifying him by name, Biden was clearly referring to a proposal by Senator Rick Scott. However, Biden was intentionally twisting the meaning of Scott's proposal to imply Republicans wanted to end Social Security and Medicare.

According to Scott, "In my plan, I suggested the following: All federal legislation sunsets in five years. If a law is worth keeping, Congress can pass it again…This is clearly and obviously an idea aimed at dealing with all the crazy new laws our Congress has been passing of late." Scott also noted that his plan fully anticipates that Congress would quickly renew popular programs such as Medicare, Social Security, and defense. He added, "This is the fake 'gotcha' BS that people hate about Washington. I've never advocated cutting Social Security or Medicare and never would."

What makes Biden's false claim even worse is that when he was a senator, Biden proposed a nearly identical bill. On July 9, 1975, Biden sponsored S.2067, "A bill to limit the period of authorization of new budget authority and to require comprehensive review and study of existing programs for which continued budget authority is proposed to be authorized by committees of the Congress."

Biden's proposal prohibited the authorization of budget authority for a period of more than four years for laws enacted after the effective date of the Act and required Congressional committees to conduct a comprehensive review and study of existing programs in considering legislation extending budget authority for such programs.

Biden's 1975 bill was not enacted, and he tried and failed again to pass the bill in 1995. In response to Biden's remark at the State of the Union, Republicans in attendance audibly voiced their objections to his claim. In turn, Biden seemed to recognize that Republicans were not going to sit idly by and listen to him repeat a false and malicious claim like this again. Biden then said, "So folks, as we all apparently agree Social Security and Medicare is off the books now…"

Observers of this exchange could be forgiven if they doubted whether this would be the last time Biden and the Democrats used this traditional attack against Republicans, claiming that they wanted to push Grandma over the cliff and take Social Security away from seniors.

Any hope that Biden would refrain from such claims was short-lived. The very next day, Biden addressed an audience in Deforest, Wisconsin, claiming, "We had a spirited debate last night with my Republican friends…They seemed shocked when I raised the plans of some of their members and their caucus to cut Social Security. A lot of Republicans, their dream is to cut Social Security and Medicare…It's your dream, but I'm with my veto pen to make it a nightmare."

Once again, Biden refused to let the truth get in the way of his political argument. Instead of acknowledging the fact that Republicans publicly rejected the notion that they supported cutting Social Security and Medicare, he simply doubled down and pushed forward with this false claim several times in the weeks and months that followed.

"As I stand here tonight, we have created a record twelve million new jobs, more jobs created in two years than any president had created in four years."

–President Joe Biden, February 7, 2023

It's important to recognize that Biden claims to have "created" twelve million new jobs in the comment above, which was made during his State of the Union address. According to the Bureau of Labor Statistics, the economy under Biden had added only 2.7 million jobs at that point. The remaining nine million jobs he references were ones that had been eliminated during the pandemic and were now reinstated. Claiming to have *created* so many *new* jobs is a pretty misleading statement but one that is typical of Joe Biden.

"It's not a major breach."

–President Joe Biden, February 9, 2023

During an interview with Telemundo, Biden was asked about a Chinese spy balloon that entered US airspace over Alaska on January 28, 2023, and was finally shot down by a US Air Force fighter jet off the coast of South Carolina on February 4, 2023.

Biden's nonchalant attitude toward the Chinese spy balloon was criticized by both Democrat and Republican members of Congress. Many asserted that Biden should have ordered the US military to shoot the balloon down as soon as it entered US airspace.

On the same day as Biden's interview with Telemundo, Democrat Senator Jon Tester, Chairman of the Senate Appropriations Subcommittee, angrily told Defense Department officials during a hearing about the Chinese spy balloon, "I don't want a damn balloon going over the United States when we could've taken it down over the Aleutian Islands."

According to the United States Air Force website, the Third Wing is the host unit for Elmendorf Air Force Base, Alaska. It is the largest and principal organization in the Eleventh Air Force. The Third Wing provides air superiority and defense for Alaska with F-15C aircraft. This forward operating base allows the F-15s a quicker response time on identifying aircraft approaching North American airspace. At Elmendorf, the aircraft stand alert twenty-four hours a day, 365 days a year. The fighter units are trained to actively engage and destroy enemy air forces in either an offensive or defensive capacity. More than 6,000 military personnel from all branches of the US and Canadian armed forces are assigned to Elmendorf. Elmendorf's annual payroll, paid to military and civilian employees, is more than $316 million.

Elmendorf Air Force Base's very existence is to stop incursions into US airspace by enemy air forces. With that in mind, many Americans were left dumbfounded as to why President Biden and the Department of Defense failed to stop the Chinese spy balloon before it began its multi-day journey across the continental United States. After all, what is the point of maintaining a base like Elmendorf if we fail to use its assets when they are needed?

The New York Times reported on February 9, 2023, "The Chinese spy balloon was equipped with an antenna meant to pinpoint the locations of communications devices and was capable of intercepting calls made on those devices, according to declassified intelligence released by the State Department."

Also, on February 9, 2023 (the same day as Biden's Telemundo interview), the US House of Representatives, in a rare example of bipartisanship, voted unanimously to condemn the Chinese Communist Party for flying the spy balloon over the United States, declaring the act a "brazen violation of United States sovereignty."

Shortly after the downing of the Chinese spy balloon, additional flying objects were shot down by the US Air Force. One was off the coast of Alaska on February 10, 2023. Another object was shot down over the Yukon Territory in Canada on February 11, 2023. Yet another object was then shot down over Lake Huron on February 12, 2023.

During this period, there was widespread concern across America regarding the sudden frequency of these encounters and the potential threat that the objects might pose. On February 16, 2023, Biden referred to the first Chinese spy balloon incursion, saying, "We waited until it was safely over water…and then we shot it down, sending a clear message, clear message, the violation of our sovereignty is unacceptable."

Given that the balloon spent a week traversing Canada and the continental United States before Biden had it shot down, and the fact that additional flying objects soon followed, many observers questioned how clear his message to the Chinese government really was.

"I can't recall that I, I don't think I've talked to the mayor. I talked to everyone else there, multiple times. Talked to both the senators, both governors. And I've talked to everyone there to talk to."

–President Joe Biden, February 24, 2023

Biden was responding to a question by ABC News anchor David Muir, who asked the president if he had talked with the mayor of East Palestine, Ohio. On February 3, 2023, a train owned by Norfolk Southern railroad derailed in East Palestine. Soon after, fire officials decided to burn five tanker cars filled with toxic vinyl chloride to avoid a major explosion. Residents then started becoming ill, and concerns were raised about contaminated soil, water, and air. Approximately half of the town's 5,000 residents evacuated the area, and many were still displaced months later as the EPA continued to monitor contaminants in the area. The train accident's impact on the community remained a top news story for weeks, but President Biden never took the time to visit the area.

Interestingly, on February 20, 2023, Biden made a surprise visit to Ukraine, causing some to question why the president would demonstrate his concern for the residents of another country before doing so for his own constituents. Referring to Biden's visit to Ukraine, East Palestine Mayor Trent Conway said, "That was the biggest slap in the face. That tells you right now he doesn't care about us."

Critics of the president speculated that his decision not to visit East Palestine was based on reporting that described the rural area as "Trump Country." They were quick to point out that in his victory speech, Biden pledged "to be a president…who doesn't see red states and blue states, only sees the United States."

On September 2, 2023, Biden was asked again why he had still not visited East Palestine, Ohio, almost seven months after the town was devastated. His answer was astonishing. He said, "Well, I haven't had the occasion to go to East Palestine. There's a lot going on here and I just haven't been able to break." Biden spent the majority of August on vacation, including an extended stay at Lake Tahoe, flying over Ohio to get there.

According to *The New York Post*, at the time of this comment, "Biden has spent all or part of 382 of his presidency's 957 days—or 40%—on personal overnight trips away from the White House." Many observers have compared the failures of the Biden administration with those of his predecessor, Jimmy Carter. While both men have been widely criticized as incompetent leaders, at least Jimmy Carter is considered by most to have been a hard worker. During his single term in office, he only spent seventy-nine days, or 5% of his time, on vacation.

Biden finally visited East Palestine on February 16, 2024, more than a year after the train derailment. He was greeted by residents holding signs that read, "Too little, too late."

"I think it goes well beyond the economy…I think things are a little out of whack and I don't blame people for being down. You know, when you had the year, two years of the pandemic, kids out of school, the mental health problems in the country are

seriously increased, especially among young people...Inflation is still higher than it should be, and, you know, everything from gasoline prices to a war going on in Ukraine. I mean, so I can't think of a time when there's been greater uncertainty."

–President Joe Biden, February 24, 2023

Biden was responding to a question from ABC News anchor David Muir, who asked, "Our latest ABC News poll shows four in ten Americans say they're worse off than when you were elected. Only 16% said they were better off. So why is that?"

According to RealClearPolitics, at the time of this interview, only 27% of voters thought the country was on the right track while 64% said the country was on the wrong track.

"My name is Joe Biden. I'm Dr. Jill Biden's husband, and I eat Jeni's ice cream, chocolate chip. I came down because I heard there was chocolate chip ice cream. By the way, I have a whole refrigerator full upstairs. You think I'm kidding. I'm not."

–President Joe Biden, March 27, 2023

This is how President Biden opened his address at the White House when hours earlier there had been a tragic school shooting at a Nashville Christian Elementary School where three nine-year-olds and three adults were killed. As television networks that had been airing continuous coverage of the tragedy cut to the president's live remarks, observers were expecting a somber president to begin his address by expressing his condolences to the victims' families. Instead, Biden began his address as if he were at an open mic night at a comedy club. After this awkward beginning, Biden eventually referenced the tragedy and concluded that section of his remarks by saying, "Sorry to start off that way, but I couldn't begin without acknowledging what happened." This left many observers confused as to why he didn't actually begin his address by referencing what happened. It's hard to understand how someone who has spent more than fifty years in the public spotlight could be so tone-deaf and have such poor political instincts.

"There's no such thing as someone else's child."

–President Joe Biden, April 24, 2023

In this statement, Biden went on to say that "Our nation's children are all our children," which sounds supportive and positive, painting a picture of a society where we all look out for the well-being of kids. However, the same quote can also suggest that no child belongs solely to their parents, implying instead that the government should be the final arbiter of what's best for children everywhere.

"And by the way, the one thing I thought when I got to be President, I'd get to give orders. But I take more orders than I ever did."

–President Joe Biden, April 27, 2023

Biden made this comment in jest. However, given many similar statements he made on prior occasions, it did raise some eyebrows. For instance, he has repeatedly joked, "I'm going to get in trouble with my staff" for taking reporter's questions. It has also been regularly observed that Biden uses a cue card advising him which reporters to call on during press conferences, even featuring a photo of them. This has led to widespread speculation as to who is really in control behind the scenes at the White House.

"I have six grandchildren, and I'm crazy about them. And I speak to them every single day, not a joke…and guess what? They're crazy about me because I pay so much attention to them."

–President Joe Biden, April 27, 2023

I thought a lot about whether this entry should be included in this book. On one hand, Hunter Biden's many faults have been widely reported, and one cannot blame Joe Biden for standing by his son. I believe a father's love for his children should be unconditional and absolute. However, on the other hand, Joe Biden has made several statements professing his belief in family and the importance of values and morals. It is for this reason that I felt compelled to shine a small light on his hypocrisy.

In a June 16, 2023, Father's Day Proclamation, Joe Biden wrote, "Fathers are critical to raising the next generation and to teaching their daughters and sons about the values that matter most…Along the way, dads help their children navigate life's most difficult challenges, nurture their confidence and character, and give them the tools to develop a moral compass.…My dad, Joseph Robinette Biden Sr., taught me values early in life…he taught me that, above all, family is the beginning, middle, and end, a lesson I have passed down to my children and grandchildren."

Biden's sentiments are beautifully written but are tarnished when one considers the reality of life in the Biden family. Not long after Joe's son, Hunter, ended an affair with the widow of his brother Beau, he had another brief affair with a former stripper named Lunden Alexis Roberts that resulted in the birth of a daughter in August 2018. Well into her pregnancy, Roberts tried to contact Hunter multiple times, but he would screen her calls and ignore her messages. Roberts finally sent

Hunter a text message on October 16, 2018, which read, "In hopes that you even read this- Baby was born Aug 28. Beautiful & Healthy. If you ever become curious and want to know more I can send pictures, details, or whatever you may request. I know that's a long shot and you'd much rather avoid the whole situation, but just wanted you to know the door is always open for you in the baby's life."

According to Hunter, he has "no recollection" of meeting Roberts, and noted in his memoir that the encounter occurred at a time when "I hit the (crack) pipe like there was no tomorrow, strolling around in my underwear and generally acting insane." After initially learning about Roberts' pregnancy, Hunter hired her at his company and provided her with health insurance. However, soon after she gave birth, he ended both her employment and health insurance.

Five months later, in May 2019, Roberts filed a paternity suit and sought child support in court. Roberts' attorney told the court at the time that Hunter "has had no involvement in the child's life since the child's birth" and "could not identify the child out of a photo lineup." Following a DNA test, Hunter was identified as the biological father in January 2020 and agreed to pay $20,000 per month in child support in March 2020.

In September 2022, Hunter petitioned the court to reduce his monthly payments. Roberts filed a counterclaim requesting her daughter's last name be changed to Biden. On June 29, 2023, a new settlement was reached. The new amount of monthly child support to be paid by Hunter is unknown, but as part of the agreement, his daughter will receive an undisclosed number of Hunter's paintings. During the court proceedings, Hunter's legal team demanded to know why changing his daughter's last name to Biden would be in her best interest. Roberts' attorneys responded by writing, "The Biden name is now synonymous with being well-educated, successful, financially acute, and politically powerful." Nevertheless, as part of the settlement, Roberts withdrew her request to change her daughter's last name.

According to a July 1, 2023, report in *The New York Times*, White House aides have been told that the President and First Lady Jill Biden have six grandchildren, not seven. Even though the existence of Hunter's daughter was one of the worst-kept secrets in Washington, it still hadn't led the first family to publicly acknowledge her existence.

Again, I hesitated to include this reference because this book is primarily focused on politics. However, the character of our politicians matters, and it is inexplicable to me how Joe Biden, who was correctly taught that "above all, family is the beginning, middle, and end," would continue to remain estranged from one of his grandchildren.

Regardless of the sad circumstances associated with her birth, there is no legitimate excuse for a father or a grandfather to pretend their offspring doesn't exist. Money and some paintings will never replace the love of a father. Finally, after receiving considerable criticism in the media, on July 31, 2023, Joe Biden acknowledged, "I have seven grandkids…I just think being there is important and makes such a difference. I think knowing that someone's going to be there for you, just to listen, just to hold you, just to hug you…Half of it is just showing up." Again, this is a beautiful sentiment, but there is still no evidence that Joe has ever spoken with or met his seventh grandchild. If "half of it is just showing up," Joe and Hunter should both receive failing grades.

"God save the Queen, man."

–President Joe Biden, June 16, 2023

It was just plain odd when Biden concluded a speech on gun control to a Connecticut audience with this remark. Apparently, in Biden's mind, this is some sort of light-hearted punch line. To many, however, it was a bizarre thing to say. Not only does it leave his audience wondering what he meant by the line, but it's particularly strange coming from a US President when we remember that the United States of America began with a Declaration of Independence from British rule. Biden's remark is even more perplexing when one remembers that the Queen of England had died nine months earlier and Biden attended her funeral.

"The Constitution says, 'We hold these truths to be self-evident that all men and women are created equal, endowed by their creator.' It's a uniqueness of America. We never fully lived up to it, we never walked away from it. And this court seems to say that no, that's not always the case."

–President Joe Biden, June 29, 2023

Biden made this remark during an interview on MSNBC in response to the US Supreme Court's six-to-three decision earlier that day to outlaw affirmative action programs at Harvard University and the University of North Carolina. In his majority opinion, Chief Justice John Roberts wrote, "Eliminating racial discrimination means eliminating all of it. Accordingly, the Court has held that the Equal Protections Clause applies without regard to any differences of race, of color, or of nationality. It is universal in its application."

Biden, on the other hand, seems to believe that the term equal somehow translates to preferential treatment for certain races. By the way, someone should probably remind the President of the United States that the line he quoted in this interview was from the Declaration of Independence, not the US Constitution. One may wonder if Biden even knows the difference.

"I think the court misinterpreted the Constitution."

–President Joe Biden, June 30, 2023

Biden was referring to a six-to-three decision by the US Supreme Court which invalidated the president's plan to have the Secretary of Education cancel approximately $400 billion in student loan debt.

In his majority opinion, Chief Justice John Roberts explained that "The basic and consequential tradeoffs inherent in a mass debt cancellation are ones that Congress would likely have intended for itself."

Clearly, Biden disagreed with the Court's ruling, but perhaps he should have listened to his close friend and colleague, former Speaker of the House Nancy Pelosi, who said on July 28, 2021, "People think that the President of the United States has the power for debt forgiveness. He does not. He can postpone. He can delay. But he does not have that power. That has to be an act of Congress."

Nevertheless, Biden remained steadfast in his determination to cancel student loan debt, saying, "Today's decision has closed one path, now we're going to pursue another."

On February 21, 2024, Biden announced that he was canceling $1.2 billion in student loan debt. When asked if he was worried that this new plan would also be overturned by the Supreme Court, Biden said, "I don't have a worry at all." The president's critics were quick to point out that Biden's preoccupation with canceling student loan debt was simply a shameful attempt to buy votes.

"I've already done that…We've passed a $368 billion climate-control facility."

–President Joe Biden, August 9, 2023

Biden's comment came in response to a reporter who asked, "Are you prepared to declare a national emergency with respect to climate change?"

There are two significant flaws in Biden's response. Not only has he not declared a national emergency with respect to climate change, but there is also no such thing as a $368 billion climate-control facility.

When faced with a difficult question, Biden's impulse always seems to be to announce that he has already addressed the issue even when it is a complete lie. He has employed this tactic on many occasions, and it seems to effectively get him through the pressure of the moment. It is then left to his communications team to clean things up afterward.

"I wish I hadn't called it that."

–President Joe Biden, August 13, 2023

Biden was referring to the Inflation Reduction Act, which passed Congress on August 16, 2022, without a single Republican vote. Despite its moniker, the act was primarily focused on Green New Deal initiatives, including energy and climate change.

According to *The Wall Street Journal*, the global investment bank Goldman Sachs projects that the many green subsidies included in the Inflation Reduction Act will total approximately $1.2 trillion, more than three times what the law's supporters claimed.

As inflation persisted into 2023, Biden and his subordinates frequently mentioned that it would take time to see the effects of the act.

However, by August 2023, Biden seemed to finally acquiesce when he made the comment above. It's ironic that although it is well understood that excessive government spending causes inflation to rise, the Biden administration and congressional Democrats decided to respond to this crisis with yet another massive spending bill.

"I don't want to compare difficulties, but we have a little sense, Jill and I, of what it was like to lose a home. Years ago, now fifteen years...lightning struck at home on a little lake outside of our home. Not a lake, a big pond. It hit the wire and came up underneath our home, into the air condition ducts. To make a long story short, I almost lost my wife, my '67 Corvette, and my cat."

–President Joe Biden, August 21, 2023

Biden shared this story with a crowd of victims of Maui's devastating wildfire. The fire, which consumed much of western Maui, took the lives of at least 115 individuals and was the deadliest wildfire in the United States in more than a century. Biden received much criticism for his story and its failure to convey a true sense of empathy.

Records show that the incident at the Biden residence was a small fire that was contained to the kitchen and was quickly placed under control by the fire department. Biden's brief visit to Maui received further criticism when he appeared to fall asleep during a memorial service for Maui wildfire victims. Biden's entire visit to Maui lasted less than six hours before he made his way back to Lake Tahoe to continue his extended vacation.

"America isn't failing. America is winning."

–President Joe Biden, August 29, 2023

Following the death of George Floyd, Democrats promoted soft-on-crime policies and anti-police rhetoric in cities across America. In addition to movements already underway to replace district attorneys with George-Soros-backed criminal advocates, the Black Lives Matter Movement popularized an anti-law enforcement platform.

The result has been a marked increase in crime, including violent crimes for sport. When combined with no cash bail policies, efforts to reduce incarceration rates, and refusals to prosecute a wide range of misdemeanors (including theft), our cities are becoming unlivable.

One can hardly be surprised to learn that when police officers arrest offenders only to find them released back on the streets before the ink is dry on their arrest sheet, morale is at rock bottom. Many of these officers are seeking early retirement or transfers to suburban areas and recruitment is down, leading to widespread shortages in police departments.

Stores are closing as a result of losses due to theft, and city residents are frequently finding themselves living in food deserts without access to essential institutions like pharmacies. Many city residents are also dealing with open-air drug markets and rampant homelessness, which is significantly reducing the quality of life in their communities.

A surge in woke ideology has also impacted public schools. While long known to be havens for liberal philosophy, public schools have recently embraced radical programs like the 1619 Project and Critical Race Theory. Meanwhile, there is an ever-tightening stranglehold by politically motivated teachers' unions that block much-needed reforms like school choice and show shockingly little concern for the students they supposedly serve. This has led droves of qualified teachers, like their counterparts in law enforcement, to leave the profession in disgust. National test scores are at record lows, and in one disturbing example, the Baltimore City Public Schools recently reported that in twenty-three of its schools, zero students demonstrated proficiency in math.

Our failure to properly educate our youth is only creating a new generation of potential criminals who will fuel our downward spiral for years to come. The collective result has been and will continue to be a rapid deterioration in the American standard of living. Joe Biden claims that America is winning, but there is ample evidence showing that America is failing in many areas. The question is, how long are we going to allow this to continue?

"When the last guy was here, he looked at the world from Park Avenue. Well, I look at it from Scranton, Pennsylvania. I look at it from Claymont, Delaware."

–President Joe Biden, September 4, 2023

Biden referred to his predecessor, Donald Trump, in a speech to Sheet Metal Workers' Union Local 19 in Philadelphia on Labor Day. Over the years, Joe Biden has referred to himself as "lunch-bucket Joe" and "middle-class Joe."

A CBS News article on November 6, 2009, listed his estimated net worth at just $27,012. Don't be too concerned, however. At the start of his 2020 presidential campaign, Joe Biden released his financial disclosures, and based on that information, *Forbes* estimated that he had reached a net worth of $9 million. Pretty interesting considering his government salary had not exceeded $230,000/year during the intervening years.

"You deserve what you've earned, and you've earned a hell of a lot more than you're getting paid now."

–President Joe Biden, September 26, 2023

Joe Biden made this comment at a United Auto Workers (UAW) picket line in Belleville, Michigan. On September 15, 2023, the UAW went on strike against the Big Three US car manufacturers (Ford, General Motors, and Stellantis, owner of Chrysler, Dodge et al.).

Unlike many past presidents, who have used their position and influence to serve as an arbiter in previous strikes, Biden chose to become the first US president to ever join a picket line of striking workers. According to NBC News, the UAW demanded a 40% raise (amounting to 46% compounded) over four years and a 32-hour work week.

According to CBS News, soon after the UAW strike began, Stellantis offered a 21% raise over four years, including an immediate 10% increase, but the union rejected the offer. One can only wonder how many non-union workers would jump at the chance to receive a non-merit-based raise of 5.25% each year. Union members, however, see this as mere peanuts. Instead, they are insisting on a 10% non-merit-based raise per year.

In his Inaugural Address, Biden said, "I pledge this to you: I will be a President for all Americans." Apparently, however, this pledge does not apply when a dispute between corporations and union workers is involved. According to White House Press Secretary Karine Jean-Pierre, "He is going to stand in solidarity at the picket line with the workers."

After concluding his speech, Biden was asked, "Mr. President, should the UAW get a 40% increase?" He responded, "Yes!"

Biden's presence at the picket line was made even more unnerving when he introduced UAW President Shawn Fain, who, after referencing the role automakers played in World War II, went on to tell a cheering crowd, "Today, the enemy isn't some foreign country miles away. It's right here in our own—in our own area. It's corporate greed."

"Seizing power, concentrating power, attempting to abuse power, purging and packing key institutions, spewing conspiracy theories, spreading lies for profit and power to divide Americans in every way, inciting violence against those who risk their lives to keep Americans safe, weaponizing against the very soul of who we are as Americans."

–President Joe Biden, September 28, 2023

During a speech in Tempe, Arizona, Biden referenced the MAGA threat with this comment—just as the US House of Representatives Oversight and Accountability Committee commenced a hearing entitled "The Basis for an Impeachment Inquiry of President Joseph R. Biden, Jr." In a classic strategy routinely used by Democrats, Biden accused his adversaries of what he and his party are doing.

"This MAGA threat is a threat to the brick and mortar of our democratic institutions, but it's also a threat to the character of our nation."

–President Joe Biden, September 28, 2023

It's interesting that Biden refers to the character of our nation in the above comment. A nation is defined as a large group of people bound together by a shared history, culture, language, religion, and/or homeland. The United States is a particularly unique example of what a nation is because it is essentially a collection of people from around the world, each of whom previously had their own shared history, culture, language, religion, and homeland. Here we have embarked on a daring experiment in world history by blending together multiple cultures into one distinctly American culture.

Sadly, however, not all Americans appreciate America for what it is. Instead, they tend to see it as a problem to be fixed. On May 14, 2008, soon-to-be First Lady Michelle Obama said, "We are going to have to change our conversation; we're going to have to change our traditions, our history; we're going to have to move into a different place as a nation."

America is unlike any other nation in the world, and for nearly 250 years it has succeeded. Unfortunately, today Democrats emphasize what is referred to as identity politics. Not only has this perspective caused Americans to focus on traits that separate us by emphasizing things like race, ethnicity, and sex, but it is also critical of America's history to the point that it threatens to destroy our common bonds.

Today, the ongoing demonization of all things American is creating a recipe for further division unlike anything we've seen before. Our unity is a delicate tapestry that can easily be unwoven, leading to a tribal society that will inevitably end with our demise. Note the dramatic difference in tone between the comment above and the following line from Abraham Lincoln's second Inaugural Address: "With malice toward none, with charity for all, with firmness in the right as God gives us to see the right let us strive on to finish the work we are in to bind up the nation's wounds." That's what a true president should sound like. Please take note, Joe.

"I was able to cut the federal debt by $1.7 trillion over the first two years...Guess what? We were able to pay for everything and

we ended up with an actual surplus."

–President Joe Biden, October 6, 2023

Joe Biden has frequently confused the terms debt and deficit, including multiple times in this speech alone. One wonders if Biden, who has been in national politics for more than fifty years, even knows the difference.

The federal deficit refers to an excess of expenditure over revenue in a single fiscal year. The federal debt describes the cumulative amount owed by the United States government to other entities.

Interchanging these two terms may just be a simple oversight on Biden's part that can be forgiven. What is unacceptable, however, is his claim that his administration "ended up with an actual surplus." This statement is ridiculous. Between Biden's inauguration in January 2021 and April 2023, his administration added more than $3.5 trillion to the national debt raising its total to approximately $31.4 trillion. In July 2023, the Congressional Budget Office announced that there was a $1.4 trillion deficit in just the first nine months of fiscal year 2024.

Biden is correct that the deficit was reduced in his first two years in office, but he never mentions why. In March 2020, Congress passed a $2.2 trillion stimulus bill called the Coronavirus Aid, Relief, and Economic Security Act (CARES), creating the largest single-year deficit in US history. It was expected that federal spending would go back to pre-COVID levels after the stimulus bill was enacted.

Although the deficit was reduced at the start of the Biden administration because of waning pandemic spending and increased revenues driven by higher inflation, what Biden fails to acknowledge is that during his first two years in office, spending was still 40% higher than the pre-COVID 2019 federal budget. It's worth noting that in January

2023, Biden called Republicans "fiscally demented," adding, "They don't quite get it."

"I think that the American people are smart as hell and know what their interests are. I think they know they're better off financially than they were before. That's a fact, and all that data, all that polling stuff shows they think they're more positive about the economy than they've been."

–President Joe Biden, October 6, 2023

A Fox News poll from September 9-12, 2023, showed that President Biden's job performance on the economy had a 35% approval rating and a 63% disapproval rating. The same poll found that 22% of Americans described the condition of the economy as "excellent/good" while 78% of Americans described the condition of the economy as "only fair/poor."

"I think you should be able to be a trillionaire, a billionaire, zillionaire if you want, but pay your taxes for God's sake."

–President Joe Biden, October 6, 2023

On numerous occasions during his presidency, Joe Biden has called for the rich to take on more of the country's financial burdens. He repeated his typical refrain on June 17, 2023, when he told union members at a political rally, "It's about time the super wealthy start paying their fair share." He never seems to acknowledge the fact that in 2020, the top 1% of earners in the United States paid 42.3% of all federal income taxes.

It seems Biden won't be content until that number is closer to 100%.

Perhaps Joe should direct the IRS to focus on his son Hunter. When Biden made the comment above, Hunter Biden was under investigation for engaging in a multimillion-dollar influence-peddling scheme. Although the IRS acknowledged that he failed to pay taxes on income connected to this alleged scheme, his father's justice department stalled the investigation long enough for the statute of limitations to expire on many of the potential charges.

In July 2023, Hunter Biden's attorneys reached a tentative deal with US Attorney David Weiss. The deal would have had Hunter plead guilty to two misdemeanor charges for failing to pay taxes in 2017 and 2018, for which prosecutors would recommend probation. In exchange, Hunter would agree to a pre-trial diversion that would dismiss an unrelated felony gun charge.

On July 19, 2023, two IRS whistleblowers testified before the House Committee on Oversight and Accountability and provided evidence of the Justice Department's politicization and misconduct during the Hunter Biden criminal investigation. Fortunately, on July 27, 2023, US judge Maryellen Norieka rejected the Hunter Biden plea deal.

In response to public criticism following the IRS whistleblower testimony and the exposure of the apparent sweetheart plea deal that had been prepared for Hunter Biden, Attorney General Merrick Garland found himself in an embarrassing position. Sadly, he demonstrated poor if not biased judgment in his response. On August 11, 2023, he announced the appointment of David Weiss as the new Special Counsel in the Hunter Biden investigation. It's worth noting that it was US Attorney David Weiss who had previously signed off on Hunter Biden's sweetheart plea deal. Nevertheless, Weiss filed three felony and six misdemeanor tax charges against Hunter Biden on December 7, 2023.

Unbelievably, after the Justice Department's misconduct was brought to light during the IRS whistleblower testimony in Congress, Hunter Biden then had the nerve to sue the IRS. As the British would say, this guy has got some cheek.

"Hamas does not represent the Palestinian people."

–President Joe Biden, October 20, 2023

On August 18, 1988, Hamas issued its Covenant on the Islamic Resistance Movement. This manifesto says that "the Liberation of Palestine is an individual duty for every Moslem wherever he may be." It also says, "In the face of the Jews' usurpation, it is compulsory that the banner of Jihad be raised." It goes on to say, "[Peace] initiatives and so-called peaceful solutions and international conferences are in contradiction to the principles of the Islamic Resistance Movement." Another excerpt says, "The Day of Judgment will not come about until Moslems fight Jews and kill them."

The Palestinian people of Gaza were well aware of this Covenant when Hamas won 76 of the 132 seats in Parliament on January 26, 2006. 78% of eligible voters in Gaza cast ballots.

For Biden to claim that "Hamas does not represent the Palestinian people" is absurd. Jerusalem Center for Public Affairs surveys taken in Gaza after the October 7, 2023 attack on Israel show that the Palestinian people overwhelmingly support Hamas, including the 75% who support the attack on Israel and the 75% who support the creation of a Palestinian State "from the river to the sea."

I'm old enough to also remember footage of Palestinians cheering in the streets when the US was attacked on September 11, 2001. For those Americans who are sympathetic to Hamas, try to remember who started this recent conflict and who kidnapped and killed American citizens in the process. I can't understand why some Americans are having trouble determining who the good guys and the bad guys are in this conflict.

> *"Donald Trump's campaign is obsessed with the past, not the future. He's willing to sacrifice our democracy to put himself in power...Our campaign is about preserving and strengthening our American democracy...Today, I make this sacred pledge to you: the defense, protection, and preservation of American democracy will remain, as it has been, the central cause of my presidency... We're living in an era where a determined minority is doing everything in its power to try to destroy our democracy for their own agenda."*

> –President Joe Biden, January 5, 2024

These remarks were part of Joe Biden's first campaign speech of the 2024 election year. The irony in this speech is so thick it could be cut with a knife. If the comment above started with the name Joe Biden rather than Donald Trump, the speech would be right on point.

After all, it was Joe Biden who used the entirety of this speech to replay the events of January 6, 2021. It seems clear that instead of running on his own record as president, Biden planned to focus his campaign on the so-called "insurrection" of January 6. Yet he says Trump is obsessed with the past.

He also says Trump is willing to sacrifice our democracy to put himself in power. Yet it was the Biden campaign who in the weeks before the 2020 election used their contacts in social media to squash reports about the Biden family's corruption found on Hunter Biden's laptop.

It was the Biden campaign that used their contacts in the intelligence community to falsely advise the American people that the information found on Hunter Biden's laptop was inauthentic and likely an example of Russian disinformation.

None of that was true, of course, but the Biden campaign managed to suppress the truth long enough to fool American voters.

Biden's speech also noted that he is committed to protecting and preserving American democracy. As he spoke these words, efforts were already underway by allies of Joe Biden to prosecute Donald Trump in both state and federal court with potential outcomes that could prohibit Donald Trump from doing business in the future and could even result in him being sent to prison for the rest of his life.

In addition, Biden allies were working to keep Trump's name from appearing on state ballots in both Colorado and Maine, with additional states contemplating similar action.

In the comment above, Biden noted that we are living in an era where a determined minority is doing everything in its power to destroy democracy for its own agenda. However, it was the Democrats who initiated a false accusation and an illegal investigation against Trump for allegedly colluding with Russia during his 2016 presidential campaign. It was also the Democrats who pushed for multiple Special Counsel investigations of Trump and impeached him not once but twice on purely political grounds.

If ever there was a determined minority doing everything in their power to destroy democracy for their own agenda, it is the Democrat Party led by Joe Biden. Ironically, three days before Donald Trump took office in 2017, former President Barack Obama warned *Bloomberg News* to keep a close eye on the new president, saying, "If there is even a hint of politically motivated investigations, prosecutions, et cetera, I think you guys have to really be on top of that."

"The only loser I see is Donald Trump."

–President Joe Biden, January 28, 2024

Biden made this comment during remarks at a political event in South Carolina to which the audience responded, "Loser Trump, loser Trump, loser Trump!" On more than one other occasion, he also referred to his political opponents as Neanderthals for challenging his policies on COVID-19 and climate change.

Joe may want to recall another comment he made on his inauguration day when he was swearing in a large group of presidential appointees. He told that audience, "I'm not joking when I say this. If you're ever working with me and I hear you treat another colleague with disrespect, talk down to someone, I promise you I will fire you on the spot." I guess the respect for others that Biden demands of his staff does not apply to him.

"Right after I was elected, I went to what they call a G7 Meeting. I was in south of England. And I sat down, and I said, 'America is back,' and Mitterrand from Germany, I mean from France, looked at me and said, said, 'You know what, why, how long you back for?' "

–President Joe Biden, February 4, 2024

Francois Mitterrand, who was President of France from 1981 to 1995, died in 1996.

Three days after this comment, on February 7, 2024, Biden was once again confused about the world leaders he met with as he referenced the same G7 Conference in 2021. This time he said, "When I first got elected president, I went to a G7 meeting with the seven heads of state in Europe and Great Britain. I sat down and I said, 'Well, America's back' and the president of France looked at me and said, 'For how long?' Then Helmut Kohl of Germany looked at me and said…" German Chancellor Helmut Kohl died in 2017.

According to an NBC News poll conducted between January 26 and 30, 2024, only 23% believe Biden has the physical and mental health to be president, a fifteen-point slip from 2020.

"My memory is fine."

–President Joe Biden, February 8, 2024

Earlier that day, the public was presented with Special Counsel Robert Hur's findings entitled "Report on the Investigation Into Unauthorized Removal, Retention, and Disclosure of Classified Documents Discovered at Locations Including the Penn Biden Center and the Delaware Private Residence of President Joseph R. Biden, Jr."

The report contained damaging references to Biden's poor memory. For example, on p. 208, Hur noted, "In his interview with our office, Mr. Biden's memory was worse. He did not remember when he was vice president, forgetting on the first day of the interview when his term ended ('If it was 2013…when did I stop being Vice President?'), and forgetting on the second day of the interview when his term began ('In 2009 am I still Vice President?'). He did not remember, even within several years, when his son Beau died. And his memory appeared hazy when describing the Afghanistan debate that was once so important to him."

Hours after the report became public, the White House announced a hastily organized evening public address by the president. Biden's main goal was to reassure the American people that his memory was still sharp. However, within minutes of making the comment above, Biden said he spoke with the President of Mexico, Abdel Fattah El-Sisi. El-Sisi is actually the President of Egypt. Needless to say, his performance that evening did not reassure the American people about his mental acuity. I'm reminded of a famous quote: "Better to remain silent and be thought a fool than to speak and to remove all doubt."

"I'll tell who did notice, Cookie Monster. He pointed out his cookies are getting smaller and paying the same price. I was stunned when I found out that actually happened."

–President Joe Biden, March 5, 2024

Biden was expressing his outrage over a problem called shrinkflation. What he failed to recognize is that food manufacturers have been left with a difficult choice in the Biden economy: either raise their prices, which wouldn't sit well with consumers, or reduce the size of their products. They have chosen the latter because the costs of raw materials and labor have increased dramatically during the Biden administration.

"My commitment to the safety of the Jewish people, the security of Israel, and its right to exist as an independent Jewish state is ironclad."

–President Joe Biden, April 21, 2024

When Biden made the statement above, media outlets praised him for his strong support for Israel. However, Biden's "ironclad" reference has proven to be more accurate than he probably intended. Ironclad simply refers to something (e.g. a ship) that is cased with an iron veneer. Although it looks impressive on the outside, it is no substitute for a solid iron hull.

On May 8, 2024, Joe Biden announced that he would be withholding weapons and ammunition from Israel. Biden said he made this decision because he disliked Israel's plans to invade the city of Rafah in the Gaza Strip as part of their attempt to rout Hamas. Many observers, however, believed Biden's decision was a gesture to placate the radical members of his party.

One day earlier, on May 7, 2024, during a speech at the US Holocaust Memorial Museum's annual Days of Remembrance ceremony, Joe Biden made another ironic statement. As he linked the horrors of the Holocaust with Hamas' attack on Israel, Biden stated, "We must give hate no safe harbor." At that very moment, US military personnel were following Joe Biden's order to build a temporary harbor/pier so humanitarian relief could be shipped to the people of Gaza.

"No president's had the run we've had in terms of creating jobs and bringing down inflation. It was 9% when I came to office, 9%."

–President Joe Biden, May 14, 2024

This was the third time Biden falsely claimed that inflation was 9% when he took office, two times in that week alone. Inflation was actually 1.4% on Biden's inauguration day, January 20, 2021. One might wonder if his confusion is rooted in the fact that during his administration, inflation reached a high point of 9.1% in June 2022. However, the fact that he has repeated this false assertion multiple times leads one to suspect that he may simply be an unapologetic liar.

"When I was vice president, things were kind of bad during the

pandemic. And what happened was, Barack said to me, 'Go to Detroit and help fix it.' "

–President Joe Biden, May 19, 2024

Didn't President Biden just assure us on February 8, 2024, that his memory is fine? How then does he explain why as vice president, Barack Obama supposedly told him to go to Detroit to fix the pandemic? Biden's vice presidency ended in 2017, and the pandemic reached the United States in 2020. With mistakes like this and his repeated references to Kamala as "President Harris," perhaps Joe should carry a business card to remind him of his job title. In his defense, do we really expect him to remember little details like who is president?

Chapter 3

Vice Presidents

"The vice presidency isn't worth a warm bucket of spit."

–John Nance Garner

"If we do everything right, if we do it with absolute certainty, there's still a 30% chance we're going to get it wrong."

–Vice President Joe Biden, February 6, 2009

Biden was referencing pending legislation known as the American Recovery and Reinvestment Act as he addressed members of the House Democratic caucus, who were gathered for their annual retreat. When he was later questioned about the vice president's comment, Barack Obama replied, "I don't remember exactly what Joe was referring to, not surprisingly."

"What I'm trying to say, without boring you too long at breakfast, and you all look dull as hell, I might add—the dullest audience I have ever spoken to—just sitting there, staring at me. Pretend you like me."

–Vice President Joe Biden, April 27, 2012

Biden was speaking to a room full of political donors during a fundraising event in Washington, D.C. This was not the last time Joe Biden awkwardly insulted his audience. During his address to the US

Coast Guard Academy's graduating class on May 19, 2021, President Biden said to the cadets, "You are a quiet, you're a really dull class. I mean, come on, man. Is the sun getting to you?"

"He's gonna put you all back in chains."

–Vice President Joe Biden, August 14, 2012

Biden was referring to Republican presidential candidate Mitt Romney when he made this remark to a crowd in Danville, Virginia, which included many African Americans. Romney campaign spokesperson Andrea Saul responded by saying, "The Obama campaign will say and do anything to win this election."

"And by the way, you know, I'd sit on the stand and it'd get hot. I got a lot of, I got hairy legs that turned, that, that, that, that, that, that turn blonde in the sun and the kids used to come up and reach in the pool and rub my leg down so it was straight and then watch the hair come back up again. They'd look at it. So, I learned about roaches. I learned about kids jumping on my lap and I love kids jumping on my lap."

-Former Vice President Joe Biden, June 26, 2017

Biden told this bizarre story at the dedication of the Joseph R. Biden Jr. Aquatic Center in Wilmington, Delaware, a facility at which Biden worked as a lifeguard in his youth. Biden claims he took the job in the predominantly Black neighborhood because he wanted to get more involved and didn't know any Black people at the time.

One of the kids Biden met during his time at the city pool was a supposed gang leader named Corn Pop. As Biden explained, "Corn

Pop was a bad dude, and he ran a bunch of bad boys." Biden recounted a time when he confronted Corn Pop after kicking him out of the pool. Supposedly Corn Pop, along with three friends armed with straight razors, waited for Biden at his car. Fortunately, our tough-as-nails hero Joe Biden met Corn Pop carrying a six-foot-long chain and told him, "You may cut me, man, but I'm gonna wrap this chain around your head." For some unknown reason, Biden often tells stories that make it sound like he was once the toughest man in Delaware.

"I looked at them and said, 'I'm leaving in six hours. If the prosecutor is not fired, you're not getting the money.' Well, son of a bitch. He got fired."

–Former Vice President Joe
Biden, January 23, 2018

Joe Biden has had many interesting and shady connections over the years with Ukraine, a country that has a long history of corruption. President Barack Obama put Vice President Joe Biden in charge of US policy in Ukraine, and Biden made six trips to Ukraine as vice president.

In April 2014, Biden's son, Hunter, became a paid board member of Burisma Holdings, a Ukrainian energy company. It's worth noting that Hunter had no experience with Ukraine and could not speak the language, nor did he have any experience in the energy industry, but he was earning up to $1 million per year as a board member.

During Hunter's service with Burisma, the Prosecutor General of Ukraine, Viktor Shokin, initiated a corruption investigation into the company. During one of his visits to Ukraine in December 2015, Joe Biden made the statement above to Ukrainian President Petro Poroshenko; he later recalled it during an interview with the Council on Foreign Relations.

Biden was referring to $1 billion in US aid to Ukraine which he planned to withhold if Viktor Shokin was not fired. One can only wonder why the Vice President of the United States would be so concerned with a prosecutor in another country that he would issue such an ultimatum. It wouldn't have anything to do with his son, would it?

At best, this represents a major conflict of interest. In an interview with Fox News in August 2023, Viktor Shokin referred to Joe Biden and his son Hunter, saying, "I do not want to deal in unproven facts, but my firm personal conviction is that, yes, this was the case. They were being bribed."

Interestingly, the final action Biden took as vice president was, you guessed it, a trip to Ukraine in January 2017. On July 25, 2019, President Donald Trump had a phone conversation with the new President of Ukraine, Volodymyr Zelensky, when he said to him, "There's a lot of talk about Biden's son, that Biden stopped the prosecution, and a lot of people want to find out about that so whatever you can do with the Attorney General would be great. Biden went around bragging that he stopped the prosecution, so if you can look into it. It sounds horrible to me."

This seemingly simple request to investigate potential corruption involving officials from Ukraine and the US had unimaginable consequences. After desperately and unsuccessfully looking to impeach Donald Trump for months, Democrats in the House of Representatives led by Speaker of the House and close Biden ally Nancy Pelosi decided to use this phone call as the basis for Trump's impeachment. They falsely claimed he was attempting to influence the 2020 presidential election and charged him with abuse of power. Trump was later acquitted by the US Senate.

Then, after Biden was elected president, Russia invaded Ukraine on February 24, 2022. Over the next two years, the Biden administration provided Ukraine with $75 billion in assistance, and Joe Biden publicly pledged to support Ukraine "as long as it takes."

Ironically, support for military aid to Ukraine was championed most by Democrats in Congress. It doesn't seem like it was that long ago when Democrats were closely associated with an anti-war platform during the Vietnam War era. Times have certainly changed.

Then in January 2023, classified documents were found in Joe Biden's Penn Center office and the garage and office at his home in Wilmington Delaware. There has been much speculation that some of these documents were related to Ukraine. Interestingly, Hunter Biden would have had unfettered access to the documents kept at Joe's home.

On January 24, 2023, President of Ukraine Volodymir Zelensky sent a recorded message to American business leaders explaining that Ukraine had already formed partnerships with American companies like Blackrock, JP Morgan, Goldman Sachs, and others and had made arrangements to receive Bradley fighting vehicles, Abrams tanks, and other items from the US government. He went on to imply that there is a lot of money to be made when American businesses partner with Ukraine. In other words, "Support our war effort and we will all get rich together in the process." All of this raises interesting questions like, how deep does the corruption in Ukraine go, and how far has it penetrated American business and government?

"This was an attempted modern-day lynching. No one should have to fear for their life because of their sexuality or color of their skin. We must confront this hate."

–Vice President Kamala Harris,
January 29, 2019, in a tweet

Harris and many other prominent people, including Joe Biden, quickly expressed their support for actor Jussie Smollett after he claimed to be the victim of a hate crime where he was attacked by two assailants who yelled racial and homophobic slurs at him. Democrats had no trouble believing Smollett because his claim fits perfectly with their perception of American society, especially when Smollett described his attackers as MAGA supporters.

The Chicago Police Department dedicated 3,000 hours to the investigation, spending a total of $130,000. In their investigation, the police concluded that Smollett had perpetrated a hoax. He was subsequently indicted by a Grand Jury on sixteen criminal counts. However, in a surprise twist, the Cook County State's Attorney's Office, led by Kim Foxx, inexplicably announced that it was dropping the charges against Smollett. However, the judge in the case did not agree that the evidence in the case supported a dismissal, and as a result, a Special Prosecutor was appointed in August 2019.

The Special Prosecutor investigation determined that the decision to drop charges against Smollett "represented a major failure of operations." New charges were filed against Smollett, and in December 2021, a jury convicted him of five felony counts of disorderly conduct. He was sentenced to 150 days in jail and thirty months of felony probation and ordered to pay $120,106 in restitution to the City of Chicago as well as a fine of $25,000.

"If you're able to, chip in now to the @MNFreedomFund to help post bail for those protesting on the ground in Minnesota."

–Vice President Kamala Harris,
June 1, 2020, in a tweet

According to the Minnesota Freedom Fund website, it advocates for "wide-scale decarceration." It also says, "We believe that our criminal justice system, like many other systems in our society, was designed to maintain and uphold White supremacy."

The riots in the Minneapolis/Saint Paul area following the death of George Floyd resulted in at least two deaths, more than 600 arrests, and in excess of $500 million in damage to roughly 1,500 properties. It is now recognized as the second-costliest civil disturbance in US history. By all means, Kamala, let's bail as many of these "protesters" out of jail as we can.

"I also look forward to working with members of the Congress who, I think, share our perspective on the need to address root causes for the migration that we've been seeing."

–Vice President Kamala Harris, March 24, 2021

Harris made this comment in a joint address with President Biden after he chose her to lead the administration's efforts to determine the root causes of immigration to the United States from Mexico and the Northern Triangle (Guatemala, El Salvador, and Honduras). The announcement came at a time when record numbers of illegal immigrants were entering the United States.

What Biden failed to acknowledge during this address was the fact that his decision to remove Trump administration policies had directly led to the surge in immigration. In typical Biden style, he chose not to take any meaningful action to curb this flow but instead appointed Harris to research the root causes of immigration.

Here's a tip, Joe: when your house is on fire, you don't respond by reading about the leading causes of house fires. The first thing you need to do is *stop the fire*!

"So, Ukraine is a country in Europe. It exists next to another country called Russia. Russia is a bigger country. Russia is a powerful country. Russia decided to invade a smaller country called Ukraine, so basically that's wrong."

–Vice President Kamala Harris, March 1, 2022

This comment was made during an interview on a radio show. The vice president was asked to describe the situation in Ukraine in layman's terms and how it affects Americans. Apparently, to Kamala Harris, using layman's terms means speaking to your audience as if they were kindergarteners. One can only hope that this statement doesn't adequately reflect the vice president's overall mastery of the crisis.

"I am Kamala Harris. My pronouns are she and her. I am a woman sitting at this table wearing a blue suit."

–Vice President Kamala Harris, July 26, 2022

I'm at a loss for words.

"We have a secure border in that that is a priority for any nation, including ours and our administration."

–Vice President Kamala Harris,
September 11, 2022

During an interview on NBC's *Meet the Press*, the vice president was asked about the crisis at the Southern border. This was not the first or last time Harris would be asked about the administration's border policy.

In a previous interview with NBC News on June 8, 2021, Harris was asked why she had not visited the border since being tasked by President Biden in March 2021 to lead the administration's efforts to stem migration to the Southern border. Harris replied, "So this whole, this whole, this whole thing about the border. We've been to the border. We've been to the border." When pressed further that she had not personally been to the border, Harris replied "I, and I haven't been to Europe and I mean, I don't, I don't understand the point that you're making."

Again, on September 13, 2022, Harris declared, "We have a secure border." Meanwhile, according to US Customs and Border Protection southwest, land border encounters increased from a total of 458,088 in fiscal year 2020 to a total of 2,378,944 in fiscal year 2022, a new record.

According to an NBC News poll conducted in June 2023, only 32% of registered voters held a positive view of Kamala Harris. Her rating was reportedly the lowest score of any vice president in the poll's history. Perhaps former Speaker of the House Nancy Pelosi described Harris' productivity or lack thereof best when she explained, "She's the Vice President of the United States. And when people say to me, 'Well, why isn't she doing this or that?' I say because she's the Vice President. That's the job description. You don't do that much."

If that's true, then Kamala Harris sure seems like the right person for the job.

"So, we are here together because we collectively believe and know America is a promise. America is a promise. It is a promise of freedom and liberty, not for some, but for all. A promise we made in the Declaration of Independence that we are each endowed with the right to liberty and the pursuit of happiness. Be

clear. These rights were not bestowed upon us. They belong to us as Americans."

–Vice President Kamal Harris, January 22, 2023

Harris made these comments on the fiftieth anniversary of the Roe v. Wade decision. The Preamble of the Declaration of Independence denotes, "We hold these truths to be self-evident, that all men are created equal, that they are endowed by their Creator with certain unalienable Rights, that among these are Life, Liberty and the pursuit of Happiness."

It's worth noting that Harris referenced the rights to liberty and the pursuit of happiness, which support the Democrat narrative when it comes to their support for abortion, but she omitted the unalienable right to life, which disrupts the Democrat narrative.

This may seem like a small oversight, but it is actually quite important, and one can be forgiven for associating actions like this with attempts by Democrats to reframe American history. It's also worth pointing out that Harris mentioned our rights were "endowed" without saying by whom. The Declaration of Independence clearly notes that the unalienable rights of Americans were "endowed by their Creator." Leaving this reference out speaks not only to the Left's growing indifference and sometimes outright contempt for God but also opens the door to an implicit assertion that our rights are instead endowed by our government.

"Well, I think that the concerns are based on what we should all be concerned about, but the solutions have to be and include what we are doing in terms of going forward."

–Vice President Kamala Harris, March 15, 2023

Harris was asked on *The Late Show with Stephen Colbert*, "Was there any discussion in the White House about what the blowback would be for approving the Willow oil project? Because people have gotten quite upset about it." Once again, the master of gibberish produced a thoughtful response.

"So, during Women's History Month, we celebrate and we honor the women who made history throughout history, who saw what could be unburdened by what had been."

–Vice President Kamala Harris, March 22, 2023

Harris appears to frequently get stuck on a single word when she is trying to make a point. The result is what many observers refer to as a *word salad*. The *Merriam-Webster Dictionary* defines *word salad* as a string of empty, incoherent, unintelligible, or nonsensical words or comments.

Another classic word salad by Harris was a comment she made during a roundtable discussion at Claflin University in South Carolina on September 20, 2022. "We invested an additional $12 billion into community banks, because we know community banks are in the community, and understand the needs and desires of that community as well as the talent and capacity of community."

On January 13, 2022, Harris was asked by NBC News about the Biden administration's COVID-19 policy and whether it was time for a change in strategy, to which she replied, "It's time for us to do what we have been doing, and that time is every day."

In another example, on July 8, 2022, Harris discussed the US Supreme Court's decision to overturn Roe v. Wade during an interview with CBS News, saying, "I think that, to be very honest with you, I do believe that we should have rightly believed, but we certainly believe that certain issues are just settled. Certain issues are just settled."

On July 6, 2023, Kamala's wisdom and eloquence were once again on display when she appeared at the 2023 Essence Festival of Culture, saying, "Culture is, it is a reflection of our moment and our time. Right? And present culture is the way we express how we're feeling about the moment, and we should always find times to express how we feel about the moment. That is a reflection of joy. Because, you know it comes in the morning."

You can't argue with that!

"I think it's very important, as you have heard from so many incredible leaders, for us at every moment in time and certainly this one, to see the moment in time in which we exist in our present. And to be able to contextualize it. To understand where we exist in the history and in the moment as it relates not only to the past but the future."

–Vice President Kamala Harris, April 24, 2023

If this had been part of an essay written by a student, I think their teacher's BS meter would have reached its limit. Nevertheless, Joe Biden's support for his running mate remains steadfast. As he once said, "I may not be much, but I know how to pick 'em."

When selecting a vice-presidential running mate, presidential candidates need to consider many things. The running mate needs to provide value (e.g., they should be from a key state, have foreign policy experience, have domestic policy experience, offset the age of the ticket, have strong popular appeal, etc.)

Traditionally, a running-mate was selected primarily to balance the ticket and fill any presumed gaps in the presidential candidate's experience or character. With all they bring to the ticket, presidential candidates must be careful, however, when selecting a running mate because it could prove to be detrimental if their party, the public, or even the opposition view the running mate as a preferable alternative to the leader of the ticket. So, a running-mate should bring enough assets to strengthen the ticket, but from the presidential candidate's perspective, they can't be too strong. By selecting someone with many strong qualities but at least one or more obvious flaws, the leader of the ticket affirms their own role.

In other words, this type of selection establishes an implicit insurance policy for the president against the threat of impeachment by the opposing party. Biden's complete failure when it comes to enforcing US immigration law is perhaps the most legitimate cause for impeachment in recent memory, yet Biden's dereliction of duty is effectively impeachment-proof because of Kamala Harris. One might even wonder whether this knowledge has emboldened Biden to take some of the actions he has.

> "A.I. is kind of a fancy thing. First of all, it's two letters. It means artificial intelligence."
>
> –Vice President Kamala Harris, July 12, 2023

Harris was attempting to explain what artificial intelligence is during a meeting with labor union and civil rights leaders. Unfortunately, once again Harris spoke to her audience as if they were kindergarteners. Rest assured, however, on March 24, 2021, Joe Biden once again expressed his support for Harris, saying, "When she speaks, she speaks for me."

"We must understand what are disparities and then accommodate and adjust for those disparities if we want equal outcomes."

–Vice President Kamala Harris,
September 14, 2023

The concept of *equal outcomes* is part of the political discord in America today. Section 1 of the 14th Amendment to the US Constitution reads, "No State shall make or enforce any law which shall abridge the privileges or immunities of citizens of the United States; nor shall any State deprive any person of life, liberty, or property, without due process of law; nor deny to any person within its jurisdiction the equal protection of the laws."

This guarantee of equal protection of the laws should be the definitive word on any questions related to equality in the United States. Unfortunately, in recent years Democrat politicians have largely ended public references to the term *equality* and have instead come to stress the need for *equity* in America.

Equity is defined as something fair. While that may sound quite reasonable, one must remember that fairness is a completely subjective term. What might be considered fair to one person may not be considered fair to another.

When this concept is taken to the extreme, we end up with what Vice President Harris is promoting here: equal outcomes. Nowhere in the US Constitution, education system, criminal justice system, or any other legal entity is it written that Americans should all have equal outcomes. To suggest so is not only ridiculous but dangerous.

In 1875, Karl Marx popularized a slogan that said, "From each according to his ability, to each according to his needs," which is widely considered to be a basic principle of communism. It is in this type of political theory that the concept of equal outcome is most relevant.

Clearly, there are disadvantaged individuals in the United States, and they should be helped. However, instead of pursuing 'equal outcomes' for all, we should be promoting greater access to opportunities. When opportunities exist, it is up to the individual to choose whether or not to take full advantage of them. Those who do so increase their odds of success and their chances to achieve the American dream.

Ronald Reagan once said, "The American dream is not that every man must be level with every other man. The American dream is that every man must be free to become whatever God intends he should become." There is no, never will, nor should there be some sort of guarantee of success. Promises to that end are a sham. Kamala Harris would do well to heed the words of Alexis de Tocqueville when he said, "Americans are so enamored of equality that they would rather be equal in slavery than unequal in freedom."

"We came into office during the height of a pandemic. Record unemployment, and because of our economic policies, we now are reducing inflation."

–Vice President Kamala Harris, October 29, 2023

At first glance, it may appear that there is nothing wrong with this statement. Look again. In addition to her false claim that unemployment was at a record high when the Biden/Harris administration took office, Harris is also trying to make the issues of unemployment and inflation interchangeable.

Harris is subtly trying to convey this message: "We came into office during the height of a pandemic. Record [inflation] and because of our economic policies we are now reducing inflation." This is a classic smoke-and-mirrors trick. Harris is trying to give the impression that because of the pandemic, inflation was at a record high level when the Biden/Harris administration took power, and that because of their economic policies, inflation is being reduced. The truth, however, is that the economic policies of the Biden/Harris administration caused the inflation rate to skyrocket in the first place.

"Don't."

–Vice President Kamala Harris, October 30, 2023

Three weeks after Hamas attacked Israel, Harris provided the comment above when she was asked during an interview on *60 Minutes*, "What's the message to Iran?"

"Don't" seems a little naïve and simplistic, doesn't it? Is that really how we describe our foreign policy now? In any case, Harris' message failed miserably.

Between October 17, 2023, and January 28, 2024, there were 160 attacks by Iranian proxies on US troops, ships, and bases in Syria and Iraq. Many of these attacks were made by Iranian-backed Houthis in Yemen.

Less than one month after taking office, on February 16, 2021, the Biden/Harris administration took the Houthis off the US list of foreign terror organizations, reversing a designation made by the Trump Administration. This was part of Biden's failed attempt to normalize relations with Iran.

Sadly, on January 28, 2024, three US soldiers were killed by a drone attack on a US base in Jordan near the borders with Iraq and Syria. More than 40 other service members were injured in the attack. Nevertheless, Joe Biden and Kamala Harris continued to champion their Don't Doctrine for months to come.

On April 1, 2024, Israel launched an airstrike on Iran's consulate in Syria. The attack killed two Iranian generals and five officers. Following that strike, there was widespread anticipation of a direct attack on Israel by Iran. On April 12, 2024, a reporter asked President Biden, "What is your message to Iran at this moment?" He replied once again, "Don't."

Two days later, on April 14, 2024, Iran launched an unprecedented attack on Israel with more than 300 drones, ballistic missiles, and cruise missiles. Perhaps the Biden/Harris administration should put a little more thought into the best way to deter aggression. "Don't" clearly hasn't worked.

"What we have done to pardon tens of thousands of people for simple marijuana possession under the federal law because frankly, nobody should have to go to jail for smoking weed, right? And so, these are some of the things that we have done that I think really do resonate with young people, with Black voters, with young Black voters, with young Black men."

–Vice President, Kamala Harris, February 2, 2024

Harris was asked by a reporter during a campaign trip to South Carolina, "Talk about what the Black vote means for you the Biden/Harris campaign." Harris could have responded by describing the administration's plans to strengthen the economy, reduce inflation, secure the border, improve foreign relations, etc. However, she decided to highlight the issue of marijuana. It's very sad that the Vice President of the United States has such a pathetic view of Black Americans that she believes the issue they care most about is greater access to drugs.

Chapter 4

First Ladies

"The first ladyship is the only federal office in which the holder can neither be fired nor impeached."

–William Safire

"People in this country are ready for change…And let me tell you something, for the first time in my adult life, I am proud of my country."

–Future First Lady Michelle
Obama, February 18, 2008

I t's pretty ironic that someone who would soon receive the title First Lady of the United States had the nerve to say she never took pride in her own country until her husband had a chance of becoming president. Since there have only been forty-six presidents in our nation's history, let's hope that most of us can find other reasons to be proud Americans.

"Every time they get into a car by themselves, I worry about what assumption is being made by somebody who doesn't know everything about them…I, like so many parents of Black kids, the innocent act of getting a license puts fear in our hearts."

–Former First Lady Michelle
Obama, May 10, 2021

Michelle Obama, who lives in an $11.5 million mansion on Martha's Vineyard and has an estimated net worth between $70 and $135 million, still claims that she and her children, who are protected around the clock by the US Secret Service, are oppressed because of their race.

Commentator Candace Owens responded to Obama's whining by saying, "They're not one of us. They're nothing like us. They don't live like us. She has nothing that goes on in her life that is similar to the average American, yet she keeps trying to use her skin color and her complexion as a way to make people believe that she's suffering, and she's absolutely not suffering."

It has been a cherished theme in American society for individuals to overcome challenges on their way to success. For example, for years college applications have asked students to describe these types of experiences. Some observers have even described this concept as "achieving the American dream." Today, however, this theme seems to have dropped its most important element: the act of actually overcoming the challenge.

Americans today seem content simply to complain about their obstacles, using phrases like oppression, systemic racism, White supremacy, etc. rather than overcome them. Terms like these provide a rationale for a growing number of Americans to identify as victims. They seem to have learned that sustained victimhood means they will continuously receive sympathy, charity, and above all, preferential treatment. This concept is sadly promoted by government leaders, mass media, entertainment, and schools.

If there is one thing I've learned in life, it is that everyone—*everyone*—has hardships and pain of their own. Just like the veteran who suffers from traumatic brain injury has been wounded as badly as one who has lost a limb, we need to understand that we all have unique challenges in life and only some of those challenges are apparent to the eye.

Instead of recognizing that fact, our culture today supports the notion that skin color or some other form of physical characteristic is the primary source of hardship in America. Democrats eagerly portray Republicans as racists and White supremacists even when Republican leadership under President Trump led to record-low Black and Hispanic unemployment.

Ignoring the data, Democrats regularly emphasize Black victimhood for a reason. It's not because they believe it's true; they don't. I believe many leaders on the Left perpetuate this narrative because they don't want Blacks to succeed. That doesn't seem plausible; why would they do such a thing you might ask. The answer is simple: to maintain power.

As long as members of the Black community see themselves as victims, it explains all of the perils they face, including poor performance in school, disproportionate numbers in jail, and inexcusable rates of fatherlessness and Black-on-Black violence. If Blacks were to escape this fate and reject the concept of victimhood, choosing instead to become more self-reliant members of society, the Democrat Party would risk losing a reliable voting block.

Democrats are not the least bit interested in the advancement of Black America. Instead, they portray themselves as empathetic only to gain their favor and in turn use this support to promote views and enact policies that perpetuate racial division and government dependence.

Organizers and followers of movements like Black Lives Matter claim that they are advancing their cause. In reality, they are yet another example of victimhood on display. Martin Luther King's vision of an America where individuals are judged by the content of their character rather than the color of their skin has been unfortunately replaced by what is commonly referred to today as *identity politics*. Simply put, this means that physical characteristics like race, ethnicity, or sex, over which we of course have no control, should be used as the defining characteristic of an individual. Among the many troubling consequences of this demeaning concept is the fact that it tries to perpetually associate Whiteness with oppression, and, worse yet, Blackness with victimhood. As long as this belief is allowed to continue, the Black community will be held down by the Democrat Party.

> *"The diversity of this community, as distinct as the bodegas of the Bronx, as beautiful as the blossoms of Miami and as unique as the breakfast tacos here in San Antonio, is your strength."*
>
> –First Lady Jill Biden, July 11, 2022

Jill Biden made this remark in a speech at the annual conference of UnidosUS, a Latino civil rights group. In addition to badly mispronouncing the word *bodega* in her speech, the First Lady's remarks prompted a response from the National Association of Hispanic Journalists, which noted that Biden's comment demonstrated "…a lack of cultural knowledge and sensitivity to the diversity of Latinos in the region. We are not tacos."

> *"No, he's not losing in all the battleground states. He's coming up, and he's even or doing better."*
>
> –First Lady Jill Biden, April 3, 2024

Jill Biden was responding to a question during an appearance on *CBS Mornings* about a recent *Wall Street Journal* poll released the day before. The poll showed that Donald Trump was leading Joe Biden in six battleground states (Michigan, Pennsylvania, Georgia, North

Carolina, Arizona, and Nevada). According to the poll, Trump and Biden were tied in the battleground state of Wisconsin. Apparently, much like her husband, Jill Biden is also reluctant to accept the truth sometimes.

> *"As time goes on and as people start to focus a little bit more about what's at stake and start to become educated on the issues and the differences between the two men, I believe that Americans are going to choose good over evil."*

–First Lady Jill Biden, May 29, 2024

This statement is a sad but common refrain from those on the Left. Once upon a time, Democrats and Republicans could disagree without being disagreeable. Joe Biden himself likes to tell stories about how he and his Republican colleagues would argue in the Senate and then socialize together afterward. Today, however, Democrats have adopted a destructive posture toward their political adversaries. Whereas most Republicans tend to think of Democrats as misguided ideologues, Democrats like Jill Biden see Republicans as "evil." The consequences of such a caustic viewpoint are equally destructive. If your opponent is truly evil, then you and your supporters are rightly justified to use any and all means to stop them.

147

Chapter 5

Members of the Cabinet and the Bureaucracy

"The first rule of a bureaucracy is to protect the bureaucracy."

–Ronald Reagan

"Guilty, your honor."

–Former US National Security Advisor
Sandy Berger, April 1, 2005

Berger, who served as National Security Advisor to President Bill Clinton from 1997 to 2001, pleaded guilty to intentionally taking and deliberately destroying classified documents from the National Archives and Records Administration.

In a story fit for a Hollywood movie, Berger visited the archives four times between 2002 and 2003. During his visits, he was given access to boxes of files, many of which were classified as Special Access Program (SAP), which is higher than top secret.

Berger was searching for material related to the Millennium After-Action Review, which was a report prepared by Richard Clarke, Director of Counterterrorism at the National Security Council. This report contained recommendations to improve national security following an Al Qaeda plot to blow up Los Angeles International Airport during the Millennium celebration in 1999.

According to the rules at the National Archives, Berger should have been required to review these documents in a secure reading room called a SCIF, where he would have been monitored by security. Because he was a former senior member of the intelligence community, however, each time he visited he was given the courtesy of reviewing the documents in the office of Nancy Kegan Smith, a senior archivist.

During his first visit, May 30, 2002, he took notes and returned the materials when he was finished. During his second visit on July 18, 2003, Berger's violation of the archive's rules became more serious. At the end of his visit, Berger was required to return not only the classified documents but also any notes he took on them that day. Because of their subject matter, Berger's notes were now considered classified as well.

While reviewing the documents, Berger asked Smith to briefly leave her office so he could make a private phone call. In her absence, he ripped out fifteen of seventeen pages of notes he had taken that day and put them in his jacket. On Berger's third visit to the archives, on September 2, 2003, his actions became even more daring. Using the same diversion with Smith, this time he stole some of the classified documents themselves.

Unfortunately for Berger, another archives employee noticed the documents protruding from the bottom of Berger's pants as he passed him in the hallway. The employee alerted Smith, and although they weren't sure if Berger had actually stolen anything, they decided to create a "sting" for his next visit. When Berger returned for the fourth and final time on October 2, 2003, Smith had prepared by numbering the back of each of the classified documents Berger was to review.

When Berger left Smith's office to visit the bathroom, her colleagues quickly reviewed the stack of documents and discovered one was missing. During his final two visits, Berger took a total of five classified documents. Two days later, when he was confronted by the archive leadership about the missing documents, Berger had already cut up three of them with scissors and disposed of them in the trash. Initially, he denied any wrongdoing and accused the Archives of losing the documents. That night, however, Berger spoke again with the archive leadership by phone and said he had found two of the documents, calling his actions an "honest mistake."

Eventually, as part of his plea agreement, Berger admitted that he had intentionally taken five classified documents and deliberately destroyed three of them. Government officials later concluded that all of the documents in question were nearly identical drafts of the same report. However, according to the archives the files Berger had gone through had never been fully cataloged, so it was impossible to know exactly what he had stolen. Many suspect Berger was trying to conceal evidence that might be critical of the Clinton administration's homeland security measures prior to the terrorist attack on September 11, 2001.

On July 19, 2004, three days before the 9/11 Commission issued its final report, news broke about the investigation into Sandy Berger's theft. Berger was eventually sentenced to 100 hours of community service, two years of probation, and a fine of $50,000. He also lost his security clearance and his license to practice law.

"This White House will do anything that needs to happen to ensure that both the president and his family are safe and secure."

–White House Press Secretary
RobertGibbs, December 1, 2009

Gibbs was referring to an incident that occurred on November

24, 2009, at a White House State Dinner for Indian Prime Minister Manmohan Singh. A married couple from Virginia, Michaele and Tareq Salahi, crashed the highly secure event. During their two-hour visit, the Salahis met with President Obama, Prime Minister Singh, Vice President Joe Biden, Chief of Staff Rahm Emanuel, and others before exiting the event just as dinner was served. This incredible breach in White House security had many observers questioning the safety of the president and his family. When he was asked about the reaction of the president and the first lady, Gibbs stated, "It's safe to say he was angry. Michelle was angry."

"One thing I'd like to point out is that the system worked."

–Secretary of Homeland Security Janet
Napolitano, December 27, 2009

Napolitano was referring to an incident that occurred on a Northwest Airlines flight from Amsterdam to Detroit on Christmas Day, 2009. Among the 279 passengers and eleven crew members was a 23-year-old known terrorist from Nigeria. During the flight, he tried to detonate a bomb he had concealed in his underwear. The device failed, and instead, the bomber was set afire. He was quickly subdued by passengers and taken into custody when the plane landed.

On February 16, 2012, the bomber, who had received support from Al Qaeda in the Arabian Peninsula, was sentenced to life in prison after pleading guilty to attempted use of a weapon of mass destruction and conspiracy to commit an act of terrorism. One can only imagine the devastation that would have resulted had the bomber succeeded. When a known terrorist comes this close to taking down a commercial jet, it should be pretty clear to everyone, especially the Secretary of Homeland Security, that the system clearly did not work.

"The Supreme Court dealt a huge blow, overturning a 100-year-old precedent that basically corporations couldn't give directly to political campaigns. And everyone is up in arms because they don't like it. The Federal Election Commission can't do anything about it. They want the IRS to fix the problem."

–Internal Revenue Service Director of Exempt
Organizations, Lois Lerner, October 19, 2010

Lerner was referring to the US Supreme Court's decision in the case of *Citizens United v. Federal Election Commission*. In a five-to-four vote, the court ruled that expenditures on political campaigns by groups such as corporations, labor unions, or other collective entities were protected speech under the First Amendment to the US Constitution.

Democrats quickly expressed their dissatisfaction with the court's decision. During his State of the Union Address on January 27, 2010, President Barack Obama stated, "With all due deference to separation of powers, last week the Supreme Court reversed a century of law that I believe will open the floodgates for special interests, including foreign corporations, to spend without limit in our elections."

As Obama made this statement, Supreme Court Justice Samuel Alito, who was in attendance, was caught on camera mouthing the words "Not true." In fact, federal law already prohibited political donations by foreign corporations, and the Citizens United decision did not overturn that ban.

Following the Citizens United decision, it was discovered that the IRS was improperly scrutinizing conservative organizations that applied for tax-exempt status.

After receiving a subpoena, IRS Director of Exempt Organizations Lois Lerner appeared before the House Oversight and Government

Reform Committee on May 22, 2013. Lerner chose to make a voluntary statement professing her innocence at the hearing before asserting her Fifth Amendment protection. It was later determined by the committee that when she delivered her public statement, Lerner had effectively waived her right to invoke her Fifth Amendment protection.

On March 5, 2014, Lerner was recalled to testify before the House Oversight and Government Reform Committee. During the hearing, she was asked several questions by Chairman Darrell Issa, but she invoked her Fifth Amendment privilege each time.

On May 7, 2014, the House of Representatives voted 231-187 to find Lois Lerner in contempt of Congress. Not surprisingly, however, the Obama Justice Department later declined to prosecute Ms. Lerner. During an interview on February 2, 2014, President Obama claimed that there was "not even a smidgen of corruption" at the IRS.

"While we are disappointed in the outcome of this particular loan, we support Congress' mandate to finance the deployment of innovative technologies and believe that our portfolio of loans does so responsibly."

–Secretary of Energy Steven
Chu, November 17, 2011

Chu was referring to $535 million in federal loans that the Department of Energy issued to a California-based solar panel manufacturer called Solyndra. The loans were part of President Barack Obama's highly touted American Recovery and Reinvestment Act of 2009. This law was informally known as the economic stimulus program, and the Obama Administration frequently cited Solyndra as a model for its clean energy initiatives.

Unfortunately, on August 31, 2011, Solyndra ceased all operations and filed for Chapter 11 bankruptcy, laying off more than 1,000 employees in the process. Secretary Chu came under fire from Congress for mishandling the loan guarantees for Solyndra. Critics claimed that the Department of Energy failed to perform due diligence and hurried through its loan process to accommodate Solyndra. There were also claims that the company received preferential treatment because large fundraisers for Barack Obama were among the company's investors.

Chu eventually resigned as Secretary of Energy on February 1, 2013. In response to Chu's resignation, President Obama said in a statement, "Thanks to Steve, we also expanded support for our brightest engineers and entrepreneurs as they pursue groundbreaking innovations that could transform our energy future."

I guess losing more than half a billion dollars on one company isn't that big a deal. After all, it's just taxpayer money, and there's always more of that to spend, isn't there?

Not to be outdone, the Biden administration took government support for green energy to a whole new level with the passage of the $1.9 trillion Infrastructure Investment and Jobs Act on November 15, 2021. As part of this law, President Biden dedicated more than $10 billion to support zero-emission transit and school buses. This investment in electric buses was lauded even though one of the Biden administration's highly touted partners, a California-based electric bus manufacturer called Proterra, embarrassed the administration when it filed for Chapter 11 bankruptcy on August 7, 2023.

Making matters even worse is the fact that Secretary of Energy Jennifer Granholm served on Proterra's board for four years prior to her confirmation as Secretary of Energy. She also owned stock in the company, which she sold for $1.6 million—but only after serving as Secretary of Energy for four months.

"I personally apologize to the American people. As the head of the agency, I'm responsible. I deeply regret this. I will mourn for the rest of my life the loss of my appointment."

–Former Chief of the US General Services
Administration Martha Johnson, April 16, 2012

Johnson made this statement during a hearing before the House Subcommittee on Accountability and Oversight. She had recently resigned from her position as head of the GSA following a financial scandal at the organization. The scandal centered around the GSA's Western Regions Conference, which was held at the M Resort Spa and Casino in Las Vegas in October of 2010.

The conference was attended by 300 federal employees at a cost of $823,000 in public funds. The lavish conference was organized by Acting Regional Administrator Jeffrey Neely, who became a poster boy for wasteful government spending when a photograph emerged of him shirtless and lounging in a bathtub at the M Resort with two glasses of red wine sitting nearby. Neely was eventually indicted on September 25, 2014, on three counts of making false claims and two counts of making false statements and using false documents.

Six months later, Neely pled guilty to one count of submitting a false reimbursement claim from the conference at the M Resort. According to a statement by US Attorney Melinda Haag, "Mr. Neely has acknowledged he violated the special trust that was placed in him as a public servant." Neely was sentenced to three months imprisonment followed by three months of home confinement. He was also ordered to pay $8,000 in restitution and a $2,000 fine in addition to serving a two-year period of supervised release. During the House hearing Democrat Congressman Elijah Cummings summed up the frustration many Americans had in response to the scandal by saying, "They disregarded one of the most basic tenets of government service: It's not your money; it's the taxpayers' money."

"Today's vote is the regrettable culmination of what became a misguided and politically motivated investigation during an election year."

–Attorney General Eric Holder, June 28, 2012

Holder was responding to a vote of 255 to 67 in the House of Representatives to hold him in criminal contempt of Congress for failing to turn over documents pertaining to the Fast and Furious scandal.

Operation Fast and Furious was a program created by the Bureau of Alcohol, Tobacco, Firearms and Explosives (ATF) to sell weapons to individuals with the hope of tracking them by GPS to Mexican drug cartel leaders so they could be arrested.

On December 14, 2010, a US Border Patrol four-man rural assault team engaged five drug traffickers late at night in difficult terrain west of the town of Rio Rico, Arizona. During a short but intense firefight, Agent Brian Terry was fatally wounded. Weapons seized following the gun battle were discovered to be part of Operation Fast and Furious. Soon after Terry's death it was determined that weapons involved in Operation Fast and Furious had been found at numerous crime scenes in the US and Mexico, damaging diplomatic relations between the two countries.

The House of Representatives launched an investigation into the operation, but it was stonewalled by Attorney General Holder. In a move that surprised no one, the White House and the Department of Justice (led by Holder) announced on July 6, 2012, that Holder would not face criminal prosecution for contempt of Congress.

"The basic principle is that you don't deploy forces into harm's way without knowing what's going on, without having some real-time information about what's taking place."

–Secretary of Defense Leon
Panetta, October 25, 2012

Panetta was referring to an attack by Ansar al-Sharia, an Al Qaeda affiliate, on the US diplomatic compound and a CIA annex in Benghazi, Libya, on September 11, 2012.

Panetta's caution meant that a small group of Americans were left to fight fiercely for their lives against approximately 150 armed Islamic militants. While Panetta waited for more information about the situation, the attack went on for hours. When it was all over, four Americans—Sean Smith, Tyrone Woods, Glen Doherty, and US Ambassador to Libya, Christopher Stevens—had been killed. Some may applaud Panetta's prudence, but I think it is shameful that the Secretary of Defense dithered while US government officials under attack overseas were left to fend for themselves.

"What difference at this point does it make?"

–Secretary of State Hillary
Clinton, January 23, 2013

Clinton was testifying before the Senate Foreign Relations Committee when she made this comment. She had been asked by Senator Ron Johnson about the causes of a September 11, 2012 attack on a US diplomatic compound and nearby CIA annex in Benghazi, Libya. The attack by Islamic militants who were affiliated with Al-Qaeda killed Ambassador Christopher Stevens, Sean Smith, Tyrone Woods, and Glen Doherty. According to the House Oversight and

Accountability Committee, prior to the attack the US mission in Libya had made multiple requests for increased security in Benghazi but were denied additional resources.

The Obama Administration was also criticized after it was learned that rescue teams waited far too long before deploying to Benghazi to help after the attack had begun. Making matters worse was that following the attack, US Ambassador to the United Nations Susan Rice tried to provide cover for the Obama administration by insisting that the attack evolved out of a spontaneous protest over an internet video that disparaged Muslims. This claim was known to be false; the attack was actually pre-planned and well-organized.

"He served the United States with honor and distinction."

–US National Security Advisor
Susan Rice, June 1, 2014

Barack Obama's National Security Advisor, Susan Rice, made this comment in reference to US Army Sergeant Bowe Bergdahl. Bergdahl voluntarily left his observation post in Paktika Province in Afghanistan in June 2009 and was subsequently taken prisoner by the Taliban and held for nearly five years.

The Obama administration negotiated a deal in 2014 in which five Taliban leaders who were being held at Guantanamo Bay were exchanged for Bergdahl. Given that Bergdahl had intentionally deserted his post, many observers were angered by this swap. They were angered even further when President Obama held a Rose Garden ceremony at the White House with Bergdahl's parents to celebrate the news of his release.

After returning to the US, Bergdahl was eventually charged with desertion and misbehavior before the enemy. During his military trial, his fellow soldiers testified that members of his unit were wounded as they searched for Bergdahl in enemy territory after his disappearance. In 2017, he pleaded guilty to both charges and was dishonorably discharged from the military and ordered to forfeit $10,000 in pay.

US Senator John McCain described the five Taliban members exchanged for Bergdahl as "the hardest of the hard-core" and "the highest high-risk people." One month after the US completed its departure from Afghanistan in August 2021, it was reported that four of the five Taliban leaders released in the Bergdahl exchange were now part of the Islamic Fundamentalist group's new hardline government in Afghanistan.

"Actually, while I was landing at the airport, I did see President Clinton at the Phoenix airport as I was leaving, and he spoke to myself and my husband on the plane. Our conversation was a great deal about his grandchildren. It was primarily social and about our travels. He mentioned the golf he played in Phoenix."

–Attorney General Loretta Lynch, June 29, 2016

Lynch had met with former President Bill Clinton on June 27, 2016. At the time, both claimed it was an unplanned chance meeting that was social in nature. However, according to journalist Christopher Sign, who authored the book *Secret on the Tarmac*, the meeting was planned in advance and Clinton waited in his motorcade for Lynch to arrive. At the time of the meeting, Hillary Clinton, Bill's wife, was the leading Democrat candidate for president, and the US Justice Department, led by Loretta Lynch, was conducting an investigation into Hillary's use of a private email server during her tenure as Secretary of State.

Republican and Democrat pundits widely admonished both Clinton and Lynch for their meeting, saying that at the very least it presented the appearance of impropriety and political influence in a high-profile federal investigation. Republican presidential candidate Donald Trump took to Twitter, writing, "The system is totally rigged." In another tweet, he added, "Does anybody really believe that Bill Clinton and the USA.G. talked only about 'grandkids' and golf for thirty-seven minutes in plane on tarmac?"

Bill Clinton later told investigators, "I thought, you know, I don't know whether I'm more offended that they think I'm crooked or that they think I'm stupid." Do we have the option to choose both, Bill?

"Although there is evidence of potential violations of the statutes regarding the handling of classified information, our judgment is that no reasonable prosecutor would bring such a case."

–FBI Director James Comey, July 5, 2016

Comey was referring to the results of a year-long investigation into Hillary Clinton's use of a personal email server during her time as Secretary of State. The investigation was focused on whether classified information was transmitted on that server.

In his comments, Comey confirmed that it is a felony to mishandle classified information either intentionally or in a grossly negligent way, and it is a misdemeanor to knowingly remove classified information from systems or storage facilities.

Clinton, who was a presidential candidate at the time and only a few months away from the 2016 election, had done all of those things. However, Comey concluded that she should not be punished.

Critics quickly pointed out that it was not Comey's responsibility to adjudicate this case, and that he significantly overstepped his authority

DID I HEAR YOU RIGHT?

by making the comment. Imagine for a moment that you took a job as a federal employee and decided that you wanted to set up a private server in your home to store all of your email correspondence. Would this be acceptable?

One has to wonder why Clinton would do something like this. She claimed it was more convenient. Really? How much did it cost to set up this server? There is really only one possible reason why someone would do something this brash: she was clearly trying to hide something. By storing her email correspondence on her own server rather than a government server, Clinton could protect her emails from disclosure requests through the Freedom of Information Act.

Again, if you or I had set up this server, and it was later discovered that some of the emails stored there contained classified documents, would we be able to justify this? Could we realistically talk our way out of this? Would we likely face prosecution?

After it was learned that Clinton had deleted 33,000 emails that were under a federal subpoena, she was asked by a reporter, "Did you wipe your server?" She responded coyly, "What, with like a cloth or something?"

This case highlights not only Hillary Clinton's devious and deceitful behavior but a larger issue as well. Some individuals in this country behave as though they are above the law. In spite of our collective belief as Americans that this isn't true, high-ranking government officials rarely face criminal prosecution even when they are found in very compromising situations.

So perhaps as disturbing as this is, some people *are* effectively above the law. We tend to rationalize or dismiss opprobrious behavior as long as it is done by a popular politician with whom we share a viewpoint.

America would be better served if we truly held our senior leaders to a higher standard. By that, I don't mean to suggest that the law should be used as a weapon to attack our opponents for purely political reasons. This practice has already been done several times in recent years, and it should be denounced. I simply mean that our standards under the law should be consistent. If you or I would face immediate prosecution for something we did wrong, doesn't it make sense that high-ranking officials up to and including the Commander-in-Chief should face the same consequences?

"It's against the policy of the United States to pay ransom for hostages."

–White House Press Secretary Josh
Earnest, August 3, 2016

Barack Obama's Press Secretary, Josh Earnest, made this statement after a deal was made to free American hostages held in Iran. As the Obama administration desperately sought a nuclear agreement with Iran, officially known as the Joint Comprehensive Plan of Action (JCPOA), it offered several concessions to the Iranian government. In the hopes that Iran would faithfully dismantle much of its nuclear program, the US and other nations promised Iran billions of dollars in sanctions relief.

On the same day the Iran nuclear deal took effect, Iran released four American prisoners. Interestingly, also on that same day, the US arranged a secret flight to transport $400 million in cash to Iran. When details of the secret flight became public, Republicans criticized the Obama administration for violating a long-standing practice not to pay for hostages. Illinois Senator Mark Kirk said, "Paying ransom to kidnappers puts Americans even more at risk."

Taking a page from the Obama playbook, the Biden administration engaged in very similar behavior seven years later. On September 18, 2023, Iran released five American prisoners and the US released five Iranians. That may sound like a reasonable swap until you learn that the US also gave Iran $6 billion in oil assets that had previously been frozen under US sanctions. Once again, Republicans criticized the practice of paying for hostages.

According to the US Department of State, the official policy of the United States reads, "The US government will make no concessions to individuals or groups holding official or private US citizens hostage. It is US government policy to deny hostage takers the benefits of ransom, prisoner releases, policy changes or other acts of concession."

Secretary of State Antony Blinken tried to justify the payment to Iran by saying it could only be used for humanitarian purposes. However, Iranian President Ebrahim Raisi was quick to point out that Iran would spend the funds "…wherever we need it."

I think today's Democrats would benefit from watching the Steven Spielberg film *Bridge of Spies*. The film chronicles the story of attorney James Donovan, who in 1962 was enlisted by the US government to negotiate a prisoner swap between the US and the Soviet Union. Donovan was asked to secure the trade of convicted Soviet spy Colonel Rudolf Abel for an American U2 spy plane pilot named Francis Gary Powers, who had been shot down over the Soviet Union. After traveling to East Germany to negotiate the exchange, Donovan was able to reach a deal in just ten days. Not only that, but he also secured the release of an American graduate student named Frederick Pryor in the process.

Recognizing Donovan's negotiation skills, President John Kennedy subsequently asked him to participate in another difficult situation, this time with Cuba. In April 1961, the CIA helped more than 1,000 Cuban exiles, referred to as Brigade 2506, invade Cuba at the Bay of Pigs in the hopes of starting an uprising that would overthrow the government of Fidel Castro. The invasion failed, and the surviving members of Brigade 2506 were taken prisoner by Castro. President Kennedy asked James Donovan to secure their release. Donovan made several trips to Cuba to build a rapport with Castro and came to the conclusion that Cuba desperately needed food and medicine. In exchange for both, Donovan was not only able to secure the release of 1,113 members of Brigade 2506 but also managed to free another 10,000 relatives of the survivors and other political prisoners held in Cuba. Barack Obama and Joe Biden, take note. That's negotiating.

"I want to believe the path you threw out for consideration in Andy's office—that there's no way he gets elected—but I'm afraid we can't take that risk. It's like an insurance policy in the unlikely event you die before you're 40."

–FBI Counterintelligence Division Deputy
Assistant Director Peter Strzok, August 15, 2016

Agent Strzok was referring to Donald Trump in this text message to his colleague FBI Legal Counsel Lisa Page. On December 13, 2017, 375 text messages between Strzok and Page were released to the media. While the two were having an extramarital affair, they were also both assigned to the investigation into potential collusion between Donald Trump's 2016 presidential campaign and Russia, which was codenamed Operation Crossfire Hurricane.

Donald Trump adamantly denied any collusion had occurred. On May 17, 2017, Deputy Attorney General Rod Rosenstein appointed former FBI Director Robert Mueller as Special Counsel for the Department of Justice. Mueller was tasked with investigating "any links and/or coordination between the Russian government and individuals associated with the campaign of President Donald Trump."

On March 24, 2019, Attorney General William Barr provided Congress with an executive summary of Mueller's findings, writing, "The Special Counsel's investigation did not find that the Trump campaign or anyone associated with it conspired or coordinated with Russia in its efforts to influence the 2016 US presidential election."

Donald Trump described the Mueller investigation as "the world's most expensive witch hunt" and repeatedly criticized the FBI's handling of the Crossfire Hurricane investigation.

On May 13, 2019, Attorney General William Barr directed US Attorney John Durham to conduct a preliminary review of the 2016 presidential campaigns. This review later evolved into a criminal investigation. Meanwhile, on December 9, 2019, the US Department of Justice Office of the Inspector General issued a report detailing its internal review of Operation Crossfire Hurricane. The report found that the FBI included several serious inaccuracies and omissions in their applications to the Foreign Intelligence Surveillance Court (FISC) to conduct surveillance on Carter Page, a foreign-policy advisor to Donald Trump's 2016 presidential campaign.

On October 19, 2020, William Barr officially appointed John Durham as Special Counsel for the Department of Justice. According to the appointment notice, as Special Counsel Durham was "authorized to investigate whether any federal official, employee, or any other person or entity violated the law in connection with the intelligence, counterintelligence, or law-enforcement activities directed at the 2016 presidential campaigns."

On May 15, 2023, Durham released a 300-page report detailing his findings from the four-year-long probe. He concluded that the FBI rushed into its investigation of the Trump campaign and relied too much on "raw, unanalyzed and uncorroborated intelligence."

The FBI relied heavily on a dossier compiled in 2016 by a former

British MI-6 Agent named Christopher Steele that alleged that Russia was working with the Trump campaign to influence the 2016 presidential election. Steele had been hired to compile the dossier by a Washington, D.C. firm called Fusion GPS, which specializes in opposition research for political campaigns. Fusion GPS was retained by a law firm called Perkins Cole. Perkins Cole was working on behalf of the Hillary Clinton 2016 presidential campaign and the Democratic National Committee.

John Durham's report concluded that at the time the Crossfire Hurricane investigation began, the FBI had no credible information that any Trump campaign officials had been in touch with any Russian officials. Durham also noted that FBI investigators showed bias during the investigation and "failed to uphold their important mission of strict fidelity to the law."

In their text messages to each other during the Crossfire Hurricane investigation, Peter Strzok and Lisa Page expressed their support for Democrat presidential candidate Hillary Clinton and repeatedly referred to Donald Trump as an idiot. On May 4, 2018, Lisa Page resigned; on August 13, 2018, Peter Strzok was fired by the FBI.

Nevertheless, on August 11, 2022, Joe Biden's Attorney General, Merrick Garland, said in a speech, "Let me address recent unfounded attacks on the professionalism of the FBI and Justice Department agents and prosecutors. I will not stand by silently when their integrity is unfairly attacked." One can only wonder if Garland was paying any attention at all to events over the past five years.

"It's deeply discouraging how unfairly he [Garland] has been treated by Republicans in the United States Senate who abdicated

their responsibility to give him a hearing and a timely vote."

–White House Press Secretary Josh
Earnest, November 9, 2016

On June 25, 1992, Senator Joe Biden stated, "Mr. President, where the nation should be treated to a consideration of constitutional philosophy, all it will get in such circumstances is a partisan bickering and political posturing from both parties and from both ends of Pennsylvania Avenue. As a result, it is my view that if a Supreme Court Justice resigns tomorrow, or within the next several weeks, or resigns at the end of the summer, President Bush should consider following the practice of a majority of his predecessors and not, and not, name a nominee until after the November election is completed."

As leader of the Senate Judiciary Committee, Joe Biden went on to say that if President George H.W. Bush were to nominate a candidate for the US Supreme Court, "The Senate Judiciary Committee should seriously consider not scheduling confirmation hearings on the nomination until after the political campaign season is over." Biden added, "Some will criticize such a decision and say it was nothing more than an attempt to save a seat on the court in the hopes that a Democrat will be permitted to fill it, but that would not be our intention."

These words would come back to haunt Joe Biden twenty-four years later. Following the death of Justice Antonin Scalia, President Barack Obama nominated Merrick Garland to serve on the US Supreme Court on March 16, 2016. That same day, Senate Majority Leader Mitch McConnell stated, "The Senate will continue to observe the Biden Rule so that the American people have a voice in this momentous decision." On November 8, 2016, Donald Trump won the presidential election, ensuring that a Republican president would fill the vacancy on the Supreme Court.

"Michelle (Obama) always says, 'When they go low, we go high.'
No. No. When they go low, we kick them."

–Former Attorney General Eric
Holder, October 7, 2018

All in all, I think Holder's view of Democrat behavior is far more accurate than the one presented by Michelle Obama.

"I know that 1,000 overwhelms the system and I cannot begin to
imagine what 4,000 a day looks like."

–Former Secretary of Homeland Security
Jeh Johnson, March 29, 2019

Johnson was referring to the number of apprehensions by US Border Patrol agents on the US Southern border.

The issue of illegal immigration was highlighted by Donald Trump during his campaign for president in 2016. According to *Newsweek*, during the Trump administration, the average number of Border Patrol encounters per month averaged just under 51,000.

By September 2022, the average number of Border Patrol encounters per month during the Biden administration averaged 189,000.

Nevertheless, referring to the border, Biden said on April 30, 2021, "Look, it's way down now. We've now gotten control."

On December 5, 2023, a new record was reached when 12,000 migrants crossed the US Southern border in one day. Underlying the severity of the situation, on that same day FBI Director Christopher Wray testified before Congress about national security, telling them that "I've never seen a time where all the threats or so many of the threats are all elevated, all at exactly the same time."

When he was asked if he saw warning signs similar to those before

September 11, 2001, Wray answered, "I see blinking lights everywhere I turn." Wray went on to say, "I am concerned that we are in an elevated threat environment, a heightened threat environment from foreign terrorist organizations for a whole host of reasons, and obviously their ability to exploit any port of entry, including our Southwest border, is a source of concern...Let's not forget, it didn't take a big number of people on 9/11 to kill 3,000 people."

Sadly, it is not likely a question of if but when the US will experience another major terrorist attack. Joe Biden has been negligent in his responsibility to keep America safe and will likely bear the blame for the next tragedy to come.

"She's the favorite of the Russians."

–Former Secretary of State Hillary
Clinton, October 17, 2019

Clinton was referring to Democrat Congresswoman Tulsi Gabbard. Gabbard, who was running for president at the time, was attacked by members of her own party, like Clinton, because she was seen as too moderate.

Previously Clinton had attempted to connect Donald Trump to Russia during the 2016 presidential campaign by falsely claiming that he colluded with them to win the presidency. Clinton and her colleagues seem to make the same accusation any time they come up against someone with whom they disagree: Russia, Russia, Russia!

Following her loss in the presidential election, Gabbard announced she was leaving the Democrat Party on October 11, 2022. She stated at the time, "The Democrats of today believe in open borders and weaponize the national security state to go after political opponents."

"We want to give the VP a talking point to use in response."

–Former Acting Director of the Central Intelligence
Agency Michael Morell, October 18, 2020

This line was part of a note sent to other officials in the US intelligence community asking them to sign on to a letter discrediting the authenticity of Hunter Biden's laptop. Without any evidence to support their claim, Morell and others provided Joe Biden with the cover he needed to convince voters that his son Hunter's laptop and the trove of incriminating material it contained was an attempt by Russia to interfere with the presidential election.

Four days later, during the final presidential debate in Nashville on October 22, 2020, Biden referred to Trump, saying, "There are fifty former national intelligence folks who said that what he's accusing me of is a Russian plant. They have said that this has all, four, five former heads of the CIA, both parties, said what he's saying is a bunch of garbage."

On August 24, 2022, the Technometrica Institute of Policy and Politics (TIPP) announced the results of a new poll. According to TIPP's president, Raghavan Mayur, "Terming the laptop 'disinformation' by the FBI, Intelligence Community, Congress, and the Biden campaign, along with Big Tech, impacted voters…A significant majority, 78%, believe that access to the correct information could have been critical to their decision at the polls."

The work of these intelligence officials would have been much harder were it not for the assistance of executives in Big Tech. Prior to 2016, social media applied few restrictions on their users' content aside from egregious examples such as criminal activity, threats of violence, etc. Unfortunately, Big Tech has since decided to censor what is allowed on social media in part because they blame the presence of free speech on their platforms for Donald Trump's 2016 victory.

Members of Congress, the FBI, and the Democrat Party have all exerted pressure on Big Tech executives and directed them to silence political expression from prominent individuals on the Right. Twitter, for example, was originally considered by many to be the modern version of the town square, where everyone could voice their opinions and share them directly with the public. Whereas traditional journalism relies on reporters to write the story, Twitter provided individuals with an opportunity to reach a potentially large audience using their own words.

As political bias in the media became more prevalent in recent years, platforms like Twitter grew in popularity because users continued to enjoy complete control over their messages. This is precisely why the Left felt the need to restrict access to Twitter, even if it meant suspending the account of President Donald Trump.

Perhaps the most egregious example of censorship by Big Tech, however, was the suppression of *The New York Post's* Hunter Biden story in October 2020. Prominent officials on the Left immediately recognized that this story had the potential to influence the outcome of the 2020 presidential election. As the quote above shows, they quickly mobilized, and like faithful soldiers, Big Tech executives fell in line behind them.

After Elon Musk's acquisition of Twitter and the subsequent release of The Twitter Files, the public witnessed clear evidence that Big Tech organizations like Twitter were arbitrarily censoring content and restricting access to individuals on the Right. With the political bias of Big Tech executives as well as their disturbing influence on the 2020 election now exposed, urgent changes are desperately needed to prevent this from happening again in 2024 and beyond.

"They can be the people that go to work to make the solar panels."

–US Special Presidential Envoy for
Climate John Kerry, January 27, 2021

This comment was made at a White House press briefing during which Kerry, as the White House Climate Czar, was asked what his message was to fossil fuel industry workers who were worried about losing their jobs as a result of a series of executive orders issued by President Biden that negatively impacted the oil and gas industry.

Kerry, a multi-millionaire, was widely criticized for being arrogant, out of touch, and lacking in empathy. Representative Dan Crenshaw responded with a tweet noting, "By the way, solar will pay on average $20k less than oil and gas jobs."

Kerry's comment reminded many of a similar remark made by Joe Biden in 2019 during his race for President. At a campaign event in Derry, New Hampshire, Biden referred to coal miners, saying, "Anybody who can go down 300 to 3,000 feet in a mine, sure in hell can learn to program as well…Gimme a break! Anybody who can throw coal into a furnace can learn how to program, for God's sake."

Chris Hamilton, co-chair of the West Virginia Coal Forum, responded by saying, "It's just inconceivable how someone, particularly in his position, could advocate putting tens of thousands of working Americans out of work. But it comes as no surprise. Former Vice President Biden has repeatedly demonstrated his disdain for mining and for our coal miners."

"It's the only choice for somebody like me, who is traveling the world to win this battle."

–US Special Presidential Envoy for
Climate John Kerry, February 3, 2021

Kerry was responding to a question from an Icelandic reporter who questioned the White House Climate Czar whether his decision to fly to Iceland by private jet to receive the Arctic Circle Award for his leadership on climate issues was an environmentally friendly way to travel.

Kerry, who went on to say, "I've been involved in this fight for years," did not explain why it was necessary to receive the award in person nor why a commercial flight was not a viable option for him.

However, on July 13, 2023, Kerry disassociated himself from using private jets in spite of his earlier justification for doing so. During a bizarre exchange at a House Foreign Affairs Committee meeting, Kerry denied owning a private jet, stating "I just don't agree with your facts, which began with the presentation of one of the most outrageously persistent lies that I hear, which is this private jet. We don't own a private jet. I don't own a private jet. I personally have never owned a private jet."

When pressed further about the issue later in the hearing, Kerry said, "Yes, my wife owns a plane…I have flown on it sure." Hypocrisy on this issue is not limited to John Kerry. In May 2022, approximately 1,040 private jets landed at airports serving Davos Switzerland so leaders from around the world could attend the World Economic Forum annual meeting to discuss ways to save the climate.

"We've seen in this past year more and more Americans interested in riding a bike."

–Secretary of Transportation Pete
Buttigieg, March 3, 2021

Buttigieg made this comment during an interview at the League of American Bicyclists National Bike Summit. Less than one month later, however, Buttigieg apparently lost some of his enthusiasm for bike riding.

On April 1, 2021, Buttigieg was seen riding his bike on his way to a cabinet meeting at the White House. However, instead of riding his bike the entire three miles from his office at the Department of Transportation, Buttigieg was filmed unloading his bike from an SUV just a few blocks away from the White House.

I'm sure the footage came as a bit of a letdown to Bill Nesper, Director of the League of American Bicyclists, who had praised Buttigieg only weeks earlier telling his members, "I'm sure you, like me, felt the surprise and excitement and the possibilities of seeing a US Secretary of Transportation riding a bike home from work, just going by bike like millions of Americans do every day, not for a photo op but for a sensible way to get around. Clearly, our new secretary knows the pleasure of riding bikes and how convenient biking can be."

"The United States of America is the wealthiest country in the world."

–Fact sheet issued by the White
House, March 31, 2021

Democrats like to use this line often to support their calls for greater spending or taxation. According to *Forbes India,* the United States has the largest economy in the world, but that doesn't mean it is actually the richest country in the world.

For decades, the standard measurement of a country's wealth has been Gross Domestic Product (GDP). GDP measures the total value of finished goods and services produced within a country during a specified period, usually a year. According to *Forbes India,* the US ranks ninth in the world in GDP per capita.

It also makes sense to consider a nation's debt when making claims about total wealth. The US has a national debt of more than \$33 trillion. Not only is this by far the largest amount of debt held by any nation on earth, but it also ranks the US fourth in the world when it comes to its debt-to-GDP ratio.

On June 8, 2022, Joe Biden appeared on *Jimmy Kimmel Live* and made yet another false claim, saying, "We have the fastest-growing economy in the world, the world, the world." According to *Global Finance*, in 2022 Guyana had the fastest-growing economy in the world with a GDP of 47.2%. The United States ranked eighty-eighth in 2022 with a GDP of 3.7%.

"There is racism physically built into some of our highways."

–Secretary of Transportation Pete
Buttigieg, April 6, 2021

On November 15, 2021, President Joe Biden signed a \$1.9 trillion infrastructure bill into law. Using funds from this Infrastructure Act on June 30, 2022, Secretary Buttigieg unveiled the Transportation Department's new Reconnecting Communities Program during an event with local leaders in Birmingham, Alabama.

In a shocking demonstration of its endorsement of such a bizarre notion as racist highways, the Associated Press reported on Buttigieg's announcement by publishing an article with a headline that read, "Pete Buttigieg launches \$1B pilot to build racial equity in America's roads." The AP article and its disconcerting headline were reiterated by news outlets across the nation.

"The major platforms have a responsibility related to the health and safety of all Americans to stop amplifying untrustworthy content, disinformation, and misinformation, especially

related to COVID-19, vaccinations, and elections."

–White House Press Secretary
Jen Psaki, May 5, 2021

The Biden administration essentially crowned themselves as the authority on what is and isn't true and decided that anyone who disagreed with them should be canceled. It remains unclear where exactly they presume to get the power to decide what is misinformation or disinformation.

During a White House press conference on July 15, 2021, Jen Psaki said, "We're flagging problematic posts for Facebook that spread disinformation." Not only has the government been wrong about many of its "truths," but it also circumvented the Constitution by exerting its influence on social media companies to restrict free speech.

Fortunately, on July 4, 2023, a federal district court issued a preliminary injunction preventing a number of executive branch agencies and employees from communicating with social media companies. According to the Congressional Research Service, "The court cited free speech concerns with prior government communications that allegedly led to the censorship of third parties on private social media platforms."

"The process beginning today is truly historic. It represents an opportunity for a historically marginalized group to more fully participate in a fairer, more equitable system of American agriculture."

–Secretary of Agriculture Tom
Vilsack, May 21, 2021

Vilsack wrote this statement as part of an op-ed featured in *USA Today*. He was touting a provision in the $1.9 trillion American Rescue Plan Act signed into law by President Joe Biden on March 11, 2021.

The law created a relief program that planned to pay up to 120% of loans to farmers who are Black, Hispanic, Latino, American Indian, Alaskan native, Asian American, or Pacific Islander. However, this provision was challenged in court by twelve White farmers from Wisconsin, Minnesota, South Dakota, Missouri, Iowa, Arkansas, Oregon, and Kentucky. Their lawsuit claimed, "Because plaintiffs are ineligible to even apply for the program solely due to their race, they have been denied the equal protection of the law and therefore suffered harm."

On June 10, 2021, Federal Judge William Griesbach issued a temporary restraining order suspending the program. In his decision, Judge Griesbach wrote, "The obvious response to a government agency that claims it continues to discriminate against farmers because of their race or national origin is to direct it to stop; it is not to direct it to intentionally discriminate against others on the basis of their race and national origin."

When the Inflation Reduction Act became law on August 16, 2022, it included a new relief program for farmers. Fortunately, this time it avoided references to race and instead, it used a new term; the Department of Agriculture was now empowered to make payments for loans or loan modifications to farmers who face "financial distress."

"Attacks on me, quite frankly, are attacks on science."

–Director of the National Institute of
Allergy and Infectious Diseases Dr.
Anthony Fauci, June 9, 2021

As the COVID-19 virus outbreak evolved into a pandemic, American citizens and government officials alike were desperate for the advice of scientific experts to help them stay safe. Beginning in the Trump administration and continuing in the Biden administration, officials turned to a small group of advisors to help them shape policy.

Chief among them was Dr. Anthony Fauci. For example, while still a candidate for president, Joe Biden said, "I would be telling governors to listen to Dr. Fauci."

On March 8, 2020, Fauci advised the public that "There's no reason to be walking around with a mask." The rationale for his guidance seemed sound when one reads an email he sent a colleague on February 5, 2020. This email and many others were obtained by *The Washington Post* and *BuzzFeed News* through the Freedom of Information Act. It reads, "Masks are really for infected people to prevent them from spreading infection to people who are not infected rather than protecting uninfected people from acquiring infection. The typical mask you buy in the drug store is not really effective in keeping out virus, which is small enough to pass through material."

The flaws associated with placing so much power in the hands of one individual were recognized when Dr. Fauci began to contradict himself. On July 15, 2020, he said, "As we try to proceed, we need to really take seriously the issue of wearing masks all the time." By January 25, 2021, Fauci, who by then was being treated like a sage, was advising the public to double-mask. "So, if you have a physical covering with one layer, you put another layer on, it just makes common sense that it likely would be more effective."

The confusing and sometimes erroneous advice provided by Dr. Fauci should be a lesson for all of us. While it is tempting to believe during times of crisis that there may be one wise old man to whom we should turn, giving so much power to a single individual is a dangerous thing to do. This problem was exacerbated when Dr. Fauci supported the censorship of average citizens, elected leaders, and esteemed epidemiologists who disagreed with his advice and White House policy on vaccinations.

Dr. Fauci was also critical of those who suggested that the pandemic originated at China's Wuhan Institute of Virology, an institute to which the US National Institutes of Health provided a grant of $599,000 for the study of coronaviruses. In defense of his actions, Dr. Fauci said, "I don't regret anything I said then because in the context of the time in which I said it, it was correct."

According to a Gallup poll in 2023, public confidence in the US medical system went from 44% in 2021 to 34% in 2023. When a new variant of COVID-19 appeared on the scene in 2023, Fauci, who is now retired, went on television again to say, "There's no doubt that masks work…I am concerned that people will not abide by recommendations."

Given the fact that he and a handful of his colleagues were primarily responsible for increasing distrust in the US medical system, it's pretty ironic that he is worried that the US public may not abide by their recommendations now like they did before. As Thomas Jefferson once warned, "Those who desire to give up freedom in order to gain security, will not have, nor do they deserve, either one."

"I said, Hell, I'll call you."

–Chairman of the Joint Chiefs of Staff
General Mark Milley, September 29, 2021

General Milley was responding to Congresswoman Vicky Hartzler, who had asked him if he informed General Li Zuocheng of the People's Liberation Army that he would give the Chinese advance notice of an impending offensive by the United States military.

His shocking answer came as part of his testimony before the House Armed Services Committee concerning conversations he had with his Chinese counterpart following the January 6 riot. In September 2023, former President Trump chastised Milley's actions by posting on Truth Social, "This is an act so egregious that, in times gone by, the punishment would have been DEATH!"

Milley, who on numerous occasions stressed his belief that the military should not be involved in domestic politics, appeared to respond to Trump's criticism during his retirement ceremony (which was attended by President Biden) when he said that the US military doesn't "….take an oath to a wannabe dictator." Well, so much for staying out of domestic politics, General.

"Obviously, given the nature of my job, when you take a job like mine, you understand and accept that you're going to have to be available 24/7, depending on what's going on, and you're going to have to engage."

–Secretary of Transportation Pete
Buttigieg, October 17, 2021

After only six months into his position as Secretary of Transportation, Buttigieg went on paternity leave for two months. The Biden administration was criticized for not publicly disclosing the Secretary's leave at a time when the country was experiencing serious logistical challenges resulting from a supply chain crisis.

On March 11, 2023, during his speech at the annual Gridiron Dinner for journalists and politicians, former Vice President Mike Pence joked to the audience, saying, "When Pete's two children were born, he took two months' maternity leave, whereupon thousands of travelers were stranded in airports, the air traffic system shut down, and airplanes nearly collided on our runways. Pete is the only person in human history to have a child and everyone else gets postpartum depression."

Buttigieg also received widespread criticism when he flew to Portugal in August 2022 for a week-long vacation at the same time the government and Union negotiators were frantically working to avoid a nationwide rail worker's strike.

His reputation for being missing in action is compounded by his general lack of experience. Prior to becoming Secretary of Transportation, Buttigieg's most prominent position was serving as Mayor of South Bend Indiana, which, according to *World Population Review,* is the sixth largest city in the state of Indiana. Buttigieg was elected mayor with fewer than 11,000 votes. This is not typically the kind of resume that lands you a position that is fourteenth in the presidential order of succession and responsible for managing a department of 55,000 employees. Then again, we need to remember that this is the Biden administration.

"Well, I'm not sure that it's in the middle of the night."

–White House Press Secretary Jenn
Psaki, October 19, 2021

Psaki was responding to a question from Fox News correspondent Peter Doocy, who asked, "Why is the administration flying thousands of migrants from the border to Florida and New York in the middle of the night?"

Instead of addressing the main point of the question, Psaki chose to quibble over the time of night when the flights occurred. Doocy then pointed out that some flights occurred at 2:30 a.m. Many local officials were caught off guard by these flights when they arrived in their communities because the Biden administration provided no advanced notice for their arrival. Some of these flights arrived at Orange County Airport in Montgomery, New York, including one flight carrying twenty-five migrant girls all under the age of 17. Montgomery is a village with a population of approximately 3,800. After learning about the flights, Orange County Executive Steve Neuhaus said, "I think most Americans are sympathetic but things being done secretly always add to suspicion and confusion."

"There are 9,000 approved oil leases that the oil companies are not tapping into currently...Do you think the oil companies don't have enough money to drill on the places that have been preapproved?"

–White House Press Secretary
Jen Psaki, March 3, 2022

Psaki was asked why the president wasn't doing more to support an increase in domestic oil production. The claim that high gas prices were the result of Putin's Price Hike and a lack of production by US oil companies was repeated frequently by the President and his staff.

According to Western Energy Alliance, thousands of the oil leases Psaki referenced have been held up in court due to litigation initiated by environmental groups and cannot be developed until the cases are adjudicated. Also, before any leases can be developed by oil companies, federal law requires that the government conduct an environmental analysis study, which often takes years to complete.

Such factors, however, are never acknowledged by the president or his team. A White House Fact Sheet released on March 31, 2022, actually noted, "The fact is that there is nothing standing in the way of domestic oil production."

In addition, Biden, the self-proclaimed capitalist, often criticizes oil companies for having the audacity to make a profit. During his State of the Union address on February 7, 2023, Biden said, "Have you noticed that Big Oil just reported its profits? Record profits. Last year, they made $200 billion in the midst of a global energy crisis. I think it's outrageous. Why? They invested too little of that profit to increase domestic production and when I talked to a couple of them, they said, 'We're afraid you're going to shut down all of the oil wells and oil refineries anyway, so why should we invest in them?' I said we're going to need oil for at least another decade."

Biden's remark that the US will still need oil for another decade drew audible laughs from the congressional audience. Biden appears to have virtually no understanding of the oil industry and how it works. Not only does he seem to think that they can simply snap their fingers and increase production, but they should also eagerly begin the steps to pursue new oil production—even though that process will likely extend beyond the next ten years when Biden claims it will no longer be needed.

According to Economic and Private Sector PEAKS, the first phase in the production of oil is the exploration phase, where geological surveys are conducted to identify potentially viable oil and gas sources. This phase typically takes one to five years to complete. Next comes the appraisal phase, where potentially viable sites are examined in more detail. During this phase, initial infrastructure may be developed, exploratory wells are drilled, and oil reserves are mapped. This phase typically takes four to ten years to complete. The next step prior to the extraction of oil is the development phase. During this phase, government contracts and permits are revised and renewed, and infrastructure projects are completed. This phase typically takes four to ten years to complete.

Oil production is not only a complex process but an expensive one as well. It can cost tens of millions of dollars to explore a single location. It's worth remembering that as a presidential candidate, Joe Biden told a young girl during a campaign rally, "I want you to look into my eyes. I guarantee you, I guarantee you, we're going to end fossil fuels and I am not going to cooperate with them."

Tim Stewart, President US Oil and Gas Association, described the current situation well when he said, "So what the White House is saying is that the federal government will begin dictating a required level of oil and gas investment designed to increase production of oil and gas via the tax code while simultaneously phasing out oil and gas investment via another part of the tax code." Is it any wonder why the oil executives Biden spoke with have expressed their reluctance to make new investments?

> *"Cat's out of the bag: here's what I've been up to the past two months."*
>
> –Department of Homeland Security
> Disinformation Governance Board Executive
> Director Nina Jankowicz, April 27, 2022

Earlier that day, Secretary of Homeland Security Alejandro Mayorkas testified before the House Appropriations Subcommittee that his department was establishing a Disinformation Governance Board to counter disinformation.

Almost immediately concerns were raised about the power and influence of this new Board. On May 5, 2022, twelve Republican members of the House Judiciary Committee formally expressed their apprehension, writing, "This board is un-American, anti-democratic, and a dangerous escalation of the Biden administration's embrace of government-endorsed censorship."

Political pundits also shared their criticism of the new board by comparing it to the Ministry of Truth in George Orwell's dystopian novel *1984*. Making matters even worse, the public soon learned that the individual chosen to lead the new board, Nina Jankowicz, had a history of spreading disinformation.

On October 22, 2020, during the final presidential debate between Donald Trump and Joe Biden, Jankowicz tweeted, "Back on the 'laptop from hell', apparently—Biden notes fifty former natsec [national security] officials and five former CIA heads that believe the laptop is a Russian influence op."

After facing an onslaught of criticism, on August 24, 2022, Secretary Mayorkas announced that the Disinformation Governance Board had been terminated.

"So, look, I think we encourage those who have done very well, right? Especially those who care about climate change, to support a fairer tax, tax code that doesn't change, that doesn't charge manufacturers' workers, cops, builders a higher percentage of their earnings; that the most fortunate people in our nation, and not let the, that stand in the way of reducing energy costs and fighting this existential problem. If you think about that as an example, and to support basic collective bargaining rights as well. Right? That's also important."

–White House Press Secretary Karine
Jean-Pierre, May 16, 2022

Jean-Pierre's incoherent rambling was in response to a simple question from Fox News correspondent Peter Doocy during a White House press briefing. Doocy had asked, "But how does raising taxes on corporations lower the cost of gas, the cost of a used car, the cost of food for everyday Americans?"

It is worth noting that this was Jean-Pierre's first briefing as White House Press Secretary. However, it should also be noted that Jean-Pierre has perhaps the most high-profile job in the entire communications industry, and as chief spokesperson for gaffe-prone Joe Biden, she has a particularly important role to play.

"It's not like somebody walks over."

–White House Press Secretary Karine
Jean-Pierre, August 29, 2022

Jean-Pierre was responding to a question from Fox News correspondent Peter Doocy during a White House press briefing. Doocy had asked, "Somebody unvaccinated comes over on a plane, you say that's not ok. Somebody walks into Texas or Arizona unvaccinated, they're allowed to stay?" After Jean-Pierre's response, an incredulous Doocy added, "That's exactly what's happening!"

"I would not be honest if I didn't say I think there was a seditious conspiracy against the government of the United States, and that's a crime...led by Donald Trump, encouraged by Donald Trump."

–Former Secretary of State Hillary
Clinton, September 6, 2022

This isn't the first time Clinton expressed her belief in conspiracies. On January 28, 1998, when she was still First Lady, she famously noted during an interview, "The great story here, for anybody willing to find it and write about it and explain it, is this vast right-wing conspiracy that has been conspiring against my husband since the day he announced for president."

On February 2, 2016, during her own campaign for president,

Clinton reaffirmed her belief in the vast right-wing conspiracy saying that it was now "…even better funded."

"In September 2022, the US Department of State awarded a grant to the Centro Cultural Ecuatoriano Norteamericano Abraham Lincoln, a US-Ecuadorian cultural center in Cuenca, Ecuador, for a program that uses the arts to raise awareness about diversity and inclusion. The program's goal is to promote tolerance, and the arts to provide new opportunities for LGBTQ+ Ecuadorians to express themselves freely and safely."

–Spokesperson for the US Department
of State, October 23, 2022

This comment was made in a statement to Fox News Digital. According to the State Department's grant, the project would include three workshops, twelve drag theater performances, and a two-minute documentary. The grant for $20,600 has caused many to question why President Biden's State Department would use American tax money to sponsor such a program in a foreign country.

A letter sent by Republican lawmakers to Secretary of State Antony Blinken advised, "Instead of funding drag theater programs, your department should focus its limited resources on advancing America's national interests, not the Left's agenda."

"Of course, high turnout and voter suppression can take place at the same time."

–White House Press Secretary Karine
Jean-Pierre, October 25, 2022

This comment was in response to a question by a reporter who asked, "Was President Biden wrong with his assessment of Georgia's voting law? Where does he stand by that Jim Crow comparison?"

Biden had previously criticized Republican attempts to secure voting integrity in several states by saying "It is the most pernicious thing. This makes Jim Crow look like Jim Eagle."

Georgia Secretary of State Brad Raffensperger advised Fox News Digital that the 2022 midterm election in Georgia is on track to "break records in terms of voter turnout in every category." The high voter turnout rate prompted Gabriel Sterling, Chief Operation Officer of the Georgia Secretary of State's Office, to ask, "How many turnout records do we have to break before Stacey Abrams and President Biden apologize to Georgia?"

"The President continues to condemn all violence."

–White House Press Secretary Karine
Jean-Pierre, October 28, 2022

This comment was made following a home-invasion attack on Speaker of the House Nancy Pelosi's husband Paul. However, Biden didn't always seem to be such a pacifist.

Referring to Donald Trump on March 20, 2018, Joe Biden said, "They asked me if I'd like to debate this gentleman, and I said no. I said, if we were in high school, I'd take him behind the gym and beat the hell out of him."

Similarly, during a campaign stop on March 10, 2020, Joe Biden spoke with a Detroit auto plant worker named Jerry Wayne. When Wayne questioned Biden about his position on the Second Amendment, Biden responded by saying, "You're full of shit." Biden then proceeded to point his finger in Wayne's face, to which Wayne responded by saying "That is not OK, all right." Biden then replied, "Don't tell me that, pal, or I'm going to go outside with you."

"Seniors are getting the largest increase in their Social Security checks in ten years thanks to President Biden's leadership."

–White House tweet, November 1, 2022

That same day, one week before the 2022 midterm election, Biden echoed this claim during an address to a community center in Hallandale Beach, Florida, saying, "On my watch, for the first time in ten years, seniors are getting an increase in their Social Security checks."

After these claims were made, observers were quick to point out that under a law passed in 1972, Social Security benefits are adjusted every year based on a formula tied to inflation and that seniors had received increases in nearly each of the preceding ten years. For some reason, the Biden administration seems to make a lot of exaggerated claims and half-true statements. The White House later took down the tweet, noting that it "lacked context."

"Unfortunately, we have seen Mega-MAGA Republican officials who don't believe in the rule of law."

–White House Press Secretary Karine
Jean-Pierre, November 2, 2022

Jean-Pierre made this comment from the White House press room less than a week before the 2022 midterm election. By using the term *Mega-MAGA Republican* in her official capacity, the US Office of Special Counsel determined that she violated the Hatch Act.

The Hatch Act is a federal law passed in 1939 that limits certain political activities of federal employees. The law ensures that federal programs are administered in a nonpartisan fashion and protects federal employees from political coercion in the workplace. President Joe Biden introduced the term *Mega-MAGA* on October 21, 2022, as a derogatory reference toward former President Trump and his supporters. Fortunately for Jean-Pierre, and perhaps not surprisingly, the Office of Special Counsel decided not to pursue disciplinary action against her. She was, however, issued a warning letter.

"The Biden-Harris Administration lowered the deficit with the single largest one-year reduction in American history."

–White House tweet, November 22, 2022

In yet another example of a Biden administration half-truth, this claim is not all that it seems to be. The White House failed to note that the deficit hit record levels between 2020 and 2021 due to emergency spending by Congress in response to the COVID-19 pandemic. The deficit in fiscal year 2020 was $3.13 trillion and the deficit in fiscal year 2021 was $2.77 trillion. The White House was accurate in that as the pandemic waned, the deficit in fiscal year 2022 was $1.38 trillion, a decrease of nearly 50% from the previous year. However, it failed to mention that Biden's fiscal year 2022 deficit was still the fourth-largest budget deficit in US history. So deceptive was this statement that even the Democrat-friendly *Washington Post* gave Joe Biden a Bottomless Pinocchio rating after he repeated this misleading claim thirty times in ten months.

"Today, the White House and the Department of Energy (DOE) announced that the Biden-Harris administration has surpassed its goal to take 100 actions in 2022 to strengthen energy efficiency

standards for a range of appliances and equipment."

–Fact sheet issued by the White
House, December 19, 2022

As the Biden administration continues its relentless push toward a Green New Deal, it has declared war on despicable and objectional items including lightbulbs, air conditioners, furnaces, clothes washers and dryers, water heaters, and gas stoves.

In his righteous fight for energy efficiency, Biden doesn't seem to care that it will be the American people who will have to pay the bill for these changes. I'm reminded of a famous line President Ronald Reagan said on August 15, 1986: "Government's view of the economy could be summed up in a few short phrases: If it moves, tax it. If it keeps moving, regulate it. And if it stops moving, subsidize it." One can only wonder the point of saving the world if you destroy the people in it in the process.

"The President's very much looking forward to seeing for himself first-hand what the border security situation looks like, particularly in El Paso."

–White House National Security Council
spokesman John Kirby, January 6, 2023

Kirby had been asked by a White House correspondent if President Joe Biden was going to see a sanitized version of El Paso during his visit to the US Southern border. Meanwhile, large migrant camps in El Paso Texas were removed by the city's mayor, and a fleet of garbage trucks cleaned up those areas in the days and hours prior to Biden's visit in an obvious attempt to hide the severity of the problem and improve the optics for the President's visit.

Similar actions were taken to present an unrealistic impression prior to visits by Homeland Security Secretary Alejandro Mayorkas and Vice President Kamala Harris. Photos taken by El Paso native and Border Security Coalition President Irene Armendariz-Jackson showed the dramatic differences before and during Biden's visit.

When asked by reporters why the president didn't meet with any migrants during his visit, White House officials stated that there were no migrants available. What a coincidence, considering that according to the City of El Paso's website, an average of 900 migrants per day were entering the city at the time.

"Look, as you've heard us say before, we will not be doing any negotiation over the debt ceiling."

–White House Press Secretary Karine Jean-Pierre, January 23, 2023

On January 27, 2023, a group of twenty-four Republican Senators sent a letter to President Biden advising him that "…any increase in the debt ceiling must be accompanied by cuts in federal spending of an equal or greater amount as the debt ceiling increase, or meaningful structural reform in spending."

Ironically, in May 2011, when Joe Biden was vice president, he led White House negotiations with Congressional Republicans over the debt limit and deficit reduction. At that time, he even expressed his frustration when Republicans resisted negotiation saying, "How can you explain the fact that grown men and women are unwilling to budge up till now, and still some of them are still unwilling to budge, by taking an absolute position: my way or no way. That's not governing. That's no way to govern. You can't govern that way."

Fortunately, a compromise was eventually reached during that dispute. In fact, in 2012, Biden seemed pleased with his ability to successfully negotiate with Republicans when he mentioned during an appearance on NBC's *Meet the Press*, "I have had the great honor of spending hours and hours and hours, as you've covered my negotiating the debt limit and other things, with the leaders of the Republican Party."

In spite of the White House Press Secretary's comment to the contrary, on May 28, 2023, President Biden and Speaker of the House Kevin McCarthy reached a negotiated deal on the debt ceiling. Biden said at the time, "The agreement also represents a compromise, which means no one got everything they want. But that's the responsibility of governing."

> *"FBI Richmond assesses the increasingly observed interest of racially or ethnically motivated violent extremists (RMVEs) in radical-traditionalist Catholic (RTC) ideology almost certainly presents opportunities for threat mitigation through the exploration of new avenues for tripwire and source development."*
>
> –Memo from the FBI's Richmond
> Field Office, January 23, 2023

On February 8, 2023, news of the FBI's Richmond memo became public after a whistleblower named Kyle Seraphin revealed its existence in internal FBI systems. Soon thereafter, the House Judiciary Committee and its Select Subcommittee on the Weaponization of the Federal Government began an investigation into the rationale behind the memo.

On December 4, 2023, the committees released an interim report entitled, "The FBI's Breach of Religious Freedom: The Weaponization of Law Enforcement Against Catholic Americans." Among its findings, the interim report noted, "The documents received pursuant to the Committee's subpoena show there was no legitimate basis for the memorandum to insert federal law enforcement into Catholic houses of worship." It also noted, "The documents received pursuant to the Committee's subpoena show that the FBI singled out Americans who are pro-life, pro-family, and support the biological basis for sex and gender distinction as potential domestic terrorists." One day after the Richmond memo was revealed by the whistleblower, the FBI publicly rescinded the memo.

Salvatore Cordileone, Archbishop of the Archdiocese of San Francisco, summed up the current climate well when he said, "In our own Catholic Church, we're in a struggle about living our faith in a world that's become very secularized but secularized not in the sense of apart from religion, but with a value system that's hostile to some basic values that we have."

In my opinion, secularism has replaced religion on the Left. The Left often mocks religion and believes it is detrimental to society because it has been associated with historical conflict. They believe a secular world would be better. Based on what? When has the quality of life in a secular society ever been better? Certainly not in Nazi Germany, Communist Russia, or Communist China.

Belief in God and the practice of religion has brought peace around the world. Think of all the charity and goodwill for which religion is responsible. Faith and religion have pacified mankind. We look to it as a moral compass. Without it, we are lost, and we degrade into chaos and violence.

Today's media likes to focus on church scandals and individual failures rather than the collective good religion has brought to the world. How often does the news report on the amazing impact people make every day around the world helping their fellow man in the name of God?

The death of Mother Teresa occurred the same week as Princess Diana's death but received a fraction of the coverage. Why? Sure, Diana's death was unexpected and controversial. She was also perhaps the most photographed person of her generation. I don't mean to disparage Diana, whom I admired and whose death was a tragedy, but why didn't Mother Teresa's death get a similar amount of coverage? What does that say about our values? What do we truly care about? Which lifestyle do we admire more?

It says a lot not only about the decision by those in the media as to what they considered more salient that week but also about our modern society.

It takes a very special person to live a life like Mother Teresa's. Why did she do it? What inspired her? God and faith! Ask yourself, who do you want to be more like? Be honest. If you choose Diana, what does that say? Why don't we aspire to be more like Mother Teresa? Could the answer simply be because it is hard? Which lifestyle asks more of us?

This type of reflection can also be applied to modern American political philosophy. The Left, for example, promotes a message that the government will take care of you throughout your life. The Right, on the other hand, advocates the need for individuals to exercise personal responsibility.

Maintaining freedom is hard. Consider those who died defending our country. Religion and faith are also hard. We don't like to feel compelled to live by example, to constantly improve, to forgive our enemies, to practice charity, to help our neighbor, to go to church, to pray, etc. That's too difficult for many of us.

Our society today sends us the message that we never have anything to apologize for and we should never be made to feel guilty. In short, today's society has completely rejected the concept of shame.

Instead, our young people are taught by some today that none of that matters and that religion is a sham. They suggest that it is ok to reject all of the morals associated with the Judeo-Christian values that were once important to us because it is much easier to live that way.

As a result, many don't just simply make an individual choice to become agnostic or atheist; rather they come to express disdain for those who display the dedication and discipline it takes to remain faithful, leading to attacks on religion itself.

Between 2018 and 2023, attacks on churches nearly tripled. There have been many other despicable acts in recent years as well. Take, for example, a 1987 photograph taken by an American "artist" called *Piss Christ*. This photograph featured a plastic crucifix submerged in the "artist's" urine. The "artwork" won awards and was sponsored by The National Endowment for the Arts, a US government agency.

Many believe examples like this are subtle attacks on our society that are intended to slowly drag all of us down with those responsible so we may share in their misery and contempt for God and our fellow man.

Like those who attack religion, those who reject American values are not content with allowing the rest of us to maintain our history and our traditions. Instead, they are committed to destroying American institutions in a similar way.

We Americans have an important choice to make. Will we sit back and idly watch our society continue to degrade at the alarming pace we have witnessed in recent years, or are American principles and values worth fighting for?

Our young people are often taught in public schools today to focus on our country's flaws and reject the things that have made America exceptional. The Left 'cancels' anyone who disagrees with them, and they have gradually and discretely taken control over critical institutions like academia, the media, and Big Tech. This has enabled them to exert greater control over our information and our language. They claim their actions are in the name of science, yet they believe that strict adherence to disciplines like biology promotes bigotry.

In the name of science, the Left has justified a shift toward authoritarianism. The Left is trying to dictate the future of the US by controlling access to things like college, medical school, and law school, as well as employment in Big Tech, academia, the media, and the federal bureaucracy.

In the public and private sectors alike, hiring and other important decisions today are heavily influenced by factors like race, gender, and sexual orientation. The Left's ideology has clearly changed significantly over the last sixty years from one that believed in equality and rejected preferential treatment of one demographic over another to one that today specifically advocates for laws and policies that promote certain races and persuasions over others. Ironically, sixty years ago, the Left chose an ordained reverend to champion their cause. Given the dramatic shift in the Left's ideology in recent years, that's not likely to occur again any time soon.

> *"As Secretary of the Navy, I can tell you that I have made climate one of my top priorities since the first day I came into office."*
>
> –Secretary of the Navy Carlos Del Toro, March 1, 2023

Del Toro made this statement as the Biden administration prepared to release a $842 billion proposed defense budget, the highest ever. However, this budget represents only a 3% increase in defense spending while Biden has proposed an increase of 14% for domestic priorities.

MEMBERS OF THE CABINET AND THE BUREAUCRACY

On March 22, 2023, *The Wall Street Journal* editorial board wrote about "Joe Biden's Weak Defense," noting, "This is a defense cut, and not from an epiphany of fiscal restraint. Mr. Biden is choosing to put welfare entitlements over national security...The Biden Pentagon wants to retire ships prematurely, such as the cruiser USS Vicksburg, which taxpayers have spent hundreds of millions of dollars to upgrade for longer service."

CBS News' *60 Minutes* produced a report about the state of the US Navy on March 19, 2023. In the story, it was noted that in the early 2000s, China's navy had approximately thirty-seven vessels. Today, China has increased that number to 350 vessels, and it is expected to have approximately 440 ships by 2030.

For several years, the US Navy has had a goal of 355 ships. However, for the third year in a row, Biden's defense budget called for a reduction in ships. At the time of Del Toro's comment, the US Navy had a total of 298 ships, but Biden's 2024 fiscal year budget proposal called for the construction of only nine new ships while simultaneously decommissioning eleven ships for a net decrease of two ships. As Joe Biden said on March 22, 2023, "My dad used to have an expression... He'd say, don't tell me what you value. Show me your budget, I'll tell you what you value."

"What we are going to promise is that we are going to do this. We're going to move forward with a, with this kind of system, this immigration system...We're gonna move forward and do it in a humane way. We're gonna do it in a safe way and we're going to do it in the way that moves us forward. And so, what we have been seeing, what we have been dealing with, again, is trying to fix the damage that the last administration do, did. What we have done is we have opened the path to, we have opened the path

to make sure that people have a way to get, you know, to come through and to do it in a legal pathway."

–White House Press Secretary Karine Jean-Pierre, March 10, 2023

Am I the only one who sometimes thinks that Karine Jean-Pierre and Kamala Harris are competing for an award for Best Word Salad?

"So, we're, we're hopeful that, you know, we can all learn from what China is doing."

–Secretary of Energy Jennifer Granholm, March 10, 2023

Granholm had been asked how we should hold China and ourselves accountable for the damage being done to the world when it comes to climate change. Granholm apparently forgot that China had quadrupled its number of coal power plants between 2021 and 2022, adding the equivalent of two new coal power plants per week.

"This attack on our books, you know, from the party that preaches freedom of speech is banning books…I have confidence in our educators and our parents to communicate what's right for our students. We don't need state governments banning books."

–Secretary of Education Miguel Cardona, March 16, 2023

What Cardona calls "banning books" is not actually a ban on any books, and he knows it. He was referencing a bill under consideration in Florida that simply attempted to stop books containing inappropriate material, including pornography, from being placed in schools. One has to wonder how any reasonable adult would oppose such a law. If they do, they should explain their argument in honest terms instead of resorting to disingenuous claims like "banning books."

"Our hearts go out to the trans community as they are under attack right now."

–White House Press Secretary Karine
Jean-Pierre, March 30, 2023

One could be forgiven for assuming a comment like this must have been made on the heels of an attack on transgender victims. However, this comment was made just three days after a trans person killed three nine-year-olds and three adult workers at a Christian school in Nashville, Tennessee, on March 27, 2023.

On the same day as Jean-Pierre's statement, Joe Biden did not try to heal the nation's wounds by visiting Nashville to console the grieving parents. No, not Joe. Instead, he decided to demonstrate an astonishing lack of compassion for the victim's families by going out of his way to express his support for the transgender community by declaring March 31 as Transgender Day of Visibility.

Of course, Biden has the right to express his support for this community just like anyone else, but as President, this proclamation demonstrates extremely poor timing and insensitivity to the victims' families. For example, Biden's proclamation noted, "Transgender Americans shape our nation's soul...As kids, they deserve what every child deserves: the chance to learn in safe and supportive schools..."

Then, as if to rub salt in the wounded hearts of the families who lost loved ones at the Nashville school massacre, Jean-Pierre said on April 6, 2023 (ten days after the shooting) "LGBTQI+ kids are resilient.

They are fierce. They fight back. They're not going anywhere, and we have their backs."

At best, Jean-Pierre's comments and Biden's proclamation show poor judgment by an administration that promised to unite the country, and at worst, they serve as a de facto endorsement of the actions taken by the transgender murderer. Soon after the school massacre, the public learned that the assailant had left behind a personal manifesto. In spite of widespread demands to publicly release the content of the manifesto, the police have not done so. On November 6, 2023, portions of the manifesto were leaked and published online.

"For all this talk of chaos. I just didn't see it. Not from my perch."

–White House National Security Council
spokesman John Kirby, April 6, 2023

Kirby was referring to the frenzied US withdrawal from Afghanistan in August 2021. In response to a classified interagency assessment of the withdrawal from Afghanistan that was shared with select committees in Congress earlier that day, Kirby addressed the White House Press Corps to provide "our perspective on the withdrawal." He went on to say, "While it was always the president's intent to end that war, it is also undeniable that decisions made and the lack of planning done by the previous administration significantly limited options available to him…Despite having his options curtailed, President Biden led a deliberate, rigorous, and inclusive decision-making process that was responsive to facts on the ground. He focused keenly on the need for proper planning."

The idea that President Biden had carefully planned the withdrawal would be laughable if it wasn't so infuriating. In addition to the Afghan civilians who ran alongside a US Air Force cargo plane and several who clung to its side as it took off from Kabul Airport only to fall to their deaths moments later, there was the devastating attack at Kabul Airport's Abbey Gate, which killed thirteen US service members and 170 Afghan civilians.

Shana Chappel, the mother of late Marine Lance Corporal Kareem Nikoui, who was killed at Abbey Gate, said it well. "What happened in Kabul was preventable, avoidable, and should never have happened... When you know you're guilty of doing something wrong, you don't talk about it, and if you get caught you blame someone else. That's exactly what Biden has done for two years."

On March 8, 2023, Marine Corps Sergeant Tyler Vargas-Andrews provided emotional testimony before the House Foreign Affairs Committee's hearing on the withdrawal from Afghanistan. Sergent Vargas-Andrews was a Marine sniper assigned to provide security at Kabul Airport's Abbey Gate on August 26, 2021. After receiving intelligence about a looming threat of an improvised explosive device, which included a detailed description of the bomber, Sergeant Vargas-Andrews spotted the suspect and requested authority to shoot him. His request was denied. A short time later, the blast occurred.

Sergeant Vargas-Andrews, who lost an arm, a leg, and a kidney in the attack and has since undergone forty-four surgeries, told the House Committee members, "Over the communication network we passed that there was a potential threat and an IED attack imminent. This was as serious as it could get. I requested engagement authority while my team leader was ready on the M110 semi-automatic sniper system. The response: leadership did not have the engagement authority for us. Do not engage."

Many attribute this indecision to the fact that the withdrawal operation was under the command of the State Department rather than the Defense Department. Vargas-Andrews continued, "Operations had briefly halted but then started again. Plain and simple, we were ignored. Our expertise was disregarded. No one was held accountable for our safety…The withdrawal was a catastrophe, in my opinion, and there was an inexcusable lack of accountability and negligence. The eleven Marines, one Sailor and one Soldier that were murdered that day have not been answered for."

After the last US military personnel left Afghanistan on August 31, 2021, Joe Biden delivered an address from the White House, saying "In April, I made the decision to end this war. As part of that decision, we set the date of August 31 for American troops to withdraw…I take responsibility for the decision. Now, some say we should have started mass evacuations sooner and 'Couldn't this have been done—have been done in a more orderly manner?' I respectfully disagree."

During the speech, Biden also described the mission to withdraw the US from Afghanistan as an "extraordinary success." Christy Shamblin, mother-in-law of late Marine Sergeant Nicole Gee, who was killed at Abbey Gate, summarized the situation well when she said, "When our leaders, including the Secretary of Defense and our commander-in-chief, called this evacuation a success, as if there should be celebration, it is like a knife in the heart for our families and for the people who came back and for every service member that served over this twenty-year war."

"Show me a school that I shut down and show me a factory that I shut down."

–Former Director of the National Institute
of Allergy and Infectious Diseases Dr.
Anthony Fauci, April 25, 2023

Although Dr. Fauci acknowledged that "something clearly went wrong" during the nation's response to COVID-19, he sternly denied any responsibility for the negative consequences closures had on education and the economy. His denunciation angered many Americans because government officials across the country decided to close schools and businesses during the pandemic based on recommendations from Dr. Fauci.

For example, on July 15, 2020, Dr. Fauci said, "As we try to proceed, we need to really take seriously the issue of wearing masks all the time and not congregating in bars. I think we can stop that by just closing them because they are certainly an important mechanism of this spread."

In a classic bureaucratic blame game, government officials point to scientific experts, including Fauci, for their decisions to close schools and businesses while Fauci insists that because he didn't physically lock the doors himself, he is not responsible for one of the biggest policy failures in our nation's history.

"When it comes to illegal immigration, you've seen it come down by more than 90%."

–White House Press Secretary Karine Jean-Pierre, May 1, 2023

In fact, the Biden administration has set one record after another when it comes to illegal immigration. In fiscal year 2021, illegal immigration into the United States hit a record of approximately 1.96 million, only to be surpassed by another record in fiscal year 2022 with 2.38 illegal immigrants entering the US.

At the time of Jean-Pierre's comment, the US was on pace to set yet another record in fiscal year 2023. One issue that often gets overlooked in the immigration data is the number of "known gotaways." These are illegal immigrants who were known to have crossed our border but were not directly encountered by US Customs and Border Protection.

From the Biden administration's open border policy, one must conclude that anyone unwilling to voluntarily surrender to Border Patrol agents must have something serious to hide. During the first three years of the Biden administration, US Customs and Border Protection confirmed over 1.7 million "known gotaways" at the Southwest border.

These are dangerous individuals. Kinney County Texas Sheriff Brad Coe described the dangers his department faced from "known gotaways" during 2023 when he said, "I've got six full-time deputies. Those guys were involved in over 260 high-speed pursuits just for that year."

House Committee on Homeland Security Chairman Mark Green provided another sobering description of the problem. "I fear the extent of the threat posed by the record number of gotaways on Secretary Mayorkas' watch won't be clear until it is too late. The number of individuals apprehended illegally crossing the Southwest border and found to be on the terrorist watchlist has increased 2,500% from fiscal years 2017-2020 to fiscal year 2023. And those are only who we've caught. How many others have slipped by as Border Patrol agents have increasingly been pulled off the line to process illegal aliens crossing the border? How many violent criminals and gang members are now at large in our communities? Border security is national security, and right now, the border is not secure."

"It's dangerous and unacceptable because you're actually putting a lot of pressure on these states and local areas."

–White House Press Secretary Karine
Jean-Pierre, June 5, 2023

Jean-Pierre made this comment during a White House press conference criticizing several border state governors for sending illegal immigrants to Democrat-led states and cities. Her comment was met with widespread ridicule for its failure to acknowledge how the Biden administration's decision to allow six million illegal immigrants into the US has created unprecedented pressure and stress on border states.

"We were as forthcoming as we should have been."

–White House National Security Council
spokesman John Kirby, June 12, 2023

On June 8, 2023, Kirby was asked to comment about an article in *The Wall Street Journal* reporting on an agreement between China and Cuba that would allow a Chinese signals and electronic intelligence station to be built in Cuba in exchange for billions of dollars.

Kirby, a retired Navy Rear Admiral, responded at the time by saying, "I've seen that press report. It's not accurate." Four days later, Kirby reversed his message and made the statement above. Why he didn't choose to use the time-honored response of "no comment" when originally asked about the story is still a mystery. Needless to say, however, Kirby clearly undermined his own credibility and that of the Biden administration by blatantly lying to the American people.

"It really does not reflect the event that we hosted to celebrate the LGBTQ+ families."

–White House Press Secretary Karine
Jean-Pierre, June 13, 2023

Jean-Pierre was referring to the behavior of a transgender activist who had recently attended a White House picnic. The activist posted a Tik-Tok video showing her on the White House lawn with her dress pulled down and her hands over her bare breasts. Jean-Pierre confirmed that the activist would not be invited to future events at the White House.

> *"President Biden and Vice President Harris came into office determined to rebuild our economy from the middle out and the bottom up, not the top down—and that strategy is working."*
>
> –Public statement Issued by the
> White House, June 28, 2023

On the same day as this press release, President Biden told a crowd in Auburn, Maine, "I'm here to talk to you about what we're doing to bring manufacturing back to America, about our progress in building an economy from the middle out and the bottom up, not the top down." Interestingly, also on the very same day during a moderated conversation on reproduction, Vice President Harris said, "Most Americans are a $400 unexpected expense away from bankruptcy." Apparently, someone didn't get the message of the day.

> *"I'm really glad you asked that question…Our policies, whether they're diversity, inclusion, and equity or whether they're about transgender individuals…or whether it's about female service members, one in five, or female family members being able to count on the kinds of healthcare and reproductive care specifically that they need to serve, that is a foundational, sacred obligation of military leaders."*
>
> –White House National Security Council
> spokesman John Kirby, July 17, 2023

Admiral Kirby made this statement in response to a reporter who asked, "The administration has been critical of Senator Tuberville with his holds on military promotions because of social policy and saying that he is harming military readiness. On the flip side of that impasse, and this is something that Republican lawmakers have raised, why is the new DOD policy on abortion critical to military readiness?"

Apparently, according to Kirby, the US Department of Defense has a "foundational, sacred obligation" to provide abortion services. I always thought the DOD's mission was to protect America. Who knew?

"These borrowers are owed this relief."

–White House Press Secretary Karine
Jean-Pierre, July 18, 2023

Jean-Pierre was referring to a $39 billion student-loan-debt-relief package announced by the White House on June 30, 2023, earmarked for approximately 800,000 student loan borrowers. That same day, the United States Supreme Court ruled in a six-to-three vote that the Biden administration had overstepped its authority when it announced an earlier plan that would have canceled approximately $400 billion in student loan debt.

In spite of the court's ruling, Joe Biden was undeterred and immediately announced a new plan to forgive student loan debt. Critics of Biden's plan were quick to point out that the student debtors knowingly and willingly borrowed this money. In doing so, they entered into a legally binding contract to repay their loan.

Joe Biden is now pushing forward a plan that would eliminate these obligations. Such a policy is clearly unfair to the taxpayers who would pay for this debt forgiveness, including many who paid for college without incurring loan debt, many who already paid off their student loan debt, and many who never even went to college. Republicans in Congress explained that Biden's student loan forgiveness plan was little more than a poorly disguised attempt to buy support from younger voters.

> *"The President has done more to secure the border and to deal with this issue of immigration than anybody else. He really has."*
>
> –White House Press Secretary Karine Jean-Pierre, August 31, 2023

What does it say about a person who is comfortable telling such a bold lie directly to the American people and why is such disrespect now considered acceptable?

> *"President Biden has brought honesty and integrity back to the Oval Office."*
>
> –Deputy White House Press Secretary Andrew Bates, August 31, 2023

If this book makes anything clear, it should be the fact that this comment is utterly ridiculous.

> *"When someone tells you Americans don't like Bidenomics, it's false."*
>
> –Chairman of the Council of Economic Advisors Jared Bernstein, September 3, 2023

According to a *Wall Street Journal* poll conducted between August 24-30, 2021, 59% of Americans disapprove of Joe Biden's handling of the economy. Apparently, 59% of Americans are liars.

"It's time for the media to ramp up its scrutiny of House Republicans for opening an impeachment inquiry based on lies. [As Republicans] choose to move forward with impeachment, it is the responsibility of the independent press to treat their claims with the appropriate scrutiny."

–Special Assistant to the President
Ian Sams, September 12, 2023

Sams wrote this statement in a memo to editorial leaders at US news organizations. Liberal bias in the media has been exposed for years now but rarely has a member of the White House staff called for the "independent press" to go after Republicans in such an overt way.

One of the hallmarks of our society is the existence of a free press. Having enshrined this concept in the First Amendment to the US Constitution, Americans have historically trusted the press to be both independent and fair. In fact, one of the duties of the Fourth Estate has always been to serve as a watchdog over the power of the government.

Unfortunately, modern media outlets have demonstrated bias for the Left with increasing frequency. The media has now committed the cardinal sin of surrendering their sacred mission to seek the truth on behalf of the American people and have sadly morphed into mere institutions of political advocacy.

We should all recognize how dangerous this is for our country's future. Many "journalists" in recent years have publicly expressed support for this new mission and have rejected any notion that the media bears a responsibility to cover both sides of a story. This perspective has sadly even found a home in the curricula of schools of journalism around the country. One can only wonder about the long-term impact this dramatic change in American culture will have. The altruistic purpose of a once respected and critical industry has now been replaced with partisan zealotry.

"I am not worried about the reserve levels at all."

–Secretary of Energy Jennifer
Granholm, September 14, 2023

Granholm made this comment during a House Science, Space, and Technology Committee hearing when she was questioned about the US Strategic Petroleum Reserve (SPR), which was at its lowest level since August 1983.

Congress established the SPR in 1975 after Arab members of the Organization of Petroleum Exporting Countries (OPEC) imposed an oil embargo against the United States following the Yom Kippur War two years earlier. The SPR was created to offset severe reductions to the US oil supply in the future such as those incurred in times of war or natural disaster.

After taking office in January 2021, Joe Biden effectively declared war on US energy. Almost immediately he canceled the Keystone XL pipeline, put a halt to new drilling leases on public lands, and ended US energy independence established under President Trump. These policies, along with trillions of dollars in reckless spending bills, caused a massive spike in oil prices as well as the overall rate of inflation.

In typical Biden style, however, he refused to take any responsibility for the crisis. Instead, he blamed Russia's invasion of Ukraine as well as oil company profits for the record-high price of gasoline in the US.

Making matters even worse was Biden's reaction to the crisis. On November 23, 2021, the White House announced that the Department of Energy would release 50 million barrels of oil from the SPR in an attempt to lower gas prices. Then on April 21, 2022, the White House proudly announced the largest-ever release of oil from the SPR. Over the next six months, the Department of Energy planned to release one million barrels of oil per day for a total of 180 million barrels.

By its own admission in a Fact Sheet released on July 26, 2022, the White House once again proudly proclaimed, "There is no precedent for this level of drawdown."

It is important to clarify what exactly the White House means when they use the term *release*. Americans might naturally assume that oil from the SPR is automatically made available to US consumers, but that isn't true. Instead, it is sold on the international market. The hope is that adding millions of barrels to the market will increase supply enough that it will lead to lower prices for oil.

Adding insult to injury, the Biden administration sold much of this oil to our leading adversary, China. In total, the Biden Administration reduced the SPR by 40% in 2022, leaving the country in a very vulnerable position. With the ever-present risk of a natural disaster and growing tensions around the world, Biden chose to sacrifice our emergency oil supply in an effort to lower the price of a gallon of gasoline by a few cents prior to the 2022 midterm election.

The use of the SPR as a political tool caused many pundits to conclude that Joe Biden was playing with fire and putting our national security at risk. In January 2023, a Republican-led bill passed the House of Representatives that prohibited future oil sales from the SPR to China and allowed future use of the SPR only when there is a "severe energy supply disruption." However, according to *Politico*, the bill stalled in the Democratic-controlled Senate, and President Biden promised to veto it if it reached his desk.

"It's not a crime to question an election."

–Attorney General Merrick Garland,
September 20, 2023

Garland made this statement during his testimony before the House Judiciary Committee. On August 14, 2023, former President Donald Trump and eighteen others were indicted by a Georgia Grand Jury on forty-one criminal counts. The case, which was brought by Fulton County District Attorney Fani Willis, charged Trump and the others with racketeering, which is a charge typically used against members of organized crime organizations and has a potential penalty of up to twenty years in prison.

According to the indictment, "Trump and the other defendants charged in this indictment refused to accept that Trump lost, and they knowingly and willfully joined a conspiracy to unlawfully change the outcome of the election in favor of Trump." Despite Garland's assurance, Trump's indictment in Georgia is viewed by many as a politically motivated prosecution based on the fact that Trump dared to question the 2020 election results.

"The Middle East region is quieter today than it has been in two decades."

–US National Security Advisor Jake
Sullivan, September 29, 2023

Eight days following Sullivan's assurance, Hamas launched a terrorist attack on Israel. In the initial attack, which many referred to as Israel's 9/11, more than 1,200 were killed and approximately 150 were taken hostage. The surprise nature of the attack led many to suggest almost immediately that there had been a major failure by the US and Israeli intelligence services.

"At some point, maybe, there needs to be a formal deprogramming of the cult members."

—Former Secretary of State Hillary
Clinton, October 5, 2023

Clinton was referring to supporters of Donald Trump and the Make America Great Again agenda. With charming comments like this, is it any wonder why she lost the presidential election in 2016?

"And I'm not calling on you today."

—White House Press Secretary Karine
Jean-Pierre, October 11, 2023

Jean-Pierre was responding to *New York Post* reporter Steven Nelson, who said to her during a press conference, "You haven't called on me in two seasons, Karine."

Jean-Pierre has a bad habit of avoiding questions from people and organizations she doesn't like. On March 20, 2023, *Today News Africa* reporter Simon Ateba criticized Jean-Pierre for not calling on him for seven months. Not only is Jean-Pierre disparaging these members of the press by not calling on them, but she appears to be doing so for either personal or political reasons. Steven Nelson said it well when he told her, "You should be ashamed of that. That shows disrespect to a free and independent media."

"So, a couple of things. Look, we have not seen any credible threats. I know there's always questions about credible threats and so I just want to make sure that that's out there. But look, Muslim and those perceived to be Muslim have endured a disproportionate number of hate-fueled attacks and certainly President

Biden understands that many of our Muslim, Arab-American, and Palestinian-American loved ones and neighbors are worried about the hate being directed at their communities. And that is something you have heard the president speak to in his address just last Thursday, and so one of the things the president has done is direct his team, Homeland Security Team, to prioritize prevention and disruption of any emerging threats that could harm the Jewish, the Muslim, Arab-Americans or any other community. And that is something that the president has sought to do since day one. As you know, the president ran on protecting communities, obviously, but bringing people together, protecting the soul of the nation. And so, that is something that the president takes very very seriously and we're going to continue to denounce any sort of hate toward any American here and so that's what we're going to continue to be steadfast on. Again, he has advised, directed, his Homeland Security Team to make sure that they're on top of this."

–White House Press Secretary Karine
Jean-Pierre, October 23, 2023

This is a particularly long quote, but I wanted to share Jean-Pierre's answer in its entirety. During a press conference, Jean-Pierre was asked the following question: "What is the level of concern right now about the potential rise in antisemitism in light of everything that's going on in Israel?"

For some reason, the Biden administration has a hard time speaking about antisemitism by itself. They always feel the need to tie it in with Islamophobia. The same people who refused to use the phrase "All Lives Matter" because it diminished their focus on "Black Lives

Matter" cannot bring themselves to speak about antisemitism without lumping it in with other examples of hatred.

According to the Anti-Defamation League, antisemitism increased by 400% in the weeks following the October 7, 2023, Hamas attack on Israel. According to FBI Director Christopher Wray, Jews comprise only 2.4% of the population in the US but make up approximately 60% of all religion-based hate crimes.

In the wake of the renewed hostilities in Israel, protests against Jews erupted across the US and around the world. In Australia, mobs chanted "Gas the Jews," and on Ivy League campuses in the US, support for Hamas and hatred toward Jews was on full display as students called for a global intifada as they protested against Israel. Others ripped down posters of Israelis and Americans held hostage by Hamas, and some posted threats to Jewish students online.

At a time when antisemitism was perhaps at its highest level since World War II, how did the Biden administration respond to this crisis? On November 1, 2023, the White House announced the establishment of the first-ever National Strategy to Counter Islamophobia. You read that right. Whatever the prevailing problem of the day, you can count on the Biden/Harris administration to pour resources into something else. I suspect if shipments of Coca-Cola were found laced with poison, the Biden administration would immediately call for a public boycott of Pepsi.

"I think it was President Reagan who said, 'We're from the government. We're here to help.'"

–Secretary of Education Miguel Cardona, November 27, 2023

Cardona made this comment to an audience at the Western Governors' Association winter meeting. He was referencing cooperation between state and federal governments around education funding.

Unfortunately, Cardona's use of Reagan's famous quote was badly misunderstood. Reagan's actual quote was, "The nine most terrifying words in the English language are 'I'm from the government and I'm here to help.'" The Ronald Reagan Presidential Foundation and Institute described the meaning behind his comment well: "Reagan refers to how the government tends to be inefficient to such a degree that instead of helping, it often causes harm instead. This view expresses the need for a more diminutive form of government where an individual or organization can complete an activity more effectively than the whole government."

"I recognize I could have done a better job ensuring the public was appropriately informed...I take full responsibility for my decisions about disclosure."

–Secretary of Defense Lloyd
Austin, January 6, 2024

On January 1, 2024, Austin was admitted to Walter Reed National Military Medical Center following complications from an elective procedure on December 22, 2023. He spent four days in the hospital's intensive care unit.

Austin delegated power to the Deputy Secretary of Defense, Kathleen Hicks, but she was on vacation in Puerto Rico at the time, and reports indicated that she was not informed of the Secretary's hospitalization. Austin also failed to notify the President, the National Security Council, and Congress that he was in the hospital. The White House and Deputy Secretary of Defense Hicks were finally informed of Austin's hospitalization on January 4, 2024.

Congress was notified the following day, just minutes before the news went public. Making matters worse, during his hospitalization the Pentagon reportedly told senior Defense officials that Austin was working from home that week. It was also later learned that the "elective procedure" Austin had on December 22 was prostate cancer surgery.

It's interesting to see that in his public statement, Austin accepted full responsibility for the failure to disclose his hospitalization. While that is an appropriate response, it is also an easy one when you remember that in the Biden administration, no one is ever held responsible for their mistakes.

On Biden's inauguration day, White House Press Secretary Jen Psaki told the press that the Biden Administration planned to "bring transparency and truth back to the government to share the truth even when it's hard to hear." The Austin debacle is a particularly troubling episode for an administration that promised to be so transparent.

> *"One of the most important ways that President Biden has added real fairness to the tax code is by providing the Internal Revenue Service (IRS) with the resources they need to reduce the tax gap and improve service delivery for taxpayers."*
>
> –Public statement issued by the
> White House, February 8, 2024

In May 2021, Joe Biden announced plans to double the size of the Internal Revenue Service by hiring an additional 87,000 employees and raising its budget by $80 billion over the next decade. I believe Ronald Reagan summed up one of the key differences between the two political parties well when he said, "Republicans believe every day is the Fourth of July, but the Democrats believe every day is April 15."

"I mean, if Russia has the ability to wage a war illegally and

invade another country, they ought to find the effort to be respon-
sible on the climate issue...Russia is one of the largest emitters in
the world. If Russia wanted to show good faith, they could go out
and announce what their reductions are going to be and make a
greater effort to reduce emissions. Maybe that would open up the
door for people to feel better about what Russia is choosing to do
at this point in time."

–US Special Presidential Envoy for
Climate John Kerry, March 6, 2024

As he stepped down from his role as climate czar, Kerry expressed his frustration with Russia's lack of commitment to climate change. Listeners were shocked, however, when Kerry seemed to imply that "people would feel better" about Russia's invasion of Ukraine if they made greater efforts to reduce their emissions levels.

" 'A bloodbath.' What would you say if you saw this in another
country?"

–Former Secretary of State Hillary
Clinton, March 18, 2024, in an X post

Clinton was referring to a comment made by Donald Trump, which included the use of the term *bloodbath*. As usual, however, Clinton and numerous other Democrats knowingly and falsely accused Trump of calling for political violence if he were to lose the 2024 election, intentionally distorting Trump's actual comment.

Here is what Trump actually said: "Let me tell you something, to China, if you're listening, President Xi, and you and I are friends, but he understands the way I deal. Those big monster car-manufacturing plants that you're building in Mexico right now, and you think you're going to get that, you're going to not hire Americans and you're going to sell the cars to us. Now, we're going to put a 100% tariff on every single car that comes across the line, and you're not going to be able to sell those guys if I get elected. Now, if I don't get elected, it's going to be a bloodbath for the whole…That's going to be the least of it. It's going to be a bloodbath for the country."

Democrats can always be counted on to never let the truth get in the way of their argument.

> *"And finally, I know there's a lot, a lot of interest in reports from the Middle East overnight, and we understand that. We get that. I'm going to say it now, though I know you all will, will certainly ask me about it, that we do not have any comment on the reports at this time."*
>
> –White House Press Secretary Karine Jean-Pierre, April 19, 2024

Jean-Pierre was referring to a strike by Israel against Iran in retaliation for an attack Iran had launched on Israel on April 14, 2024. Although the retaliatory strike by Israel had occurred the night before her press conference, Jean-Pierre didn't feel it was necessary to provide any updates or information to the press corps.

Her dereliction prompted one reporter to ask, "Why is it that you don't have any comment at this time? It's been several hours since the reported strike. Certainly, that's enough time for the administration to investigate and come up with something to say."

Jean-Pierre's lack of engagement that day was typical behavior for her. She seems to have a few standard responses to most questions she is asked. She frequently refers questions to other offices, avoids answering a question by saying she has already been "very clear" about that issue in the past, and, as in this instance, she often refuses to answer questions on a wide variety of subjects by saying things like "I can't speak to that."

This not only projects incompetence but outright disrespect for the American people to whom she answers. Through our representatives in the press, we have a right to know what the president and his administration think about critical issues facing our country.

Chapter 6

Members of the US Senate

"If you ever live in a country run by a committee, be on the committee."

–William Sumner

"Hell, I might be president now if it weren't for the fact I said I had an uncle who was a coal miner. Turns out I didn't have anybody in the coal mines. I tried that crap. It didn't work."

–Senator Joe Biden, July 28, 2004

Biden made this remark during an interview on *The Daily Show with John Stewart*. It turns out there was a little more to Biden's lie than just a mistaken description of his family tree. He was referring to a statement he made at the Iowa State Fair during his first campaign for president in 1987.

At the time, Biden said, "Why is it that Joe Biden is the first in his family ever to go to a university? Is it because they didn't work hard, my ancestors, who worked in the coal mines of Northeast Pennsylvania and would come up after twelve hours and play football for four hours?"

What he didn't say during the *Daily Show* interview was that he had plagiarized this line from British politician Neil Kinnock. After revelations were made about repeated acts of plagiarism by Biden, he suspended his campaign for president.

Ironically, on August 8, 2019, speaking once again at the Iowa State

Fair, this time during his third campaign for president, Biden famously said, "We choose truth over facts"—which apparently makes sense in his mind.

> *"Well, they can call it whatever they want. Romney didn't win, did he?"*

–Senate Majority Leader Harry
Reid, March 31, 2015

In an old-fashioned act of mudslinging, Reid made a speech on the Senate floor on August 2, 2012, saying, "When we're talking about trust, we need no look no further than the person that Mitt Romney wants to, my friend the Republican Leader wants to be President of the United States. He's refused to release his tax returns, as we know. So, the word's out that he hasn't paid any taxes for ten years. Let him prove that he has paid taxes because he hasn't."

After announcing his retirement, Reid was asked by CNN's Dana Bash if his methods toward then-presidential candidate Mitt Romney in 2012 were reminiscent of McCarthyism. Reid responded with the statement above, proving that to him, trust apparently isn't as important as winning in politics.

> *"Let me tell you, you take on the intelligence community, they have six ways from Sunday to get back at you."*

–Senate Minority Leader Chuck
Schumer, January 3, 2017

Schumer was referring to President-elect Donald Trump's skepticism about the intelligence community's claim that Russia had engaged in a hacking plot to interfere with the 2016 presidential election.

Schumer's ominous warning to Trump reinforced a belief held by many Americans in a "deep state." According to the *Oxford Languages*, a *deep state* is defined as a body of people, typically influential members of government agencies or the military, believed to be involved in the secret manipulation or control of government policy.

"I know in my heart that nothing I have done as a senator, nothing has brought dishonor on this institution."

–Senator Al Franken, December 7, 2017

On January 2, 2018, Franken left the Senate following his resignation. In the preceding weeks, he had been accused by half a dozen women of groping or forcibly trying to kiss them. The most damaging evidence came when a radio broadcaster named Leeann Tweeden released a photo of Franklin pretending to grope her while she slept aboard a C-17 cargo plane flying back from Afghanistan during a USO tour in 2006.

"This is about the closest I'll probably ever have in my life to an 'I am Spartacus' moment."

–Senator Corey Booker, September 6, 2018

Booker made this comment during the Senate Judiciary Committee's confirmation hearing on Judge Brett Kavanaugh's nomination to the US Supreme Court. "Spartacus" refers to the title role played by actor Kirk Douglas in a 1960 Oscar-winning movie about the leader of a slave revolt against the Roman Empire.

Booker was referring to the fact that he had publicly leaked documents written by Kavanaugh that were previously categorized as confidential by the Judiciary Committee. He apparently did not know that the documents in question had subsequently been declassified and that they included no controversial information. He made the statement after he was criticized for his leak by Senator John Cornyn, who said it was grounds for expulsion from the US Senate, to which Booker replied, "Bring the charges."

One can't help but wonder if Booker had recently seen the movie *Spartacus* and was anxious for an opportunity to use the classic line himself. Too bad his attempt at melodrama fell flat.

> *"Are you aware that there's a perception that, that ICE is administering its power in a way that is causing fear and intimidation, particularly among immigrants and specifically among immigrants coming from Mexico and Central America?"*

> –Senator Kamala Harris, November 15, 2018

Harris was questioning President Trump's nominee to lead Immigration and Customs Enforcement (ICE), Ronald Vitiello, during his confirmation hearing before the Senate Committee on Homeland Security and Government Affairs.

Moments earlier, she had asked Vitiello why the Ku Klux Klan would be called a domestic terrorist group. He responded by saying, "Because they tried to use fear and force to change the political environment." Harris then asked, "And what was the motivation for the use of fear and force?" Vitiello responded, "It was based on race and ethnicity." Harris agreed saying, "Right. Are you aware of the perception of many about how the power and the discretion at ICE is being used to enforce the laws and do you see any parallels?"

Harris' comparison between ICE and the Ku Klux Klan was widely

MEMBERS OF THE US SENATE

criticized. On April 4, 2019, President Trump withdrew Vitiello's nomination as Director of ICE.

> *"I want to tell you, Justice Kavanaugh and Justice Gorsuch, you have unleashed a whirlwind, and you will pay the price. You won't know what hit you if you go forward with these awful decisions."*

–Senate Minority Leader Chuck
Schumer, March 4, 2020

Schumer delivered this inappropriate and disgusting comment while addressing a pro-abortion rally outside of the US Supreme Court while a case was being argued inside. The case, *June Medical Services, LLC v. Russo,* involved a Louisiana state law that required abortion providers to have admitting privileges at local hospitals.

Schumer's comment was met with a rare public rebuke by Chief Justice John Roberts, who wrote, "Justices know that criticism comes with the territory, but threatening statements of this sort from the highest levels of government are not only inappropriate, they are dangerous. All members of the Court will continue to do their job, without fear or favor from whatever quarter." Schumer later denied that he was threatening the two justices. In the early morning hours of June 8, 2022, a man was arrested near Justice Kavanaugh's Maryland home after he called 911 and told the dispatcher that he had traveled from California to kill Justice Kavanaugh. When police arrested the 26-year-old man, he was found to have pepper spray, a knife, and a gun with him.

At the time of this arrest, protesters had been regularly demonstrating outside the homes of Supreme Court justices following the leak of a draft opinion written by Justice Samuel Alito regarding another case on abortion, *Dobbs v. Jackson Women's Health Organization.* On June 24, 2022, the Supreme Court released its official opinion on the case. The

227

Court's six-to-three judgment found that the US Constitution did not confer a right to abortion, overturning the 1973 *Roe v. Wade* judgment.

Justice Samuel Alito later told *The Wall Street Journal*, "Those of us who were thought to be in the majority, thought to have approved my draft opinion, were really targets of assassination…It was rational for people to believe they might be able to stop the decision in Dobbs by killing one of us."

"Nobody is taking away your gas stove."

–Senate Majority Leader Chuck Schumer,
February 3, 2023, in a tweet

Schumer went on to tweet, "Shameless and desperate MAGA Republicans are showing us they will cook up any distraction to divert from real issues the American people want solved, like the debt ceiling." Exactly one month later, on May 3, 2023, Schumer's home state of New York passed a budget that prohibits gas hookups in smaller residential buildings by 2026 and in larger residential buildings by 2029.

"I haven't made that decision. I haven't released anything."

–Senator Dianne Feinstein, February 14, 2023

Senator Feinstein responded to a question asking about her retirement. A staffer then explained to the Senator that a statement announcing her retirement had been released earlier that day. Feinstein replied, "You put out the statement? I didn't know they put it out."

The Senator's apparent confusion about her own retirement announcement seemed to epitomize the significant decline in her mental health that had been noted by many reporters and colleagues in recent years. Only one hour before her exchange with this reporter, the eighty-nine-year-old Senator commented on her retirement, "Oh, no. I'm not announcing anything. I will one day."

This is reminiscent of the announced retirement of Supreme Court Justice Stephen Breyer, who also denied it at the time. These actions have led some to believe that this is a political tactic by the Democrat party to force the hand of elderly leaders in the party to retire even when they don't want to do so. That way, party leaders can use their organization and its financial resources to support younger replacements.

Interestingly, after announcing her candidacy for president on the same day as Feinstein's retirement announcement, fifty-one-year-old Nikki Haley, former South Carolina Governor and former US Ambassador to the United Nations, delivered a speech the next day in which she called for mental competency tests for politicians over 75 years old.

"The Republicans want to give a work requirement for SNAP [Supplemental Nutrition Assistance Program]. You know for, a hungry family has to have these kind of penalties or some kinds of working requirement. Shouldn't you have a working requirement after we sail [sic] your bank billions for your bank because they seem to be more preoccupied than SNAP requirements for works for hungry people but not about protecting the taxpayers that will bail them out of whatever does about a bank to crash it."

–Senator John Fetterman, May 16, 2023

Fetterman was questioning witnesses during a Senate Banking Committee hearing about the collapse of Silicon Valley Bank. The panel of banking executives appeared thoroughly confused by Fetterman's incoherent attempt at a question. Following his statement, there was an awkward silence before Fetterman finally said, "Chair," returning his time back to the committee chairman.

Interestingly, when Fetterman's office released an "official" record of the above statement, it read, "Shouldn't you have a working requirement after we bail out your bank? Republicans seem to be more occupied with SNAP requirements for hungry people than protecting taxpayers that have to bail out these banks." Quite a difference, don't you think?

"This is the whole reason why the 14th Amendment exists, and we need to be prepared to use it."

–Senator John Fetterman, May 18, 2023, in a tweet

Senator Fetterman was referring to the US debt ceiling and expressing his frustration with demands by Speaker of the House Kevin McCarthy and fellow Republicans to require an agreement to limit spending before allowing the debt limit to be raised.

Fetterman and some other Democrats in Congress argued that the following reference in the 14th Amendment to the US Constitution gives the president the power to raise the debt ceiling without congressional approval: "The validity of the public debt of the United States, authorized by law, including debts incurred for payment of pensions and bounties for services in suppressing insurrection or rebellion, shall not be questioned."

Most constitutional scholars agree that Fetterman's interpretation is completely wrong. His argument is only made worse by his claim that "this is the whole reason why the 14th Amendment exists." Had he paid a little more attention in school, he might remember that the 14th

Amendment, which was ratified in 1868 (three years after the end of the Civil War), also granted former slaves citizenship and established due process and equal protection as tenets of American democracy.

Former Senior Advisor to President Trump Stephen Miller put it well when he responded to Fetterman by tweeting, "How about this: we will take you seriously as a constitutional scholar when you stop dressing like an eleven-year-old at a skate park?"

"This MAGA Supreme Court is continuing to erode our country's environmental laws."

–Senate Majority Leader Chuck
Schumer, May 25, 2023

Senator Schumer was critical of the "MAGA Supreme Court" for its decision in the case of *Sackett v. Environmental Protection Agency*. The court ruled that the EPA overstepped its authority to protect wetlands when it tried to regulate property owned by the plaintiffs, Michael and Chantell Sackett, near Priest Lake Idaho.

Schumer said the "MAGA" court's ruling would lead to more polluted water and the destruction of wetlands. What he never bothered to mention, however, was that the court's decision in this case was unanimous, meaning that all nine justices, including Sonia Sotomayor, Elena Kagan, and Ketanji Brown Jackson, voted together. Senator Schumer has never let the facts get in the way of a good argument.

"We passed the Inflation Reduction Act to put us on track to reduce our greenhouse gas emissions by 50% by 2030. But we must do more."

–Senate Majority Leader Chuck
Schumer, June 7, 2023, in a tweet

Really! That's why you passed the Inflation Reduction Act? What does this have to do with inflation? As is often the case, the Democrats gave a massive spending bill for their favorite pet projects an attractive name so it would foster public support even though it did practically nothing to actually address that issue.

Schumer seems to be pleased with this deceit. This tweet was written on a day when winds from the north caused smoke from wildfires in Canada to blanket much of the Northeastern US, including New York City (Schumer's hometown). He was taking advantage of this event to call for more climate change legislation as if somehow wildfires are examples of climate change.

According to *Science News*, the earth's oldest known wildfires raged 430 million years ago. Wildfires are a natural part of the environment. They are nature's way of clearing out the dead litter in the forest so important nutrients can return to the soil and new plants can grow. Some plants even rely on wildfire for their reproduction. The lodgepole pine, for example, has cones that are sealed with resin, and the seeds within are only released after the resin has been melted by a wildfire. Of course, wildfires can be destructive to human habitats as communities continue to expand into the countryside. It is worth noting however, that according to the National Interagency Fire Center, 87% of wildfires each year are caused by humans, including the approximately 20% that are caused by arsonists.

"Now, I'm standing next to the president again, next to a collapsed bridge here. And he is here to commit to work with the governor and the delegadation [sic] to make sure that we get this fixed quick, fast, as well too. This is a president that is committed to infructure [sic] and on top of that, the jewel kind of it law, of

the infration [sic], infric [sic], yeah infration [sic] bill."

–Senator John Fetterman, June 17, 2023

Fetterman made these remarks following a tragic accident in Philadelphia that destroyed a heavily traveled bridge on Interstate 95. Wearing shorts, a hoodie, and sneakers, the senator from Pennsylvania appeared to refer to the President of the United States as a collapsed bridge. You can cut the irony here with a knife.

"America...it's about freedom and choice. It's like [a] Burger King 'You Rule' kind of a thing."

–Senator John Fetterman, September 18, 2023

Fetterman was referring to a decision by Senate Majority Leader Chuck Schumer to no longer enforce the Senate's informal dress code. Schumer's decision may seem like a trivial issue to many, but it is a perfect example of the incremental decline of our society.

Have you ever watched a commercial on TV and thought to yourself, "There is no way something like this would have been allowed to air when I was younger?" If you haven't, try watching (if you dare) a musical act during next year's Grammy Awards, and you will quickly see what I mean.

I suspect that one day even traditional liberals will wake up and say, "How did we get here?" Allowing shorts, sneakers, and hoodies on the Senate floor is just another example of what former US Solicitor General Robert Bourke described as "slouching toward Gomorrah."

Fortunately, in this case, the dress code change was met with widespread criticism by the public and senators alike. Forty-six Republican senators wrote in a letter to Senator Schumer, "Allowing casual clothing on the Senate floor disrespects the institution we serve and the American families we represent." Within only a few days of Schumer's decision to remove the informal dress code, the Senate unanimously passed the SHORTS (Show Our Respect To the Senate) Act, which requires business attire for men. It looks like John Fetterman will have to put on his big-boy pants and grow up after all.

"Those behind this campaign simply cannot accept that a first-generation Latino American from humble beginnings could rise to be a US senator."

–Senator Bob Menendez, September 22, 2023

New Jersey Senator Bob Menendez made this statement following his federal indictment on bribery charges. Menendez is accused of secretly giving sensitive US government information to the government of Egypt and using his influence to aid businessmen friends of his between 2018 and 2022.

A search of Menendez's home found $100,000 in gold bars and $480,000 in cash stuffed into envelopes and hidden inside jackets. Menendez was also charged with conspiracy, bribery, and honest services fraud in a separate case in 2015. His prosecution at that time ended in a mistrial when his jury was deadlocked.

Following his second indictment in eight years, many of Menendez's colleagues, including fellow Democrats, called for him to resign his position as senator, but he refused to do so. When Menendez appeared to have no real defense for his actions, he turned to an old tried and true tactic like many others before him: he played the race card.

"Sometimes you literally just can't believe like, these people are

*making the decisions that are determining the government here.
It's actually scary."*

–Senator John Fetterman, October 11, 2023

Fetterman made this comment during an appearance on *The Late
Show with Stephen Colbert*. He also stated, "You all need to know that
America is not sending their best and brightest to Washington, D.C."
For once, I can honestly say I agree wholeheartedly with Senator
Fetterman. As evidence of how scary our elected officials can be, I sub-
mit a comment Fetterman made in February 2020: "We could release a
third of our inmates and not make anyone less safe."

*"We should control the border (which our bill does), not close
it."*

–Senator Chris Murphy, February
5, 2024, in an X post

The Biden administration significantly exacerbated the problems
associated with illegal immigration into the United States and openly
encouraged illegal immigrants, creating an unprecedented level of
crisis at the border. Border security was even the number one issue
of concern to voters in both the Iowa caucus and the New Hampshire
primary of 2024.

In response to this border crisis, the Democrat-led US Senate
drafted a bill entitled the Emergency National Security Supplemental
Appropriations Act, 2024. Senator Chris Murphy was the co-author
of the immigration provisions of the bill. The bill was heralded by
Democrats and the media as a major step forward in securing our
Southern border.

So how did it presume to do this? Did it reduce illegal immigration to zero? Did it reduce illegal immigration to only a few hundred encounters per day? Hardly. According to the bill, "The Secretary shall activate the border emergency authority if during a period of seven consecutive calendar days, there is an average of 5,000 or more aliens who are encountered each day; or on any one calendar day, a combined total of 8,500 or more aliens are encountered."

In other words, if this bill were to become law, it would codify and normalize more than 1.8 million illegal immigrants crossing our Southern border each year. This is apparently what Senator Murphy thinks a secure border should look like. Senator Murphy was telling the truth about one thing for sure; this bill certainly does not close the border.

Two days later, Murphy responded to a reporter who pointed out that the proposed Act did not contain a path to citizenship for illegal aliens. Murphy said, "Well, I mean, Chris, that's been a failed play for 20 years. So, you are right that that has been the Democratic strategy for thirty years, maybe, and it has failed to deliver for the people we care about most, the undocumented Americans that are in this country." Are you kidding me? Did Murphy really admit that the people Democrats care about the most are not US citizens but undocumented Americans?

"Can I make a suggestion? I move that every newspaper in America quits doing any fact-checks on Joe Biden until they fact-check Donald Trump every morning on the front page. It is ridiculous that The New York Times fact-checked Joe Biden on something."

–Former US Senator Claire
McCaskill, February 22, 2024

She's right. How dare an organization like *The New York Times* fact-check the sitting president of the United States? Don't they know they're supposed to be working for the Democrat Party?

Chapter 7

Members of the US House of Representatives

"I have wondered at times what the Ten Commandments would look like if Moses had run them through the United States Congress."

–Ronald Reagan

"We have to pass the bill so that you can find out what is in it."

–Speaker of the House of Representatives
Nancy Pelosi, March 9, 2010

Pelosi was referring to the Affordable Care Act, which later became known as Obama Care. The Act, which was nearly 11,000 pages long, would be approximately three feet tall if printed. It's probably a good bet that no one in Congress actually read the bill in its entirety before it was passed, and who could blame them?

That's the problem. Congress regularly relies on what are known as *omnibus spending bills*. These bills typically include a wide range of appropriations that are all passed in one large bill requiring only one passing vote. These bills are often thousands of pages long and include a huge number of dubious items.

One example is *earmarks*. These are passages inserted into a large appropriations bill directing funds to a specific project without following a merit-based allocation process. Earmarks are often associated with the term *pork* or *pork barrel*, which are funds directed toward a specific representative's district (as if they were "bringing home the bacon" to their constituents).

There is nothing wrong with a representative securing funding for a local project, but when dozens of these provisions are included in a large bill, the representatives avoid the need to separately justify those expenditures.

Making matters worse, these earmarks often come in the form of *riders*. A rider is a provision added to a piece of legislation that may have absolutely nothing to do with the subject matter of the bill. Forty-one state governments have tried to address these problems by adding single-subject rules to their state constitutions that prohibit these types of tactics.

Unfortunately, Congress has yet to seriously consider such a change at the federal level. If I had my way, I would not only require the single-subject rule, but I would also limit any bill in Congress to a maximum of 100 pages in length. If a representative can't clearly communicate their bill in 100 pages, then they should reconsider what they are asking the American people to accept. After all, the entire US Constitution was written in only four pages. One can only imagine how long that document would be if it were to be written today.

"Hey, if I was you, I may want me to go away, too. I am not going away. I am here."

–Congressman Charles Rangel, August 10, 2010

Beginning in 2008, Rangel faced several ethics complaints, including an accusation that he had accepted an apartment at below-market value.

During an investigation of his personal finances, it was discovered that he had also misused office resources and failed to pay taxes on $500,000 worth of assets. In March 2010, the House Ethics Committee found Rangel in violation of eleven of thirteen charges that had been brought against him. Nevertheless, Rangel continued to assert his innocence. On November 18, 2010, he told the House Ethics Committee, "My actions may have been sloppy, or even stupid, but never corrupt." On December 2, 2010, the House voted 333 to 79 to officially censure Rangel. Rangel eventually retired in 2017 after serving forty-six years in Congress.

"Look, this is a prank and not a terribly creative one. I was hacked. It happens to people. You move on."

–Congressman Anthony Weiner, May 30, 2011

Weiner claimed that a hacker broke into his social media accounts and posted a lewd photo sent to a 21-year-old female college student in Seattle who followed Weiner on Twitter.

Weiner joked about the hack, writing, "Is my blender gonna attack me next?" After vehemently denying any responsibility for the photo for a week, Weiner eventually admitted on June 6, 2011, that he had posted the photo himself. During a press conference he explained, "Last Friday night, I tweeted a photograph of myself that I intended to send as direct message as part of a joke to a woman in Seattle. Once I realized I posted it to Twitter, I panicked. I took it down and said that I had been hacked. I then continued with that story to stick to that story, which was a hugely regrettable mistake."

He also added, "Over the past few years, I have engaged in several inappropriate conversations conducted over Twitter, Facebook, e-mail, and occasionally on the phone with women I have met online." On

June 16, 2011, Weiner, who was married, announced his resignation from Congress.

"It's so pathetic."

–House Minority Leader Nancy
Pelosi, January 11, 2018

On December 22, 2017, President Trump signed a $1.5 trillion tax cut into law, which included a reduction in the corporate tax rate from 35% to 21%. In response to the new tax reform, AT&T and many other corporations across America began giving their workers bonuses often in excess of $1000 per employee.

During a news conference on Capitol Hill, Nancy Pelosi referred to these bonuses as pathetic "crumbs." Ironically, in 2011 Pelosi praised a payroll tax cut during the Obama administration, when she tweeted "Forty dollars each paycheck will make a difference."

"If you see anybody from that Cabinet in a restaurant, in a department store, at a gasoline station, you get up and you create a crowd and you push back on them and you tell them they're not welcome anymore, anywhere."

–Congresswoman Maxine Waters, June 23, 2018

Waters was referring to members of the Trump administration as she spoke during a rally in Los Angeles. Just in case anyone believes she may have misspoken, Waters doubled down on her hostility toward Trump administration officials later that day during an interview on MSNBC, saying, "The people are going to turn on them. They're going to protest. They're going to absolutely harass them until they decide that they're going to tell the president, 'No, I can't hang with you.'"

"The world is going to end in twelve years if we don't address climate change, and your biggest issue is how are we gonna pay for it?"

–Congresswoman Alexandria Ocasio-Cortez, January 21, 2019

On February 7, 2019, Ocasio-Cortez and Massachusetts Senator Ed Markey introduced a framework for legislation to transition the US to 100% renewable, zero-emission energy sources within ten years in a plan they dubbed The Green New Deal. In a study co-authored by the former director of the non-partisan Congressional Budget Office, the Green New Deal was estimated to cost as much as $93 trillion. Given that astronomical price tag, perhaps it isn't totally absurd to discuss how we plan to pay for this transition before we blindly rush to implement it.

"They were taunting five Black men before they surrounded Phillips and led racist chants."

–Congresswoman Ilhan Omar, January 22, 2019, in a tweet

Omar was referring to an encounter in Washington, D.C. four days earlier when a group of students from Covington Catholic High School (Kentucky) were confronted by a Native American activist named Nathan Phillips. The students were in Washington to attend the March for Life, an anti-abortion event. Phillips was in Washington attending a simultaneous Indigenous Peoples March.

As the students waited for their buses near the Lincoln Memorial, they were taunted by a group of five Black Hebrew Israelites. In response, the students began to cite sports chants. Phillips then approached the students and began to chant and beat a drum. Video clips of the encounter quickly went viral.

Because several of the students were wearing items showing their support for President Trump, including MAGA hats, it was assumed by many observers of the video that the students were the instigators and that they were deriding Mr. Phillips. The students were quickly denounced by an unrelenting media mob that described them as racists.

Eventually, longer video recordings of the encounter showed that it was the students who were actually being harassed. In spite of these new revelations, Congresswoman Omar still tweeted her attack on the students.

The student most widely criticized by the media was Nicholas Sandmann. Phillips stood directly in front of Sandmann and seemed to focus his attention on him. Sandmann remained still and silent as he stared back at Phillips throughout the encounter. In response to the media's criticism of him, Sandmann eventually filed multimillion-dollar defamation lawsuits against CNN, NBC Universal, and *The Washington Post*, reaching settlements with each of these outlets.

> *"Anything is possible: today was the day a group of dedicated, everyday New Yorkers & their neighbors defeated Amazon's corporate greed, its worker exploitation, and the power of the richest man in the world."*
>
> –Congresswoman Alexandria Ocasio-Cortez, February 14, 2019, in a tweet

Ocasio-Cortez was celebrating the decision of Amazon to abandon plans for a new headquarters in Long Island City. Earlier that day, Amazon released a statement that read, "A number of state and local politicians have made it clear that they oppose our presence and will not work with us to build the type of relationships that are required to go forward."

New York Governor Andrew Cuomo and New York City Mayor Bill de Blasio had been brokering the deal with Amazon, but Ocasio-Cortez was an outspoken critic of the plan. After Amazon's decision to back out, Governor Cuomo estimated that at least 25,000 to 40,000 well-paying jobs and nearly $30 billion in new revenue for New York had been lost. This is a classic example of what happens when a misguided politician puts their personal ideology above the best interests of their constituents.

"Some people did something."

–Congresswoman Ilhan Omar, April 11, 2019

Omar was referring to the September 11, 2001, terrorist attack on the United States. She was trying to explain that CAIR (the Council on American Islamic Relations) was founded in response to the attacks because in their aftermath Muslims in America were starting to "lose access to our civil liberties."

Not only was Omar wrong about the founding of CAIR, which was actually established in 1994, but she also received widespread criticism for her absurd description of the 9/11 terrorist attack. Terrorists murdered a total of 2,977 innocent victims that day in the worst terrorist attack in our nation's history. You might think that an elected representative of the United States would show proper respect to those killed and their families by referencing their loss with a little more reverence.

"This is the essence of what the president communicates: We've been very good to your country, very good. No other country has

done as much as we have. But you know what, I don't see much reciprocity here. I hear what you want. I have a favor I want from you, though, and I'm going to say this only seven times, so you better listen good. I want you to make up dirt on my political opponent, understand, lots of it. On this and on that. I'm going to put you in touch with people, not just any people. I'm going to put you in touch with the Attorney General of the United States, my Attorney General, Bill Barr. He's got the whole weight of the American law enforcement behind him. And I'm going to put you in touch with Rudy. You're going to love him, trust me. You know what I'm asking, and so I'm only going to say this a few more times in a few more ways. And by the way, don't call me again. I'll call you when you've done what I asked."

–Congressman Adam Schiff, September 26, 2019

Schiff, who was Chairman of the House Intelligence Committee at the time, made this speech during his opening remarks at a committee hearing. He was referring to what was said during a phone call between President Donald Trump and Ukrainian President Volodymyr Zelenskyy on July 25, 2019.

Based on this conversation, Schiff called for President Trump to be impeached. There is one major problem however with Schiff's account of the call; it was completely made up. Schiff described the conversation as if he was reading a transcript of the call. Instead, he was giving his own version of what he believed was said.

I believe Schiff's remarks are among the most outrageous I've ever witnessed by a public official. Schiff's false retelling of the phone call was one of several ethics violations he was accused of by the House Ethics Committee. Another included his repeated claims that he possessed evidence that Donald Trump had colluded with Russia to interfere with the 2016 presidential election.

Reports by Special Counsel Robert Mueller, Special Counsel John Durham, and Justice Department Inspector General Michael Horowitz proved this evidence never existed. On June 21, 2023, the House of Representatives voted 213 to 209 to officially censure Schiff for knowingly misleading the American public.

Unbelievably, on March 1, 2023, Schiff told a crowd in Santa Barbara, California, "I think of all the corrosive things that we saw there in the last administration, perhaps none was as corrosive to democracy as this relentless assault on truth." Schiff made this comment soon after announcing his candidacy for US Senate.

"I don't hate anybody. I was raised in a Catholic house, we don't hate anybody."

–Speaker of the House of Representatives
Nancy Pelosi, December 5, 2019

A visibly angry Speaker Pelosi had just been asked by a reporter whether she hated Donald Trump. In spite of her objection, one might wonder whether someone who wasn't motivated by hate would rip up a copy of President Trump's State of the Union speech immediately following his address on national television.

When asked about her callous action, Pelosi responded, "It was the courteous thing to do, considering the alternative." Pelosi also led House Democrats in their decision to impeach Republican President Donald Trump an unprecedented two times based on partisan and dubious evidence. If she doesn't actually hate Trump, she has done a good job of imitating it. It's worth noting that some observers also took issue with Pelosi's reference to her Catholicism in her defense. Pelosi has been a longtime champion of abortion, which is considered a mortal sin in the Roman Catholic Church.

"We cannot rely on an election to solve our problems."

–Congressman Jerrold Nadler, December 18, 2019

Nadler made this comment during a House Judiciary Committee debate on articles of impeachment for President Donald Trump. The congressman was making the case that Trump had to be impeached because Democrats couldn't take the risk knowing that millions of American voters might reelect him to office in 2020. This is a good example of the Democrat party's view toward democracy in the twenty-first century.

"That's a myth that's being spread only in Washington D.C."

–Congressman Jerrold Nadler, July 26, 2020

Nadler was asked, "Do you disavow the violence from Antifa that's happening in Portland right now?"

At the time of Nadler's comment, there had been sixty consecutive nights of protests and violence in Portland, Oregon, including attacks on police officers, destruction of property, looting, and arson.

According to Fox News, "Antifa has no defined organizational hierarchy or membership process. The collection of autonomous Antifa groups in mostly left-wing cities sees itself as a descendant of the European anti-Nazi movements and generally agrees that the best way to combat ideas they find odious is not through speech or debate but by direct action and physical confrontation."

Congressman Jim Jordan responded to Nadler's comment by

saying, "Go tell the officers who have been blinded, the officers who have been attacked, ask them if Antifa is a myth or an imaginary organization. Ask Andy Ngo, the journalist who was attacked in Portland over a year ago, if they're an imaginary organization or some kind of myth. They are very real. They are very dangerous."

"The president is, shall we say, in an altered state right now."

–Speaker of the House of Representatives
Nancy Pelosi, October 8, 2020

In 2018, following intense pressure from congressional Democrats, President Donald Trump agreed to take a cognitive test. White House Physician Rear Admiral Ronny Jackson administered the Montreal Cognitive Assessment to Trump and later announced that the President received a perfect score of thirty out of thirty.

Nevertheless, in 2020 Pelosi once again questioned Trump's fitness for office with the above comment. The next day, Pelosi and Congressman Jamie Raskin introduced a bill to establish The Commission on Presidential Capacity to Discharge the Powers and Duties of Office.

To counter her critics, including Trump himself, who believed this was yet another attempt by Democrats in the House to challenge his leadership, Pelosi pointed out that "This is not about President Trump. He will face the judgment of voters. But he shows the need to create a process for future presidents."

In spite of this logic and calls by many Republicans (including Ronny Jackson, who is now a member of Congress), for Joe Biden to take a cognitive assessment similar to Trump's, Biden has not done so.

Democrats only seem interested in questioning a president's mental acuity when it involves a Republican. During the 1964

DID I HEAR YOU RIGHT?

presidential race between Democrat Lyndon Johnson and Republican Barry Goldwater, the editors of *Fact Magazine* posed the following question to thousands of psychiatrists across the US: "Do you believe Barry Goldwater is psychologically fit to serve as President of the United States?"

Although none of the psychiatrists had ever personally met with Goldwater, their responses were striking. One said, "I believe Goldwater to be suffering from a chronic psychosis." Others claimed he was a paranoid schizophrenic. So disturbing were the results of this exercise that the American Psychiatric Association responded by establishing Section 7.3 in the Principles of Medical Ethics in 1973. The new guidance, which applied to public figures, reads, "It is unethical for a psychiatrist to offer a professional opinion unless he or she has conducted an examination and has been granted proper authorization for such a statement." This has been known ever since as the Goldwater Rule.

"Democrats single-handedly saved the economy."

–Congresswoman Jahana Hayes, March 16, 2022

In addition to this absurd comment, Hayes also asserted that the American Rescue Plan Act of 2021 stabilized the economy. Really? The inflation rate was 1.7% when the American Rescue Plan Act of 2021 was passed in March 2021. This $1.9 trillion act was described at the time as an economic stimulus package. However, one year later in March 2022, the inflation rate was 8.5%. Is that the Democrats' idea of how to save the economy?

"Well, I grew up in a family where if the gas price went up, the food price went down, so by this time of the week we'd be eating

Chef Boyardee if that budget wasn't gonna change, right. So, that's what families have to do."

–Congressman Sean Patrick
Maloney, November 5, 2022

Maloney made this comment when he was asked during an interview, "Hudson Valley residents are feeling pain at the pump and at grocery stores. What have you done and what do you plan to do to help solve our inflation problem?"

Perhaps not surprisingly, Maloney who also served as Head of the Democratic Congressional Campaign Committee (DCCC), lost his bid for re-election four days later on November 9, 2022. It was the first time in over forty years that the DCCC Chair lost a re-election. After losing his job, Maloney and his family may have to get used to eating Chef Boyardee once again.

"I think, you know, the average American person can see what is going on. We have these right-wing conservatives who are, you know, we have domestic terrorists in the House of Representatives. These people are extremists."

–Congresswoman Maxine
Waters, January 28, 2023

I think Donald Trump described Maxine Waters best when he called her a "low IQ individual."

"Being a Republican witness today certainly casts a cloud over your objectivity."

–Congresswoman Debbie Wasserman-
Shultz, March 9, 2023

251

Wasserman-Shultz made this comment to Matt Taibi and other journalists who were testifying before the House Government Weaponization Subcommittee. One can only wonder if Democrats would feel the same about witnesses they call to testify before Congressional committees.

"No one is above the law, and everyone has the right to a trial to prove innocence."

–Congresswoman Nancy Pelosi,
March 30, 2023, in a tweet

Pelosi wrote this tweet following the indictment of Donald Trump by a New York City Grand Jury. In the United States, any person accused of a crime is presumed innocent until proven guilty beyond a reasonable doubt. It's funny how Pelosi's message about Donald Trump seemed to twist that critical element of the US judicial system.

"I believe that the Biden administration should ignore this ruling."

–Congresswoman Alexandria
Ocasio-Cortes, April 9, 2023

Ocasio-Cortez was responding to a CNN correspondent who questioned her about a decision by a federal judge in Texas that put an injunction on the abortion drug mifepristone.

Ocasio-Cortes went on to say, "You know, I think the interesting thing when it comes to a ruling is that it relies on enforcement. And it is up to the Biden administration to enforce, to choose whether or not to enforce such a ruling."

The Congresswoman's disturbing recommendation is reminiscent of a famous line attributed to President Andrew Jackson. In 1832, the US Supreme Court, under the leadership of Chief Justice John Marshall, ruled in the case of *Worcester vs. Georgia* that Georgia's attempt to seize Cherokee lands had violated federal treaties. In response, President Jackson is purported to have said, "John Marshall has made his decision, now let him enforce it."

Fortunately, Jackson soon had a change of heart. Later that year, he issued a proclamation upholding the US Supreme Court's power to decide constitutional questions and confirmed that its decisions had to be obeyed.

Nearly two hundred years later, Ocasio-Cortes doesn't seem to agree. Her statement is a clear attempt to sidestep the federal system of checks and balances by encouraging the executive branch to simply not enforce any federal court decisions with which it philosophically disagrees. One has to wonder: is she just that ignorant about the federal court's status as a coequal branch of government, or is she actively trying to thwart it?

> *"It has come to my attention that information foundational to your testimony that day has since been revealed to be false and misleading... Under the federal perjury statute, 18 USC. § 1621, providing false information is punishable by up to five years imprisonment."*

–Delegate Stacey Plaskett, April 13, 2023

Plaskett is the nonvoting delegate from the Virgin Islands to the US Congress. She is also the ranking member on the House Judiciary Select Subcommittee on the Weaponization of the Federal Government. Plaskett made this notation in a letter to Matthew Taibbi, who was one of the journalists associated with the publication of the Twitter Files.

These files referenced internal documents from Twitter showing the attempts by the social media platform's executives to censor the speech of its users. The documents were made available to journalists by Elon Musk after he took control of Twitter.

In her letter, Plaskett referred to an error Taibbi had made in one of his tweets: he confused CISA, the Cybersecurity and Infrastructure Security Agency, a government agency, with CIS, the Center for Internet Security, a nonprofit organization. Taibbi later clarified in writing, "I did in a tweet conflate the Center for American Security (CIS) with the Department of Homeland Security's Cybersecurity and Infrastructure Security Agency (CISA), saying that CISA was so close to Stanford's Election Integrity Project (EIP) that Twitter staffers didn't really distinguish between them. This happened precisely because the agencies were hand-in-glove partners and I'd seen so many communications about their cooperation that I lost track of some acronyms."

Referring to Delegate Plaskett's assertion that his mistake may be punishable by up to five years imprisonment, Taibbi wrote, "Have they all gone mad?"

"You also plan to make important investments to address the roadway safety crisis, including the critical funding that would accelerate the development, and this is an area that I've written to you about, of the use of female dummies in crash testing."

–Congresswoman Laura DeLauro, April 20, 2023

DeLauro was speaking with Secretary of Transportation Pete Buttigieg about the department's budget during a hearing of the House Appropriations Committee. Instead of focusing on ways to improve the supply chain or strategies to deal with a number of recent near-accidents by commercial aircraft or how to prevent tragedies like the devastating train derailment in East Palestine, Ohio, Congresswoman DeLauro chose to focus on the all-important issue of crash-test dummy equity.

For some reason, the same people who can't define what a woman is are so concerned about gender inequity in mannequins that they are willing to allocate $20 million to correct the problem. Fear not, however; I have it on good authority that many of the male crash test dummies used by the Department of Transportation identify as female, so we should be OK for now.

"Nay."

–Congresswoman Rashida Tlaib and
Congresswoman Cori Bush, May 15, 2023

These two members of "the squad" were the only members of Congress to vote "no" on House Resolution 363, which expressed support for recognizing National Police Week. The Resolution was intended to memorialize police officers killed in the line of duty and express condolences to their families. Two days before this vote, 224 names of officers who died in the line of duty in 2022 were added to the National Law Enforcement Memorial in Washington, DC. With those additions, a total of 23,785 names are engraved on the memorial.

"Whereas financial reparations must be paid by the Federal Government for an amount that respected economists have estimated totals, at minimum, $14,000,000,000,000 to eliminate the racial wealth gap that currently exists between Black and White Americans."

–Congresswoman Cori Bush, May 17, 2023

Yes, you read that correctly. Representative Bush introduced a bill (H.R. 414) in Congress demanding that the federal government pay $14 trillion in reparations to Black Americans. To help put that in perspective, the federal government collected $5 trillion in revenue in fiscal year 2022. Also, the US national debt reached $34 trillion on December 29, 2023.

Without even getting into the many political, legal, ethical, historical, and logistical flaws in Bush's argument, how on earth does a member of Congress think that $14 trillion in reparations is a reasonable request?

Bush is not alone, however, in her delusion. On June 29, 2023, California's Task Force to Study and Develop Reparation Proposals for African Americans delivered its final report to the California legislature. This 1,200-page report included more than 100 recommendations that could cost the State of California (a non-slave state) approximately $800 billion, more than 2.5 times its annual budget.

In addition, during their visit to Al Sharpton's National Action Network convention, nearly every Democrat candidate for president in 2020 publicly pledged to support a bill in Congress that would create a commission to study reparations.

According to the University of Minnesota, in 1861 there were 365,216 slave owners in the US.

According to the US Census Bureau, in 2021 there were approximately 331,500,000 people in the US, 13.6% of whom were Black, equaling approximately 45,000,000 people.

So in essence, proponents of reparations would like 286,500,000 Americans to pay reparations for the sins of 365,216 individuals (.11% of today's non-Black population in America), all of whom died more than 100 years ago.

According to Congresswoman Bush, "The reason why the United

States is where it is economically is because of enslavement." It is worth remembering that slavery became illegal in the US in 1865. Sadly, slavery has existed throughout human history in cultures all over the world. Instead of focusing on compensating for a problem that ended nearly 160 years ago, Democrats might want to take a moment to consider the harsh realities of the world at large both past and present.

In 2023, a powerful film entitled *Sound of Freedom* was released. The film tells the story of two siblings from South America who were stolen by human traffickers and the remarkable efforts of an American official to rescue them. The film sheds light on a very dark and disturbing industry—human trafficking and child sex slavery. At the film's conclusion, credits on the screen reveal, "Human trafficking is a $150 billion-dollar-a-year business. There are more humans trapped in slavery today than any other time in history, including when slavery was legal. Millions of these slaves are children. The United States is one of the top destinations for human trafficking and is among the largest consumers of child sex."

As despicable as Black slavery in America was, our time, energy, and treasure would be much better used, in my opinion, to stop the atrocities that are happening at this very moment.

"No person or business should be given a license to discriminate."

–House Minority Leader Hakeem
Jeffries, June 30, 2023

Jeffries, the House of Representatives Democrat Leader, was referring to the six-to-three decision by the US Supreme Court in the case of *303 Creative LLC v. Elenis*. The court ruled in this case that the First Amendment to the US Constitution prohibited the state of Colorado from compelling a website designer to create designs that contradicted her personal beliefs.

Interestingly, one day earlier, the US Supreme Court announced another six-to-three decision, which effectively ended the use of affirmative action in college admissions. The court ruled in this case that Harvard University and the University of North Carolina admissions programs violated the Equal Protection Clause of the 14th Amendment. Once again, Congressman Jeffries disagreed with the court, tweeting this time that "extremists just obliterated consideration of racial diversity in college admissions."

It's funny that Congressman Jeffries views the protection of one's personal or religious beliefs as "a license to discriminate" while simultaneously viewing discrimination by college admissions officers under the heading of affirmative action as simply racial diversity.

"Many of these people couldn't win elections for dogcatcher."

–Congressman Ro Khanna, June 30, 2023

Khanna was referring to justices on the US Supreme Court, whom he called "out of touch." His comments were made after the court issued what Democrats called a series of "hard-right decisions." Khanna went on to call the court "regressive" and stated, "It's exactly why we need term limits on these Supreme Court Justices."

Perhaps someone should remind the Congressman that Supreme Court Justices are not politicians, so their ability to win elections is irrelevant. According to the Supreme Court's website, "To ensure an independent Judiciary and to protect judges from partisan pressures, the Constitution provides that judges serve during 'good Behaviour', which has generally meant life terms." Khanna's suggestion is typical of Democrats who frequently call for a change in the rules whenever they find themselves on the losing side.

"The Supreme Court is far overreaching their authority, and I believe frankly that we really need to be having conversations about judicial review as a check on the court as well."

–Congresswoman Alexandria
Ocasio-Ortez, July 2, 2023

Ocasio-Cortez was expressing her frustration with the court after it concluded its 2022-2023 term with a number of decisions that were criticized by Democrats. However, she did not provide any rational explanation as to how the Supreme Court exceeded its authority by doing so. Instead, the fact that the court did not side with the prevailing view of Democrats seems to be reason enough for the Congresswoman to suggest a need for greater oversight and even impeachment.

In her statement, the congresswoman called for "judicial review as a check on the court." Judicial review is a concept that was established in 1803 following the landmark Supreme Court case of *Marbury v. Madison*. Ironically, it is a term used to describe the power of the federal courts to declare legislative and executive acts as unconstitutional. I guess A.O.C. missed that lesson in school.

"This July 4th, we must remember that we stand on stolen land toiled by enslaved Africans."

–Congressman Jamaal Bowman,
July 4, 2023, in a tweet

Instead of expressing his pride in being American, this is how one Democrat Congressman chose to recognize the birth of our great nation. Compare the sentiment expressed by this Congressman with that of

John Adams. In a letter to his wife Abigail on July 3, 1776, Adams wrote about how future Americans should commemorate the signing of the Declaration of Independence. "I am apt to believe that it will be celebrated, by succeeding Generations, as the great anniversary Festival. It ought to be commemorated, as the Day of Deliverance by solemn Acts of Devotion to God Almighty. It ought to be solemnized with Pomp and Parade, with Shews, Games, Sports, Guns, Bells, Bonfires and Illuminations from one End of this Continent to the other from this Time forward forever more. You will think me transported with Enthusiasm, but I am not. -- I am well aware of the Toil and Blood and Treasure, that it will cost Us to maintain this Declaration, and support and defend these States. -- Yet through all the Gloom I can see the Rays of ravishing Light and Glory."

I think our leaders today need to spend less time vilifying America and more time recognizing how lucky they are to represent our country and to be counted among great Americans like John Adams.

"I'd like to address the way my Republican colleagues are attempting to co-opt the phrase 'two-tiered justice system' to make it sound like Trump and his cronies are somehow the victims here when the reality is that the term two-tiered system of justice is meant to refer to the very real system that exists in the United States which affects Black and Brown folks."

–Congresswoman Summer Lee, July 19, 2023

This quote is a good example of how Democrats fiercely attempt to control our vocabulary. They use terms like *extremist, collusion, hate speech, election denier*, and others to serve their specific political purpose, and they become outraged when someone has the audacity to use one of their proprietary phrases in a different context.

"It was all casual conversation, niceties, the weather, what's going on."

–Congressman Daniel Goldman, July 31, 2023

Representative Goldman made this comment during a press conference following the testimony of Hunter Biden's former business associate, Devon Archer, before the House Committee on Oversight and Accountability.

Hunter Biden and Devon Archer both served as board members for Burisma, a Ukrainian energy company. During the hearing, Archer stated that Joe Biden spoke with his son Hunter and Hunter's business associates approximately 20 times. However, because Joe Biden did not openly discuss business on these occasions, Democrats like Goldman have claimed that Joe Biden played no role in his son's business deals.

In the same press conference, Congressman Goldman also stated, "There is not a shred of evidence of a single conflict of interest of President Biden ever doing anything in connection or in relation to Hunter Biden's business ventures."

However, Republican Chairman of the House Committee on Oversight and Accountability James Comer reached a different conclusion following Archer's testimony. Comer released a statement the same day noting, "Devon Archer's testimony today confirms Joe Biden lied to the American people when he said he had no knowledge about his son's business dealings and was not involved. Joe Biden was 'the brand' that his son sold around the world to enrich the Biden family. When Joe Biden was Vice President of the United States, he joined Hunter Biden's dinners with his foreign business associates in person or by speakerphone over 20 times. When Burisma's owner was facing pressure from the Ukrainian prosecutor investigating the company for corruption, Archer testified that Burisma executives asked Hunter to 'call D.C.' after a Burisma Board meeting in Dubai."

Following Congressman Goldman's statement that Joe Biden only discussed the weather with Hunter Biden's business associates, there was widespread incredulity. Even casual observers recognized that Hunter's ability to engage his father at will was the real purpose behind the conversations Joe had with Hunter's business associates. It didn't matter what they spoke about; the interaction was merely a demonstration of Hunter's influence. Ironically, the first interview Joe Biden granted following Devon Archer's House testimony was to the Weather Channel, of all places. Coincidence? You decide.

"And, at the end of its investigation, the bipartisan January 6th Select Committee turned over to the Justice Department its evidence of an extensive plot by the ex-President to overturn the Presidential election on January 6th and prevent the peaceful transfer of power."

–Congressman Bennie Thompson, August 1, 2023

Thompson served as Chairman of the January 6th Select Committee.

Following the 2004 Presidential election, there was a controversy over the electoral votes in Ohio. After George W. Bush defeated John Kerry 51% to 49%, rumors began to circulate that electronic voting machines in Ohio changed votes from Kerry to Bush. In spite of a lack of evidence, some members of Congress supported this claim and believed that Republicans were involved in a plot to suppress Democrat votes.

In the name of election integrity, Democrats in Congress decided to take action. Using the *Electoral Count Act of 1887*, thirty-one

Democrats in the House voted against certifying Ohio's electoral votes. While they did not have enough votes to win, if they had, they would have succeeded in overturning a presidential election.

Guess who was among the thirty-one Democrats? That's right, Congressman Bennie Thompson. Not surprisingly, Thompson failed to mention that fact during his chairmanship of the January 6 Committee.

"Today is the 9th anniversary of Mike Brown's killing. He would be alive today if the institutions of racism and White supremacy were eradicated. He should be alive today. We will never forget."

–Congresswoman Cori Bush,
August 9, 2023, in an X post

Michael Brown was a Black resident of Ferguson, Missouri, who was stopped by a police officer after he had committed a strongarm robbery at a convenience store. Brown then assaulted the officer and attempted to take his pistol before he was fatally shot by the officer. Because the officer was White, activists on the Left immediately portrayed the incident as an example of racism and police brutality. Adding fuel to the fire was false testimony that claimed Brown had his hands in the air when he was shot. The incident led to numerous riots where protestors introduced the disingenuous chant, "Hands up, don't shoot."

Even after the officer involved was cleared of any wrongdoing following an investigation by the Obama Justice Department, activists on the Left continued to reference Brown as a martyr in the fight for equal justice. This tactic blatantly rejects the facts of the case and advances a narrative that Black men are being hunted all over the country by White police officers. Reckless and malicious comments by elected leaders like this one by Cori Bush only serve to perpetuate division and mistrust across America.

"Now more than ever, our city needs us to advance San Francisco values."

–Congresswoman Nancy Pelosi,
September 8, 2023, in an X post

Pelosi made this comment when she announced her intention to run for re-election at age 83. Pelosi's use of the term "San Francisco values" was obviously meant to be an accolade. However, many Americans still dread the idea of spreading "San Francisco values" nationwide. Some even refer to the term as an oxymoron.

What exactly is it that Pelosi wishes to advance on the rest of us? Is it high taxes, open-air drug markets, rampant homelessness, rising crime rates, exceedingly high property values, or just a steady decline across the board in our standard of living?

In June 2022, San Francisco Mayor London Breed was asked what San Francisco's values were. She replied, "I think San Francisco values really consist of pushing the envelope and [being] willing to try things that may make people uncomfortable."

I'm sure both Breed and Pelosi would think that this definition is a good thing. I happen to disagree. Democrats have pushed the envelope farther than many of us ever imagined in recent years, and yes, a lot of us are uncomfortable with that trend.

The bottom line is that what a San Francisco politician describes as values is quite different than what most of the country would say. Sadly, we were forewarned about this problem several years ago, but it didn't prevent the spread from happening. Prior to the midterm election of 2006, when Nancy Pelosi first took control of the gavel as Speaker of the House of Representatives, then Speaker of the House J. Dennis Hastert cautioned, "Do we really want Nancy Pelosi's San Francisco values leading the culture war?" Likewise, former Speaker of the House Newt Gingrich also warned, "Will everything you've worked so hard to accomplish be lost to the San Francisco values of would-be Speaker Nancy Pelosi?"

It's a pity we didn't take their observations more seriously.

"You didn't talk to the right people, apparently."

–Congressman Hank Johnson, September 27, 2023

Representative Johnson was asked about the illegal immigration crisis at the Southern border by Fox News correspondent Hillary Vaughn. He replied by asking her, "Have you ever been to the border before to see what's happening?" After Vaughn confirmed she had been to the border, Johnson replied with the quote above.

Oscar Lee, Mayor of El Paso Texas, said on September 23, 2023, that his city was at "a breaking point" due to the immigration crisis. On September 25, 2023, Border Patrol Chief Jason Owens said, "In terms of flow and the threats that we're seeing with fentanyl and with criminal organization that are our adversary, it's about as bad as I've ever seen." He went on to say, "This isn't sustainable. Up and down the system, everybody is overwhelmed."

Apparently according to Congressman Johnson, Democrats are more careful about whom they speak with. One can only wonder who Johnson considers "the right people" to be.

"I thought the fire alarm would open a door."

–Congressman Jamaal Bowman,
September 30, 2023

With about twelve hours before a looming government shutdown was expected to start, Congressman Bowman pulled a fire alarm in the Cannon House Office Building, causing its evacuation. When confronted by a reporter that same day, Bowman said, "I was rushing to get to a vote. I was trying to get to a door. I thought the fire alarm would open a door."

The reporter asked, "So you pulled a fire alarm to open a door?"

"Yes," Bowman replied.

The reporter continued, "How does that make sense?"

Bowman responded, "What do you mean?"

The reporter asked again, "I mean when have you ever pulled a fire alarm…it says fire on it."

Bowman replied again, "I was just trying to get to my vote. The door that's usually open wasn't open. And you know, I didn't mean to cause confusion…I didn't know it was going to trip the whole building. I thought it would help me open the door."

Many observers accused Bowman of trying to delay Republican efforts to avert a government shutdown by pulling the alarm, believing if a shutdown occurred it would largely be blamed on House Republicans. They also cite the fact that Bowman walked past several US Capitol Police Officers responding to the "emergency" without telling them that he pulled the alarm.

Bowman was eventually charged with one misdemeanor count of pulling a fire alarm, and he pleaded guilty. He was fined $1,000 and was sentenced to three months of probation. His critics argued that Bowman should have been charged with violating 18 US Code 1505 (obstructing a Congressional proceeding), the same offense many January 6 protesters were charged with.

I'm reminded of a famous dictum by US Supreme Court Justice Oliver Wendel Holmes in his opinion in the case of *Schenck v. United States*. Holmes wrote, "The most stringent protection of free speech would not protect a man falsely shouting 'fire' in a theater and causing a panic." Holmes went on to say that this type of speech presents a "clear and present danger."

In the situation involving Bowman, we have a US Congressman (and former middle school principal) who pulled a fire alarm knowing there was no fire. His actions sound like they created a "clear and present danger" to me. Of course, Bowman's fellow squad members were quick to come to his defense. Congresswoman Alexandria Ocasio-Cortez claimed Bowman "panicked" as he was trying to "escape" a vestibule. Her comment made it sound like Bowman was trapped in an actual fire. On December 7, 2023, Bowman was officially censured by the US House of Representatives for his actions.

" 'From the river to the sea' is an aspirational call for freedom, human rights, and peaceful coexistence, not death, destruction, or hate."

–Congresswoman Rashida Tlaib,
November 3, 2023, in an X post

Earlier that day, Tlaib posted a video on X that featured protesters marching in several states with some chanting the slogan, "From the river to the sea." Tlaib received immediate and widespread criticism for featuring the antisemitic phrase. She posted the quote above in an attempt to defend herself.

However, her explanation was also quickly refuted. The Anti-defamation League responded by writing, "It is fundamentally a call for a Palestinian state extending from the Jordan River to the Mediterranean Sea, territory that includes the State of Israel, which would mean the dismantling of the Jewish state." On November 7, 2023, the House of Representatives voted 234 to 188 to censure Tlaib. Censure is the formal disapproval of a House member's conduct. It is one step below expulsion. Tlaib was the twenty-sixth member of the House to have been censured.

> *"It is just unquestionable at this point that that man cannot see public office again. He is not only unfit, he is destructive to our democracy, and he has to be, he has to be eliminated."*

> –Congressman Daniel Goldman,
> November 19, 2023

Goldman was referring to former President Donald Trump during an interview on MSNBC. After receiving widespread criticism for what many considered a call for violence against Trump, the next day Goldman apologized for using a "poor choice of words."

> *"The big news here is that there was a special counsel appointed to investigate President Biden and it came back and exonerated him completely."*

> –Congressman Jamie Raskin, February 9, 2024

Raskin was referring to Special Counsel Robert Hur's investigation into Joe Biden's possession of classified documents. Let's be clear here. To be exonerated means to be cleared from accusation or blame. Biden was *not* exonerated.

According to Hur's report, "Our investigation uncovered evidence that President Biden willfully retained and disclosed classified materials after his vice presidency when he was a private citizen." Clearly, Biden did break the law and was not exonerated.

Why, then, did Hur choose not to recommend prosecuting Joe

Biden? According to his report, "We have also considered that, at trial, Mr. Biden would likely present himself to a jury, as he did during our interview of him, as a sympathetic, well-meaning, elderly man with a poor memory. Based on our direct interactions with and observations of him, he is someone for whom many jurors will want to identify reasonable doubt…We decline to recommend prosecution."

In other words, the main reason why Hur chose not to prosecute Biden is because he is too old and his memory is too poor. Is that really an acceptable defense for breaking the law years earlier when Biden was presumably more competent? Furthermore, are those really the qualities we want in a sitting president?

"Very, very few stood at Super Bowl for Lift Every Voice and Sing. The Negro national anthem. Not a pretty picture of Super Bowl crowd."

–Congressman Steve Cohen, February 11, 2024, in an X post

Cohen was referring to the recitation of the song *Lift Every Voice and Sing* prior to the start of Super Bowl LVIII in 2024. This song was originally written as a poem by NAACP leader James Weldon in 1900. It has come to be known as the Black national anthem and has been performed at every Super Bowl since 2001.

Congressman Cohen's complaint that "very, very few" fans stood for the song raises some interesting questions. First, what is the purpose of a Black national anthem? Doesn't a national anthem for Blacks only serve to further divide our nation? Do we need separate national anthems for every race in the US? What about mixed-race Americans—which anthem should they recognize? Do they need one of their own as well?

Will each of these anthems be welcomed and played before all sporting events in the future? How many could we end up with? Will we be expected to stand for each of them or only for the one(s) we recognize as ours? Where will this end? *The Star Spangled Banner* has been the official national anthem of the United States of America since 1931. Shouldn't it be recognized and honored by every American regardless of race?

It is a sign of respect to stand when the national anthem is played. We all know, however, that in recent years several professional athletes have politicized sports by kneeling in protest during the national anthem.

Why, then, does Congressman Cohen assume all Americans should naturally rise for a song that supposedly represents only a fraction of the population? If it is acceptable for Black athletes to kneel in protest during *The Star Spangled Banner*, isn't it also acceptable for non-Black fans to sit during the Black national anthem?

It's pretty easy to see how we unnecessarily open a can of worms when we start recognizing more than one national anthem. We should all take a moment and remember the most important word in the name of our country; we are the *United* States of America. Every time we highlight our differences and promote identity politics, we only weaken the bonds that hold us all together.

In my humble opinion, there is and should only be one national anthem.

The first time I recall hearing the phrase "Diversity is our strength" was on my first day as a teacher. Our school's athletic director would read the morning announcements over the public address system each day, and he always concluded his remarks with that line. I worked at a very diverse high school, and it seemed like a heartwarming way to acknowledge the uniqueness of each student.

More than twenty years later, however, I have a slightly different view of this well-intentioned phrase. Over the past two decades, our country appears to have become more and more polarized. There are many reasons for this division, but I believe a greater emphasis on our differences may be partly to blame. I have respect for every culture and creed and believe everyone deserves a seat at the table, but when we focus only on our differences, we seem to lose sight of a more important point. That such a diverse population can live and prosper together in harmony makes us uniquely American. It's for that reason that "E Pluribus Unum" has been used as the traditional motto of the United States.

Like most Americans, my ancestors emigrated to this country, and I still take pride in my heritage. Nevertheless, I consider myself 100% American. We may never reach a consensus as a nation on topics like politics or economics, nor perhaps should we, but we should strive to always honor the gifts and privileges associated with being Americans. Perhaps a more appropriate slogan for the next two decades would be something like: "Diversity is our essence and unity is our strength."

P.S. By the way, Congressman Cohen, for someone who acts like a champion for Black Americans, maybe you should update your vocabulary. The term *negro* has not been a common part of the American vernacular for decades.

"Just do the math. Of course, we have national minimum wages that we need to raise to a living wage."

–Congresswoman Barbara Lee, February 12, 2024

Lee made this comment during a candidate debate for a US Senate seat from California. She cited the extremely high cost of living in the San Francisco Bay Area as she defended her call for a $50 federal minimum wage. I'm not sure which concept is more ridiculous—the fact that it costs a single individual more than $104,000/year just to survive in California, or the notion that raising the minimum wage to $50 wouldn't utterly devastate small businesses.

"You've heard the word 'full moon.' Sometimes you need to take the opportunity just to come out and see a full moon is that complete rounded circle, which is made up mostly of gases and that's why the question is why or how could we as humans live on the moon. Are the gases such that we could do that?...What you will see today will be the closest distance that the moon has ever been in the last twenty years, which means that's why they will shut the light down because they will be close to the earth...And Dr. Simmons, I didn't go too far away from the scientific explanation, is that correct?"

–Congresswoman Sheila Jackson
Lee, April 8, 2024

Jackson Lee made these comments during an address to students at Booker T. Washington High School, where they were gathered to view a solar eclipse. After it was pointed out to the Congresswoman that her speech contained several factual errors, including one line where she referred to the moon as a planet, she posted a correction on X, writing, "Obviously I misspoke...Republicans are focused on stupid things instead of stuff that really matters."

According to Fox News, this was not the first time Jackson Lee seemed confused about our solar system. During a 1997 visit to NASA, Jackson Lee, a member of the House Science Committee, apparently asked to see the American flag that our astronauts had planted on Mars.

"On Memorial Day, we honor the heroic men and women who served our country. We owe them more than our gratitude; they have more than earned access to quality mental health services, job opportunities, housing assistance, and the benefits they were promised."

–Congresswoman Ilhan Omar,
May 27, 2024, in an X post

While this statement is considerate and very appropriate for Veteran's Day (November 11), it doesn't make a whole lot of sense as a Memorial Day tribute.

Memorial Day, previously known as Decoration Day, was first observed on May 30, 1868, following the end of the Civil War. It is a federal holiday to honor and mourn US military personnel who died while serving the United States of America.

Representative Omar was not alone in her misunderstanding of the holiday. Congresswoman Cori Bush posted a similar comment that day as well. Perhaps the members of "the squad" should brush up on their American history. Mistakes like this may seem trivial to some, but I assure you that Memorial Day has deep significance to many Americans. I don't think it's too much to ask that members of Congress have a basic understanding of the purpose behind our federal holidays.

Chapter 8

The Courts

"Judges are like umpires. Umpires don't make the rules. They apply them. The role of an umpire and a judge is critical. They make sure everybody plays by the rules. But it is a limited role. Nobody ever went to a ballgame to see an umpire."

–John Roberts

"There's nothing honorable, ever, in violating a court order. It would undermine the integrity of the entire system."

–Circuit Court Judge Victoria
Brennan, March 20, 2014

In 2013, Lissette Alvarez was arrested for possession of cocaine. The arrest was made following an anonymous tip to Miami-Dade/Florida Keys Crime Stoppers. The defense counsel demanded to know the source of the tip to assist their case. Crime Stoppers refused to identify the source. Judge Victoria Brennan asked Richard Mastin, Executive Director of Miami Crime Stoppers, to appear in court. While sitting in the gallery of the court, he was filmed eating paperwork that identified the source of the tip to Crime Stoppers. For refusing to identify his source, Mastin was eventually sentenced by the court to probation and ordered to complete a written assignment about anonymous tip laws. Ironically, the charges against Alvarez were dropped.

In my opinion, this case raises an intriguing question. Why do we allow courts to compel an organization like Crime Stoppers to identify their partner, and punish them if they don't, but we don't compel defendants to identify their partner(s)/accomplice(s)?

Of course, many of our laws are designed to protect the individual against the power of the government for good reason, and defendants should always be given the presumption of innocence.

The Sixth Amendment to the US Constitution, for example, states that "In all criminal prosecutions, the accused shall enjoy the right to….be confronted with the witnesses against him."

I am certainly not suggesting that we rewrite this amendment. However, it is important to reflect on the importance of an anonymous tip in the pursuit of criminal justice. First of all, a tip to the police or an organization like Crime Stoppers is just that, a tip. In high-profile cases, police sometimes receive thousands of tips from the public, many of which are anonymous.

If an anonymous tip helps the police identify a suspect and make an arrest, by all means, the defendant should have the right to confront the arresting officer, who should assume the role of the accuser or the witness against him.

If we compel groups like Crime Stoppers to identify members of the public who wish to remain anonymous, we will only make the work of law enforcement more difficult. Take, for example, high-crime districts in urban communities. Police are often frustrated when the public provides little or no assistance in their investigation of a crime. Two factors are often associated with this predicament.

First, there is a norm in some communities that anyone cooperating with a police investigation is considered a snitch or rat, having broken an unwritten but well-established code of silence. Second, there is a very legitimate fear of repercussion if a witness' identity were to become known.

Compelling a defendant to identify their accomplice, however, would not imply that either individual is guilty. It would simply provide law enforcement officials as well as crime victims the opportunity to identify all of the suspects potentially involved in the commission of a crime. If there is sufficient evidence that a defendant did not act alone, the court should compel them to identify their accomplice. If the defendant refuses to do so, they should face an additional charge of obstructing justice.

We should not accept the fact that when two suspects flee a crime scene and only one is caught by police, the second suspect may potentially escape justice simply because he was faster.

"I had all the facts. Most people don't. They just don't understand."

–Retired Presiding Judge 323rd District Court of
Texas Jean Hudson Boyd, February 22, 2016

Boyd was referring to her sentencing of Ethan Couch, who, on June 15, 2013, killed four people while driving his father's truck in Burleson, Texas, with a blood alcohol content over three times the legal limit and under the influence of marijuana.

Couch, who was sixteen at the time, was estimated to be driving seventy miles per hour in a forty-mile-per-hour zone when he lost control of his truck and slammed into a stalled vehicle. In addition to killing the driver of the stalled vehicle, Couch killed three good Samaritans who were trying to help that driver.

One of the seven teenage passengers Couch had with him at the time also suffered a serious brain injury and can no longer speak or move. Couch was charged with four counts of intoxication manslaughter and two counts of intoxication assault, and prosecutors sought the maximum sentence of twenty years in prison.

His criminal case made national news when his lawyers claimed that Couch was a product of "affluenza," meaning his affluent and irresponsible parents had not set proper boundaries for him, leading him to live a reckless and consequence-free lifestyle. (Affluenza is not a recognized diagnosis by the American Psychiatric Association.)

Although Couch had entered a plea of guilty, instead of sentencing Couch to time in prison, Judge Boyd decided to sentence Couch to ten years of probation and ordered him to seek treatment at a rehabilitation facility. The judge reportedly said at the time she believed Couch would be better served by treatment than prison.

Family members of the victims and critics across the country were outraged by the sentence. On December 2, 2015, an unrepentant Couch was caught on video drinking and playing beer pong at a party—the same game he played the night of his fateful crash.

Drinking was prohibited under the conditions of Couch's probation. After the video went public, Couch's probation officer was unable to reach him, and a warrant was issued for his arrest. Meanwhile, Couch and his mother had fled to Mexico after withdrawing $30,000 from her bank account. A manhunt for Couch and his mother was then initiated by the US Marshals Service, and several weeks later the two were arrested by Mexican police.

After returning to Texas in January 2016, Couch appeared in adult court for the first time and was sentenced to 720 days in jail. In January 2020, Couch was arrested yet again for testing positive for THC during probation. Couch's mother, Tonya, was sentenced to five years in prison for her role in hindering her son's apprehension but was released from prison after serving less than three years.

This case should serve as a cautionary tale to all judges. While Judge Boyd believed that Couch would be best served with treatment rather than prison, perhaps she should have considered what was best for the public instead. It is abundantly clear that he had no remorse for his actions then, and still appears incapable of acting like a responsible human being. When she was asked whether she had any regrets about her sentencing of Ethan Couch after learning he had fled to Mexico, Judge Boyd responded, "No. I have nothing else to say."

"The history of the Constitution, its structure, and the Supreme Court's interpretation of the pardon power make clear that President Trump's decision to pardon Mr. Flynn is a political decision, not a legal one. Because the law recognizes the President's political power to pardon, the appropriate course is to dismiss this case as moot. However, the pardon does not, standing alone, render [Mr. Flynn] innocent of the alleged violation."

–United States District Judge Emmet
Sullivan, December 8, 2020

Former Lieutenant General Michael Flynn was chosen by President Donald Trump to serve as US National Security Advisor at the start of Trump's administration. Four days after the inauguration, on January 24, 2017, FBI Director James Comey directed two agents to interview Flynn at his West Wing office.

Comey later acknowledged, "If the FBI wanted to send agents into the White House itself to interview a senior official, you would work through the White House counsel and there would be discussions and approvals of who would be there." Comey, however, decided to ignore those procedures, saying, "I thought, 'It's early enough, let's just send a couple guys over.'"

Flynn's attorneys later noted that the FBI persuaded Flynn not to bring a lawyer to the meeting and did not reveal their motives for questioning him. Flynn was asked about a conversation he had had with former Russian Ambassador to the United States Sergey Kislyak in December 2016. Flynn told the agents he had not discussed sanctions imposed on Russia by the Obama Administration with Kislyak.

FBI wiretaps, however, confirmed that he had spoken with Kislyak about those sanctions. Flynn was subsequently charged by the FBI and resigned as National Security Advisor on February 13, 2017. Flynn later pleaded guilty to one count of lying to federal authorities, acknowledging that he had given "incomplete information" during his meeting with the FBI.

Flynn later asked the court to withdraw his guilty plea. The Justice Department moved to dismiss the charges against him, noting, "(1) Mr. Flynn's false statements to the FBI agents were not 'material' to any investigation; (2) the government is doubtful that it could prove the falsity of Mr. Flynn's statements; and (3) the government has 'no substantial federal interest in penalizing a defendant for a crime that it is not satisfied occurred and that it does not believe it can prove beyond a reasonable doubt.'"

Nevertheless, Judge Sullivan wanted the case against Flynn to continue. Meanwhile, Flynn was forced to sell his house to pay for his legal bills. On November 25, 2020, President Donald Trump provided Flynn with a full and unconditional pardon. Two weeks later, Judge Sullivan officially dismissed the case but felt compelled to take some parting shots at both Flynn and Trump in his decision, as noted above.

"I can't...I'm not a biologist."

–Judge for the US Court of Appeals for the D.C. Circuit Ketanji Brown Jackson, March 22, 2022

Judge Jackson was nominated by President Joe Biden to serve as an associate justice of the Supreme Court of the United States.

In the comment above, Jackson was responding to a question by Senator Marsha Blackburn, who asked the judge during her confirmation hearing with the Senate Judiciary Committee, "Can you provide a definition for the word *woman*?"

Jackson graduated *magna cum laude* from Harvard University and cum laude from Harvard Law School, where she was an editor of the *Harvard Law Review*. Nevertheless, she was unable to define the word *woman*.

Senator Blackburn responded to Judge Jackson by saying, "The fact that you can't give me a straight answer about something as fundamental as what a woman is underscores the dangers of the kind of progressive education that we are hearing about."

"Yes, Senator, I do."

–Judge for the US Court of Appeals for the D.C. Circuit Ketanji Brown Jackson, March 22, 2022

Jackson was responding to a question from Senator Ted Cruz during her confirmation hearing before the Senate Judiciary Committee for her appointment to the US Supreme Court.

Cruz had just presented a chart showing Judge Jackson's sentencing patterns in child pornography cases. Cruz then asked the judge, "Do you believe the voice of the children is heard when 100% of the time you're sentencing those in possession of child pornography to far below what the prosecutor's asking for?"

Jackson's appointment to the Supreme Court was ultimately confirmed by the Senate by a vote of fifty-three to forty-seven.

"Article V is not coming to mind at the moment."

–Judge Charnelle Bjelkengren, January 25, 2023

This statement was made by Bjelkengren, Judge of Spokane County Superior Court in Washington State, during her confirmation hearing before the US Senate Judiciary Committee. Judge Bjelkengren was being questioned by Senator John Kennedy following her appointment by President Biden to serve on the US District Court for the Eastern District of Washington.

Kennedy said to the judge, "Tell me what Article V of the Constitution does."

Of course, we have all experienced occasions, even during important moments, when we were unable to recall information we know well. Perhaps with that in mind, Kennedy tried again by asking the judge, "How about Article II?"

Sadly, the judge was still unable to provide any description at all. It's worth noting that Senate confirmation hearings are not scheduled at the last minute. The judge was well aware she would be questioned about her professional and educational experience, her command of the law, and her judicial philosophy. As someone being considered for a position as a United States Federal Judge, it may have been prudent for her to have spent at least a little time preparing for the session. It is also a reasonable cause for concern when a sitting judge is unable to answer basic questions about the US Constitution that many high school students would be capable of answering.

"In every respect, the court today exceeds its proper, limited role
in our Nation's governance...And then, perchance, it wonders

why it has only compounded the 'sharp debates' in the country?"

–Associate Justice of the Supreme Court of the
United States Elena Kagan, June 30, 2023

Kagan was referring to the Supreme Court's majority opinion in the case of *Biden v. Nebraska*. In the opinion written by Chief Justice John Roberts, the court concluded that the Biden administration overstepped its authority in its attempt to forgive student loan debt.

Roberts explains in his decision that the Secretary of Education's authority to "waive or modify" provisions of the law does not mean he has the authority to "completely rewrite" the law. He goes on to write that "Our precedent—old and new—requires that Congress speak clearly before a Department Secretary can unilaterally alter large sections of the American economy."

Justice Kagan, however, clearly felt differently. The comment above was part of her dissenting opinion in the case. Dissenting opinions are common in the Supreme Court, but Chief Justice Roberts took exception to Kagan's criticism of the court itself. He ended his written opinion with the following comment. "It has become a disturbing feature of some recent opinions to criticize the decisions with which they disagree as going beyond the proper role of the judiciary...Reasonable minds may disagree with our analysis...We do not mistake this plainly heartfelt disagreement for disparagement. It is important that the public not be misled either. Any such misperception would be harmful to this institution and our country."

"It strikes me that you are singling out a group that is exposed to a clear and present danger."

–Judge Thomas Garza, September 6, 2023

The Chino Valley Unified School District passed a policy that would require parental notification if a student decided to use a different gender identity while at school. The policy was met with a lawsuit by California Attorney General Rob Bonta.

In his decision to issue a temporary restraining order against the school district's policy, San Bernadino County Superior Court Judge Garza made the comment above. Critics complained that Garza was essentially referring to parents as a clear and present danger to their own children.

In a similar case in New Jersey, three school districts passed policies requiring parental notification if children were to request a change to their gender identity. The policies were immediately met with emergency lawsuits by New Jersey Attorney General Matt Platkin. During their argument before the court, Deputy Attorney General James Michael said, "There will be irreparable harm if the policy is implemented. Once a school outs a student to their parent, the harm is done. It's irreversible." Apparently, according to the Left, allowing parents to raise their own children now is considered an act of irreparable harm. You just can't make this stuff up.

"I'm not here to hear what he has to say."

–Judge Arthur Engoron, November 6, 2023

Engoron, who is an elected Judge on the New York State Supreme Court, was presiding over Donald Trump's civil fraud trial. Engoron made this ridiculous statement after Trump provided an extended answer to a question during his court testimony.

Trump has repeatedly claimed that the civil suit brought against him by New York Attorney General Letitia James was politically motivated.

Adding fuel to Trump's claim, on September 26, 2023, before Trump's trial even began, Judge Engoron granted James a partial summary judgment in the case.

James' lawsuit against Trump claims that he engaged in fraudulent business practices and inflated the value of his businesses on loan applications. On February 16, 2024, Judge Engoron announced his verdict. The Trump Organization was ordered to pay $364 million in penalties and approximately $100 million in prejudgment interest. Trump was also barred from serving as an officer or director of any New York corporation for three years and is banned from seeking loans in New York for three years. Trump has repeatedly claimed that the case against him amounts to election interference and has called the Attorney General "corrupt" and the judge "crooked."

"Through no fault of her own, the defendant was out of touch with reality."

–Ventura County Superior Court Judge
David Worley, January 23, 2024

Judge Worley was referring to Bryn Spejcher, who was convicted by a jury of involuntary manslaughter in the death of her friend, Chad O'Melia.

On May 27, 2018, Spejcher was visiting O'Melia, age 26, at his condominium in Thousand Oaks, California, when the two began using marijuana. Sometime after midnight that night, Spejcher claimed to have an out-of-body experience. She then proceeded to stab her friend, whom she had only known for about three weeks, 108 times.

Judge Worley believed that the defendant had suffered what is known as marijuana-induced psychosis and was therefore not responsible for her actions. The judge sentenced Spejcher to two years of probation and 100 hours of community service.

After the judge announced his sentence, Sean O'Melia, the victim's father, stated, "I really don't believe that I have found any justice here in Ventura County, nor has my son been given any justice." I strongly agree. After all, why do individuals take drugs? One can only assume that they do so to become intoxicated. Wouldn't that imply that they wish to be out of touch with reality?

Of course, no one assumes they are going to experience a seriously adverse medical reaction to the drugs they take, but that should not excuse them for their actions. No one forced Spejcher to take drugs, and she should be held accountable for her actions after doing so. I wish I could understand why officials in states like California turn such a blind eye to the evils of drug use. A sentence of probation and community service in response to a cold-blooded murder is nothing short of outrageous.

"My biggest concern is that your view has the First Amendment hamstringing the government in significant ways in the most important time periods."

–Associate Justice of the Supreme Court of the United States Ketanji Brown Jackson, March 18, 2024

Jackson's comment was made during oral arguments in the case of *Murthy v. Missouri*, which alleges that the Biden administration pressured social media companies to remove content with which they disagreed.

Jackson's concern that the First Amendment to the US Constitution could be seen as "hamstringing" the government led many to question her understanding of its intended purpose. The First Amendment reads,

"Congress shall make no law respecting an establishment of religion or prohibiting the free exercise thereof; or abridging the freedom of speech, or of the press; or the right of the people peaceably to assemble, and to petition the Government for a redress of grievances." The phrase "Congress shall make no law" should make it clear to all Americans that the First Amendment was specifically written to "hamstring" the government.

> *"That law upends the federal-state balance of power that has existed for over a century, in which the National Government has had exclusive authority over entry and removal of noncitizens."*

–Associate Justice of the Supreme Court of the United States Sonia Sotomayor, March 19, 2024

Sotomayor was referring to the court's decision to allow Texas to implement *Texas Senate Bill 4.* "Senate Bill 4 looks to prohibit 'sanctuary city' policies that prohibit local law enforcement from inquiring about a person's immigration status and complying with detainer requests." It also "Authorizes a peace officer to arrest an undocumented person."

Sotomayor's comment about the federal-state balance of power is a reference to federalism. Federalism is the distribution of power between the national government and the state governments, and it is an essential component in the structure of government in America. The problem with Sotomayor's claim is that there is effectively no balance of power when it comes to immigration enforcement. As she correctly points out, "The National Government has had exclusive authority over entry and removal of noncitizens." The question at hand is, what recourse does a state have when the national government abdicates its responsibilities?

Chapter 9

State and Local Leaders

"All politics is local."
–Thomas P. O'Neill

"We have learned something important since the days that I served in Vietnam, and you exemplify it. Whatever we think about the war, whatever we call it, Afghanistan or Iraq, we owe our military men and women unconditional support."

–Connecticut Attorney General
Richard Blumenthal, March 2008

Blumenthal made this comment during a ceremony in Norwalk, Connecticut, honoring veterans. It was one of many times when Blumenthal referred to his service in Vietnam. For years, newspapers across Connecticut also referred to him as a Vietnam veteran.

After receiving five military deferments between 1965 and 1970, Blumenthal eventually enlisted in the Marine Reserves. He was stationed in Washington, D.C., where his responsibilities included collecting and distributing toys as part of regular Toys for Tots campaigns. He later clarified to the press that he should have used the word "during" Vietnam rather than "in" Vietnam in previous statements, saying, "I served during the Vietnam era." Blumenthal's false claims are part of what is commonly referred to as "stolen valor." He was elected to the US Senate on November 2, 2010.

"I've got this thing and it's f***ing golden, and uh, uh, I'm just not giving it up for f***in' nothing. I'm not gonna do it. And, and I can always use it. I can parachute me there."

–Illinois Governor Rod Blagojevich,
November 5, 2008

Blagojevich was caught on an FBI wiretap making this statement in reference to his opportunity to fill a US Senate seat after it was vacated by Barack Obama following his election as President the day before.

After he was impeached and removed from office, Blagojevich was convicted for illegally attempting to trade the senate seat for $1.5 million in campaign contributions and other personal benefits. On December 7, 2011, Blagojevich was sentenced to fourteen years in federal prison following his conviction on eighteen total counts of corruption during his time as governor.

As he imposed the sentence on the disgraced former governor, US District Judge James Zagel said, "When it is the governor who goes bad…the harm here is not measured in the value of money or property . . . the harm is the erosion of public trust in government."

"Earlier today, I learned from multiple credible sources that the US Immigration and Customs Enforcement (ICE) is preparing to conduct an operation in the Bay Area, including Oakland, starting as soon as within the next 24 hours."

–Oakland (CA) Mayor Libby Schaaf,
February 24, 2018, in a tweet

Schaff delivered this message to the public in the hopes of thwarting an upcoming ICE operation. Oakland is a so-called Sanctuary

City, whose municipal laws try to protect illegal immigrants from deportation and prosecution.

On January 25, 2017, shortly after taking office, President Donald Trump signed Executive Order 13768, which restricted federal funding to jurisdictions that limit cooperation with ICE. The order explained, "Sanctuary jurisdictions across the United States willfully violate Federal law in an attempt to shield aliens from removal from the United States. These jurisdictions have caused immeasurable harm to the American people and to the very fabric of our Republic."

With her post on Twitter, Mayor Schaaf took the concept of a Sanctuary City to an unprecedented level. She was not just refusing to cooperate with ICE and federal authorities; she was now actively trying to obstruct their work. In response to her actions, many officials criticized Schaaf, and some called for her arrest, pointing out that she put ICE agents' safety at risk with her post. Schaaf responded saying, "I have no regrets, none."

"We're not going to make America great again, it was never that great."

–New York Governor Andrew
Cuomo, August 15, 2018

In a rebuke of President Donald Trump's presidential campaign slogan, Make America Great Again, Cuomo claimed America had never reached greatness due to its history of discrimination and stereotyping against women. Cuomo was seeking re-election for a third term as governor at the time and was considered by many to be a potential presidential candidate in 2020. It's worth contrasting Cuomo's view of America with that of President Ronald Reagan, who proclaimed, "How can we not believe in the greatness of America? How can we not do what is right and needed to preserve this last best hope of man on Earth?"

That's what a true American leader should sound like.

"I can tell you exactly what would happen. The infant would be delivered. The infant would be kept comfortable. The infant would be resuscitated if that's what the mother and the family desired. And then a discussion would ensue between the physicians and the mother…We want the government not to be involved in these types of decisions. We want the decision to be made by the mothers and their providers."

–Virginia Governor Ralph
Northam, January 30, 2019

Northam, who is also a pediatric neurosurgeon, made this comment during an Ask the Governor segment on WTOP radio while voicing his support for a Virginia bill that would ease restrictions on late-term abortions. His description led to widespread outrage across the nation for his casual attitude toward infanticide.

On September 18, 2023, California Governor Gavin Newsom was asked by CNN's Dana Bash about abortion "up to and after birth." He responded by saying, "What does that mean, after-birth abortion? It's made up. It's a political thing…The reality is it's a canard. It's a political frame. It's total B.S." Is it really, Gavin?

"We need to get radical revolutionaries elected…Stay ready for the revolution, 'cause that's the only solution."

–New York State Assembly Member
Charles Barron, April 5, 2019

Barron, who was previously a member of the Harlem branch of the Black Panther party and the National Black United Front, once called for a portrait of Thomas Jefferson that hung in New York City's City Hall to be replaced with a bust of Malcolm X.

To justify the removal of Jefferson's portrait, he said, "The man is a pedophile." Barron, who does not salute the American flag and does not recognize the pledge of allegiance, is also an antisemite who stated, "The biggest terrorist in the world is the government of Israel." Barron also said, "[Moammar Khadafy] is a hero. He is a freedom fighter. And America doesn't like him because they can't control him."

Barron, who is also a racist, previously demanded clemency for individuals he described as political prisoners, including Anthony Bottom, who was convicted in 1971 for killing two New York City police officers. In addition, following the shooting death of Sean Bell, a Black man killed by the NYPD in November 2006, Barron said, "If we don't get an indictment, there's going to be an explosion. We're not the only ones who can bleed. Maybe the rest of us need to get a shot off."

One of Barron's most infamous comments came during a demonstration on slavery reparations when he said, "I just want to go up to the closest White person and say, 'You can't understand this, it's a Black thing' and then slap him just for my mental health." In 2012, *The New York Times* wrote an article about Barron entitled, "A Candidate Known for His Unconventional Views." *Unconventional* is certainly an understatement.

"It's really been unfortunate the amount of work we and other state attorneys general have had to do in this space to hold the line."

–Massachusetts Attorney General
Maura Healey, May 16, 2019

In February 2019, President Donald Trump used the National Emergencies Act to declare a national emergency at the US Southern border. Under the declaration, Trump intended to use $3.6 billion in military construction funds to construct a border wall.

Trump's declaration was met with a multistate lawsuit filed by twenty state attorneys general, including Maura Healey. This response should come as no surprise given that Healey's office sued the Trump administration nearly 100 times. There was a total of 138 multistate lawsuits filed against the Trump administration in just four years. All but six of these lawsuits were filed by Democrat attorneys general, leading critics to denounce them as politically motivated. In contrast, during the eight years of the Obama presidency, there were a total of seventy-eight state lawsuits filed against his administration.

Ironically, on August 8, 2023, Maura Healey, who was now governor of Massachusetts, declared a state of emergency in Massachusetts "due to rapidly rising numbers of migrant families arriving in Massachusetts in need of shelter and services and a severe lack of shelter availability in the state."

"Clean and sober is one of the biggest damn mistakes this country has ever made."

–California Governor Gavin
Newsom, January 15, 2020

For decades, Democrats have had a lax attitude toward drug use. It was widely embraced en masse by the baby boom counterculture and has been promoted and validated in feature films and popular culture ever since. Sadly, today drugs are more prevalent and powerful than ever before.

Politicians were once scorned for admitting drug use during their youth. Today, however, leaders like Barack Obama and Kamala Harris openly write about their frequent use of drugs in the past and even joke about it in interviews with no sense of shame or fear of harm to their reputations. On the contrary, such admissions seem to resonate positively with many in today's society.

Our nation's collective attitude toward drug use has taken some dramatic and dangerous turns in recent years. As a youngster during the Reagan administration, I distinctly remember the recommendation promoted by First Lady Nancy Reagan to "just say no to drugs." Influencers today refer to ideas like this as antiquated and ridiculous concepts that are best used as a punchline for a joke.

Democrats are also quick to cite "the failed war on drugs" as justification for the acceptance and legalization of drugs. This argument implies that because drugs haven't been successfully eradicated from the planet, we should completely reverse public policy and actually encourage their use.

How such a position can be taken seriously is astonishing to me. From the teen who moves from marijuana to harder drugs only to fall victim to a lifetime of addiction to the children who are neglected by their drug-addicted parents; the homeowner who was robbed by a stranger looking for money to feed their addiction; the parents who lost a child to an overdose; the family that lost a loved one to an impaired driver; the residents who once lived in a beautiful city but are now confronted daily with open-air drug dens and homeless encampments; the residents of small towns who are dealing with gang violence in what they once believed were safe communities; the law enforcement officers who risk their lives trying to protect the public from drug-related crimes; the disturbing power and devastating impact international drug cartels have had on countries like Mexico and their affiliated crimes, like human trafficking; to the billions of tax dollars and countless hours spent treating drug addiction and its long-term consequences, there is absolutely no redeeming value in the use of illicit drugs.

There is overwhelming evidence of drugs' devastating impact on individuals, families, and communities. Can anyone identify a community where drugs have been legalized and the quality of life there has improved? If you're not sure, take a closer look at recent changes to cities like Portland, Oregon. When are we going to recognize and accept that drugs are a scourge on the planet? If we don't change our collective opinion about them, we will continue to witness the gradual decline of our great nation. It's worth noting as a sad postscript that marijuana was discovered in the White House twice in 2022. In 2023, the US Secret Service also found cocaine near the Situation Room in the West Wing of the White House. No one was ever charged in these incidents.

"No resident shall be denied re-admission or admission to the NH solely based on a confirmed or suspected diagnosis of COVID-19."

–New York Governor Andrew Cuomo,
March 25, 2020, in an Executive Order
to Nursing Home Administrators

During the COVID-19 pandemic, many Americans found the televised press conferences by New York Governor Andrew Cuomo reassuring. At a time when there was much uncertainty about the virus and the best procedures to combat it, Cuomo seemed to portray an image of command and control.

However, his executive order on March 25, 2020, significantly changed the public's perception of the governor. The purpose of the order was to require nursing homes to take back residents who had been discharged from hospitals after being treated for COVID-19 so hospitals would not become overwhelmed with patients.

Critics soon pointed out, however, that the order increased the number of COVID-19-related deaths in nursing homes. By the summer of 2021, 15,000 residents and employees of nursing homes in New York had died of complications from COVID-19, more than any other state. Cuomo said he was following federal guidance, but that was later contradicted by Seema Verma, Head of the Centers for Medicare and Medicaid (the federal government's top official overseeing nursing homes).

Verma said, "Under no circumstances should a hospital discharge a patient to a nursing home that is not prepared to take care of those patients' needs." Making matters worse, the Cuomo administration was accused of altering state data by only including residents who had died of COVID-19 inside a nursing home and excluding nursing home residents who died at a hospital. This practice effectively hid the true number of nursing home deaths. A report by the New York State Department of Health later concluded that the actual number of deaths was approximately 50% higher than the figure the Cuomo administration was citing publicly at the time.

"I take my personal hygiene very seriously. I felt like I needed to have a haircut. I'm not able to do that myself. So, I got a haircut."

–Chicago Mayor Lori Lightfoot, April 6, 2020

This statement seems pretty straightforward and even insignificant until you realize that Mayor Lightfoot made this comment at a time when salons and barbershops were closed across Illinois following a stay-at-home order by Governor J.B. Pritzker.

Apparently Lightfoot believes she is entitled to disobey this order because, unlike her constituents, she takes her personal hygiene very seriously.

"We are going to dismantle the Minneapolis Police Department. Say it with me. Dismantle the Minneapolis Police Department."

> –Second Vice-Chairwoman Minnesota
> Democratic-Farmer-Labor Party
> Shivanthi Sathanandan, June 5, 2020

In September 2023, Sathanandan was carjacked in her home driveway in North Minneapolis. She received lacerations to the head, bruising, and a broken leg. Shortly thereafter she posted on Facebook, "Catch these young people who are running wild creating chaos across our city and hold them in custody and prosecute them. Period."

Perhaps there is some truth to the old line that is often attributed to former Mayor of Philadelphia Frank Rizzo: "A liberal is a conservative who hasn't been mugged yet." A lifelong Democrat, Rizzo switched to the Republican party in 1986.

"I want to make it clear that I believe strongly in defunding the police and reducing the number of officers on our force."

> –San Francisco District Supervisor Hillary
> Ronen, August 26, 2020, in a tweet

Under pressure from Ronen and other officials, San Francisco Mayor London Breed announced on July 31, 2020, that $120 million would be redirected from law enforcement agencies to be spent addressing discrepancies in the Black community.

According to *The Washington Post*, the San Francisco Police

Department was down more than 600 officers in 2023, almost 30% of its allotment. Interestingly, Supervisor Ronen said on March 15, 2023, "I've been begging this department to give the Mission [a city district] what it deserves in terms of police presence all year long, and I have been told time and time and time and time again there are no officers that we can send."

Some people just don't seem to have a basic grasp of the concept of cause and effect.

"We're looking at ways in which we can provide incentives."

–San Francisco Mayor London
Breed, September 1, 2021

Mayor Breed was referring to a new program in the city called the Dream Keeper Fellowship. Sounds intriguing, doesn't it? Is it a new college scholarship program? Is it a new community service project? Nope. This new pilot program planned to give ten individuals in the city considered to be at high risk for committing a gun crime a $300 gift card each month that they refrain from participating in a shooting. Is this really what we've come to in America? We are now paying our citizens not to kill each other.

"I'm not going to let parents come into schools and actually take books out and make their own decision...I don't think parents should be telling schools what they should teach."

–Virginia Governor Terry McAuliffe,
September 28, 2021

This comment was made during McAuliffe's Virginia Gubernatorial Debate with Republican candidate and businessman Glenn Younkin.

McAuliffe was referencing *Virginia House Bill 2191*, which would require schools to notify parents if their child is enrolled in a course in which the instructional materials or related academic activities include sexually explicit content or the potential for sexually explicit content. The legislation would also require teachers to provide alternative instructional materials if requested by a parent.

McAuliffe vetoed the bill in 2017. Meanwhile, parents across Virginia voiced their disapproval to school boards over books such as *Lawn Boy*, which was described as containing pedophilic sex between men and boys, and *Beloved*, which was described as featuring scenes of bestiality, sex, violence, and infanticide.

On November 2, 2021, Glenn Younkin was elected Governor of Virginia, defeating McAuliffe 50.8% to 48.4%. On January 23, 2024, President Joe Biden addressed an audience in Manassas, Virginia, saying, "Hello, Virginia, and the real governor, Terry McAuliffe." It's funny that President Biden doesn't seem to have any problem denying the results of an election but Donald Trump has been impeached and indicted for doing likewise.

"I do believe education is under assault."

–California Governor Gavin
Newsom, July 13, 2022

Newson made this remark while addressing the Education Commission of the States after receiving the Frank Newman Award for State Innovation. That year, Newsom's education budget became the highest in state history after closing schools for nearly two years. Meanwhile, approximately half of the public school students in California failed to meet the state standards in English, and only 40% were proficient in math. California also ranked fiftieth in the nation in literacy. Sounds like plenty of justification for an innovation award, doesn't it?

> *"And we're here to say that the era of Trump and Zelden and Molinaro, just jump on a bus and head down to Florida where you belong. OK, get out of town, get out of town because you don't represent our values. You are not New Yorkers."*

–New York Governor Kathy
Hochul, August 22, 2022

It's pretty rare for a sitting governor to tell her own constituents to leave their state, but that's what Hochul did in this public address. Apparently, in Hochul's mind, there is no room in New York for anyone with a dissenting opinion. According to US Census Bureau data, more than 100,000 residents left New York State between July 2022 and July 2023, a rate higher than any other state in the nation. In a strange twist, during Hochul's inaugural address on January 1, 2023, she said, "We must reverse the trend of people leaving our state in search of lower costs and opportunities elsewhere."

> *"Anyone who wants to question how I protect myself just doesn't understand the world Black women walk in...My travel accommodations are a matter of safety, not of luxury."*

–New Orleans Mayor LaToya
Cantrell, September 8, 2022

Cantrell was responding to criticism that she charged the City of New Orleans for tens of thousands of dollars in first-class airfare upgrades. Her explanation fell short to many, who wondered how a first-class airline seat provided more safety than an economy seat, especially when it was learned that on her July 2022 flight to France, Cantrell's security official was seated in the economy section while she sat in first class.

The city's travel policy notes, "Employees are required to purchase the lowest airfare available…Employees who choose an upgrade from coach, economy, or business class flights are solely responsible for the difference in cost."

Nevertheless, Cantrell initially refused to reimburse the city for her airfare upgrades, saying, "All expenses incurred doing business on behalf of the City of New Orleans will not be reimbursed to the City of New Orleans." However, after the Louisiana Board of Ethics filed charges against her for her use of first-class airfare, and after New Orleans' Chief Administrative Officer concluded that the city's travel policy applied to the mayor, Cantrell reluctantly agreed to reimburse the city.

This controversy was just one of many that followed the New Orleans Mayor. Cantrell was also criticized for inappropriate use of a city-owned apartment which she frequented with a New Orleans Police Officer and member of her protective detail named Jeffrey Vappie. It has been alleged that the two were having an extra-marital affair. On August 24, 2023, the New Orleans City Council voted to override Cantrell's veto and discontinue the use of the city-owned apartment.

"We are a community that comes together to support immigrants."

–Massachusetts State Representative Dylan
Fernandes, September 14, 2022, in a tweet

Fernandes represents Martha's Vineyard, the island known as a popular playground for the rich and famous. It received a flight of approximately fifty illegal immigrants on September 14, 2022. The flight originated in Texas and was funded by Florida Governor Ron DeSantis.

Along with Texas Governor Greg Abbott, DeSantis was frustrated by the overwhelming numbers of illegal immigrants entering the US across the Southern border. The two governors transported thousands of migrants to so-called sanctuary cities and states across the country. Martha's Vineyard, which proclaimed itself to be a sanctuary destination and is dominated by Democrats, seemed like a reasonable location for a small group of migrants to relocate. However, barely forty-eight hours after their arrival on the island, arrangements were made to move the migrants to Joint Base Cape Cod.

According to the *Martha's Vineyard Times*, the average home sale on the island reached $2.3 million in April 2023. It's too bad that the Obamas, who live in a 7,000-square-foot mansion on twenty-nine acres on the island, couldn't find any room to board a few of the migrants. In spite of their proclamations of support, in the end, I suppose this is simply a case of "not in my (very expensive) backyard."

"We're not a border town. We don't have an infrastructure to handle this type of and level of immigration to our city...We're not Texas."

–Washington D.C. Mayor Muriel Bowser, September 15, 2022

Bowser was responding to the arrival of two busloads of illegal immigrants who had arrived outside the US Naval Observatory, the home of Vice President Kamala Harris. The buses were sent to D.C. by Texas Governor Greg Abbott.

According to the US Census Bureau, Washington D.C. had a population of 670,000 in July 2022 while El Paso Texas, a border town, had a population of 677,000. At the same time Mayor Bowser was complaining about two busloads of migrants arriving in D.C., El Paso, Texas was receiving approximately 1,000 illegal migrants per day. Apparently, Mayor Bowser believes that, unlike D.C., border towns somehow have the infrastructure to handle that.

"I am concerned about the chilling effect other potential laws may have on physicians and surgeons who need to be able to effectively talk to their patients about the risks and benefits of treatments for a disease that appeared in just the last few years."

–California Governor Gavin
Newsom, September 30, 2022

This was part of a letter from Newsom to the members of the California legislature after he signed California Assembly Bill 2098 into law. The bill, entitled "Physicians and surgeons: unprofessional conduct," designates the dissemination of misinformation or disinformation related to the SARS-CoV-2 coronavirus, or COVID-19, as unprofessional conduct.

It also notes that existing California law requires the applicable California state medical board to take action against any licensed physician and surgeon charged with unprofessional conduct. The law further defines *misinformation* as false information that is contradicted by contemporary scientific consensus and is contrary to the standard of care.

Ironically, the law also notes, "The safety and efficacy of COVID-19 vaccines have been confirmed through evaluation by the federal Food and Drug Administration (FDA) and the vaccines continue to undergo intensive safety monitoring by the CDC."

Bearing in mind that this bill, which reaffirms the "safety and efficacy of COVID-19 vaccines," was signed into law on September 30, 2022, it is interesting to note that major news organizations had already been reporting on the declining efficacy of the vaccines for more than a year at that point.

For example, on August 18, 2021, CBS News Correspondent Alexander Tin reported that a study by CDC researchers found that during the surge in Delta variant cases in the summer of 2021, the effectiveness of the Pfizer and Moderna vaccines dropped to 53.1%, down from 74.7%, in nursing home residents.

In the same article, a separate study is referenced that analyzed data from millions of fully vaccinated adults across health databases in New York. In it, researchers found that overall vaccine effectiveness for all adults appeared to drop to 79.8% through late July 2021. Given the findings of these studies and the dissemination of this information by a mainstream news organization like CBS News, wouldn't it be reasonable to conclude that the California law's assertion about the vaccine's safety and efficacy could be interpreted as misinformation by the law's own definition?

Moreover, by requiring physicians to adhere to "contemporary scientific consensus," which is also undefined in the law, how can there be any realistic expectation that medical science will advance with time? If physicians are denied the freedom to question and challenge contemporary scientific understanding, we are effectively destroying the scientific method, which has served as the foundation of scientific discovery since the scientific revolution.

One might wonder if such a law had passed 200 years ago, would physicians today still be treating patients by bleeding them simply because they were denied the ability to challenge contemporary scientific consensus?

Furthermore, the California law clearly violates the free speech and due process rights of physicians. A lawsuit filed against the Newsom administration by five California physicians correctly noted, "The First Amendment applies not only to expression of majority opinions but to minority views as well."

This is precisely why laws like this pose such a danger if left unopposed. In their ongoing effort to seize control over language and thought, Democrats are actively working to criminalize opinions and speech that differ from their perspective. This particular law may have only targeted physicians in California and their ability to communicate freely with their patients, but if laws like this are allowed to stand, there should be no doubt that Democrats will confidently pursue additional encroachments on civil liberties, citing laws like this as precedent.

For this reason, the above quote by Gavin Newsom should serve as a warning to all of us about the slippery slope laws like this create. One has to wonder, however, if his concerns were truly sincere. After all, they didn't stop him from signing the bill into law.

However, in October 2023, Governor Newsom quietly acknowledged that the law would be repealed effective January 1, 2024. Dr. Mark McDonald, one of the physicians who filed a legal challenge to the law, said, "Obviously, I am delighted that we will no longer be threatened with license suspension for speaking to our patients honestly. I'm still hoping though, that there will be a ruling because it would be wonderful to have a legal precedent to stop this from happening again."

"It was quite a journey to get here."

–New York Governor Kathy
Hochul, January 25, 2023

Hochul was referencing the opening of New York City's new Grand

Central Madison terminal. The terminal links Long Island Railroad trains to Manhattan's East Side.

Unbelievably, proposals for this stretch of track and the new terminal were first submitted back in 1963 but changes to plans and delays plagued construction for decades, and responsibility for the project was passed along between nine different governors. The 3.5-mile-long subway tunnel and adjoining station eventually cost more than $11 billion to construct.

In 2017, *The New York Times* called the project the "most expensive mile of subway track on earth." In comparison, Manhattan's Empire State Building, which was the tallest building in the world when it opened on May 1, 1931, was built in just fourteen months at a cost in today's dollars of less than $600 million.

Why is it so hard for America today to build things as efficiently as it once did?

"Those who made the determination that, you know, no, I still want to come into a work environment and I'm not going to be vaccinated, no, I want to still ride the train, I want to do whatever I want, that just wasn't right. That wasn't right."

–New York City Mayor Eric
Adams, February 10, 2023

New York Governor Kathy Hochul shared a similar perspective about the unvaccinated when she announced on January 24, 2023, that she would not rehire unvaccinated medical workers who were fired during the pandemic, even after the state Supreme Court struck down the mandate.

There is no rationale for such a position, and one can easily understand why some might see comments like this as pure retaliation against Americans who refused to obey political leaders even at the risk of losing their jobs. Political leaders like Adams and Hochul may lead us to conclude that Democrats believe dissension—and by that I mean personal freedom—is not to be tolerated and will be punished.

"This bill…would include a parent's affirmation of the child's gender identity or gender expression as part of the health, safety, and welfare of the child."

–California Assembly Member Lori
Wilson, February 14, 2023

Wilson introduced an amendment to Section 3011 of the California Family Code, which relates to family law. According to Wilson's amendment, "Existing law governs the determination of child custody and visitation in contested proceedings and requires the court, for purposes of deciding custody, to determine the best interests of the child based on certain factors, including, among other things, the health, safety, and welfare of the child."

If enacted into law, the assemblywoman's amendment would mean that parents in California would be required by the state to affirm their child's gender expression or risk losing custody of their child. There was a time when individuals who made comments like "The state is coming for your kids" were chastised as conspiracy nuts. Bills like this, however, may be a wake-up call that perhaps those fears aren't as far-fetched now as they once were.

"Any vote coming out of the South Side for somebody not named Lightfoot is a vote for Chuy Garcia or Paul Vallas. If you want them controlling your faith and your destiny, then stay home.

Then don't vote."

–Chicago Mayor Lori Lightfoot, February 18, 2023

Lightfoot received widespread criticism for essentially telling her constituents to either vote for her or not to vote at all. I guess that's how they practice democracy in Chicago.

"I see access as a problem. I see parents being able to direct their child's education, and they are already in the lower twenty-fifth percentile, meaning a lot of those parents did not finish high school and cannot direct their, could not finish their own education. I am extremely concerned that we would put money in their hands and that entire piece of life in the hands of parents who are not qualified to make those decisions."

–Georgia State Representative Lydia Glaize, March 20, 2023

Representative Glaize made this comment at a Georgia House Education Subcommittee on Policy during a discussion about the Georgia Scholarship Act, which would create a state-funded scholarship in the amount of $6,000 per year per student that parents could use to cover approved education expenses.

Let's take a moment to dissect her point. It is like she's saying, "Our public schools are so bad that they have failed a large number of students for generations, and many of those students have never graduated high school as a result. Therefore, because these people are undereducated, they should now be denied the power to direct their child's education and the state should be allowed to force their children to stay in the very same failed public schools."

If this argument makes any sense at all and policies like these are allowed to persist, how will we ever break the cycle of failed education? Sadly, Democrat state legislators all over the country are fighting hard against the concept of school choice. On February 10, 2022, Wisconsin State Representative Lee Snodgrass tweeted, "If parents want to 'have a say' in their child's education they should homeschool or pay for private school tuition out of their family budget." This tweet was later deleted.

"I also don't get what's going on in this country. I don't get why everybody's not doing what we're doing."

–California Governor Gavin
Newsom, April 9, 2023

Governor Newsom, who once described the Biden administration as a "masterclass" on government, was referring to his home state of California during an interview on MSNBC with Biden's former White House press secretary, Jen Psaki.

According to the US Census Bureau, between 2021 and 2022, 818,000 residents moved out of California. It is the second most expensive state in the country to live in after Hawaii. It also has more than 4.7 million residents living below the poverty level (the most in the nation), more than 170,000 homeless people (the most in the nation), as well as the nation's largest population of illegal immigrants, and a massive housing shortage. California also has the highest income tax rate of any state, the highest sales tax rate of any state, and the highest gasoline prices of any state.

According to *US News and World Report,* in 2023 California ranked thirty-eighth in the nation for K-12 education and fiftieth in affordability and opportunity. In addition, California has the most households (nearly 1.2 million) receiving SNAP (Supplemental Nutrition Assistance Program, formerly known as Food Stamps.)

According to the National Association of Realtors, the median price for an existing home in the US was $387,600 in November 2023. No surprise, California had the highest median house price in the nation at $793,600. According to ABC News San Diego, so many people were fleeing California in 2021 that the state actually ran out of U-Hauls to rent. U-Haul reported that their top destinations from California were Texas followed by Florida.

Based on his comment above, Newsom forgot about his visit to Los Angeles on January 20, 2022. He was there to inspect a portion of the Union Pacific railroad, the site of recent train robberies where thieves made off with millions of dollars in merchandise, including packages from FedEx, Amazon, and the US Postal Service. As he surveyed the area, which was strewn with hundreds of empty boxes, he said to a film crew, "I'm asking myself, what the hell is going on? We look like a third-world country." Well, Gavin, you're not the only one who thinks so.

"No one has the right to take the life of another person."

–New York Governor Kathy Hochul, May 4, 2023

Hochul was referencing a tragic incident that occurred on a New York City subway when a belligerent 30-year-old homeless man by the name of Jordan Neely threw garbage at a passenger and proceeded to yell at and harass other passengers until a 24-year-old ex-Marine subdued him by placing him in a chokehold, which sadly resulted in Neely's death.

Officials on the Left immediately called the confrontation a murder, and demonstrators in New York City took to the streets and clashed with police with some protesters chanting, "What do we want? Justice! When do we want it? Now! If we don't get it? Burn it down!"

Hochul began her public statement by saying, "I do want to acknowledge how horrific it was to view a video of Jordan Neely being killed for being a passenger on our subway trains." Statements like this provide cover to all those who believe that Black men are randomly being hunted by White men in the US.

Hochul failed to acknowledge a critical fact, which is that the instigator in the incident was Neely. He was not simply a passenger on our subway like millions of others. Neely was intentionally creating a disturbance, which, in the absence of police, led other passengers to take action when they feared for their physical safety.

I think we all agree with Hochul's statement that "No one has the right to take the life of another person" in spirit. However, we can't forget that it has always been a fundamental human right to protect yourself and others from harm. If that right is dissolved, as some politicians would prefer, public safety will be in peril.

For some inexplicable reason, in recent years politicians on the Left have repeatedly defended the actions of the criminal instigator over the law-abiding citizens who are involuntarily put in difficult situations. Hochul even had the audacity to say that "...he [Neely] was not going to cause harm to these people," as if she could somehow know what would have happened. It is worth noting that Neely had been arrested forty-two times in the past, including four arrests for assault. At the time of the incident, he had an active warrant for assault.

Does anyone believe for a minute that Neely would have been harmed that day if he was simply just another passenger on the subway? Self-defense is not a trivial issue.

"I'm declaring this a state of emergency."

–North Carolina Governor Roy
Cooper, May 22, 2023

Governor Cooper was referring to his concerns about a Republican bill in the North Carolina legislature that he feared would hurt the state's public schools. In a special address, Cooper said, "Their plan would expand private school vouchers so anyone…can get taxpayer money for their children's private school tuition."

Is that supposed to be a bad thing? The public schools are failing many of our students. According to the US Department of Education, the percentage of eighth-grade students in North Carolina who performed at or above the National Assessment of Educational Progress (NAEP) proficiency level was 26% in 2022.

Why, then, is the idea of school vouchers resisted? The answer is clear: it would diminish the control and power of the teacher's unions, which are firmly supportive of Democrats.

Cooper went on to say that Republicans want to bring culture wars into public school classrooms. This is another joke. Anyone who is familiar with public education knows that it is overwhelmingly influenced by Democrat ideology. If Republicans are successful, this type of indoctrination would not be allowed. Worse yet in the minds of Democrats, perhaps students might learn alternative points of view. This is what Governor Cooper refers to as culture wars. It's clear that he and the teacher's unions would prefer an atmosphere without war, where every student would hear only one point of view as they have for many years now.

"@RonDeSantis you small, pathetic man. This isn't Martha's Vineyard. Kidnapping charges?"

–California Governor Gavin Newsom,
June 5, 2023, in a tweet

In this tweet, Newsom was referring to Florida Governor Ron DeSantis' decision to send planes with illegal immigrants to Sacramento, California.

It should be noted that in his 2019 inaugural address, Governor Newsom reaffirmed California as a sanctuary state, saying, "Together, let us build a house stronger than the coming storms, yet open to the world. A house that provides shelter to all who need it and sanctuary to all who seek it."

In response to Newsom's tweet, Governor DeSantis said during a news conference, "These sanctuary jurisdictions are part of the reason we have this problem because they have endorsed and agitated for these types of open border policies. They have bragged that they are sanctuary jurisdictions…When they have to deal with some of the fruits of that they all of a sudden become very, very upset about that."

"The DA's role has really no impact on crime."

–Alameda County (CA) District Attorney
Pamela Price, July 18, 2023

Few comments in this book are more blatantly false than this one. According to Law.com, a district attorney is defined as "an elected official of a county or a designated district with the responsibility for prosecuting crimes." To say that a DA has no impact on crime is to ignore the obvious.

However, it is not totally surprising that DA Price would make such a comment. She is part of a wave of prosecutors across the United States that have received campaign funds from billionaire Hungarian-American businessman George Soros. By 2023, Soros was estimated to have spent $40 million in support of progressive candidates for DA roles nationwide.

Historically, the role of a DA has been to represent "the people" in the prosecution of criminals. While it may be hard to claim that any candidate for public office is completely apolitical, DA candidates were often like-minded in their approach to law enforcement. Regardless of the candidate, their priorities were traditionally focused on pursuing justice and community safety.

In recent years, however, George Soros has developed a strategy that has transformed the office of District Attorney in many communities. The progressive candidates he supported have promoted a new approach to law enforcement that has dramatically reduced criminal accountability. These radical DAs have been widely criticized for showing more concern for the accused than the victims of crime. This dangerous new perspective effectively means a criminal defendant now has two advocates in court while "the people" have been left with none. These DAs have pursued alternatives to incarceration, ended the practice of cash bail, and reduced, dismissed, or failed to pursue charges against criminals in a variety of crime categories.

By instituting policies like these, DAs have effectively claimed a fiat to eliminate criminal laws with which they disagree. Senator Josh Hawley described the situation well when he said, "Everywhere Soros-backed prosecutors go, crime follows. These legal arsonists have abandoned their duty to public safety by pursuing leniency even for the most heinous crime, and they often flat-out refuse to charge criminals for shoplifting, vagrancy, and entire categories of misdemeanors." At a meeting with Oakland residents on September 9, 2023, District

Attorney Price was publicly criticized for her approach to crime. She responded by saying, "That's racism. I'm calling it for what it is."

> *"Let me tell you something, New Yorkers. Never in my life have I had a problem that I did not see an ending to. I don't see an ending to this. I don't see an ending to this. This issue will destroy New York City, destroy New York City. We're getting ten thousand migrants a month."*

–New York City Mayor Eric
Adams, September 6, 2023

New York City is so overwhelmed by the influx of illegal immigrants that the Adams administration has even distributed flyers to migrants at the Southern border encouraging them to go elsewhere. It is certainly unusual for a mayor to warn people about how lousy life in their city really is.

The flyers tell migrants, "Housing in NYC is very expensive" and "The cost of food, transportation, and other necessities in NYC is the highest in the United States." It's worth noting that during his campaign for Mayor of New York, Eric Adams tweeted the following: "Yes, New York City will remain a sanctuary city under an Adams administration."

For some reason, the proponents of sanctuary cities seem very confident in their righteousness right up to the point when illegal immigrants start arriving in their communities.

> *"No constitutional right, in my view, including my oath, is intended to be absolute."*

–New Mexico Governor Michelle Lujan
Grisham, September 9, 2023

The governor was referring to her decision to issue an emergency public health order and the impact it would have on Second Amendment rights. Following a violent shooting, the order temporarily suspended the right of citizens to carry guns in public areas in Albuquerque. Critics said the governor was exceeding her authority by issuing the order.

I'm reminded of a famous quote by Lord Acton in 1887. As he explained why moral standards should be applied to everyone equally, especially politicians, he noted: "Power tends to corrupt and absolute power corrupts absolutely."

"To me, what is goofy and normal to other folks seems inappropriate."

–Burbank (CA) Mayor Konstantine
Anthony, September 13, 2023

Anthony made this comment at a City Council meeting. He was addressing a controversy that arose after he was seen on video receiving a spanking with a paddle from a drag queen during a Bingo event.

"Some of the misinformation is presented with artistic quality, mental acrobatics, such that it might be tempting to believe those alternative facts if only they weren't automatically discredited by a myopic analysis and bigotry that follows them."

–Oregon State Board of Education Chair
Guadalupe Martinez Zapata, September 21, 2023

On October 19, 2023, the Oregon State Board of Education voted unanimously to extend the removal of a graduation requirement that students should be proficient in reading, writing, and math for another five years. The decision was supported by the Oregon Department of

Education, which described proficiency standards as "burdensome to teachers and students."

In her comment above, the State Board Chair attempted to justify the decision by criticizing those who opposed it. One can only wonder how anyone truly dedicated to educating students would believe that removing standards will lead to increased competency.

> *"I know folks are saying, 'Oh, they're just cleaning up this place because all those fancy leaders are coming into town.' That's true because it's true."*
>
> –California Governor Gavin Newsom, November 9, 2023

Newsom was referring to efforts to clean up San Francisco prior to the Asia-Pacific Economic Cooperation leader's summit, which was taking place there between November 11 and 17, 2023. Among those attending the summit were President Biden and China's President Xi Jinping.

In advance of the summit, Newsom unveiled a program to plant new trees across the city. In addition, homeless encampments were cleared, streets were cleaned, and graffiti was removed. The swift action to transform San Francisco provided ample evidence to its residents that city and state leaders were capable of improving living conditions there all along; they simply chose not to do so.

Perhaps we should schedule similar summits regularly in Democrat-run cities all over the country. The Newsom administration's attempt to sanitize San Francisco is disturbingly similar to actions taken by the Nazis prior to the 1936 Olympic Games in Berlin Germany. They too removed evidence of their destructive policies in an attempt to hide the truth from visiting dignitaries.

"I did send that to everyone by accident."

–Boston Mayor Michelle Wu, December 12, 2023

Mayor Wu was referring to an email that was sent earlier that day by aide Denise DosSantos. The email read, "Honorable members: On behalf of Mayor Michelle Wu, I cordially invite you and a guest to the Electeds of Color Holiday Party."

This email was accidentally sent to all members of the City Council but was intended only for councilors of color. An embarrassed Mayor Wu apologized for the errant email but did not apologize for her intent to exclude White members of the City Council from the party.

Democrats frequently preach about inclusion and unity, but their actions routinely divide the people of the United States by focusing on identity politics. This perspective sees people only through primitive lenses like race, ethnicity, sex, etc.

There was a line in Martin Luther King Jr.'s historic "I Have a Dream" speech that read, "I have a dream that my four little children will one day live in a nation where they will not be judged by the color of their skin but by the content of their character." This aspiration was lauded for decades as the standard toward which America should strive. Put differently, it stressed that we should seek a color-blind society.

Unfortunately, today's Democrats have completely rejected that notion. Democrats now emphasize color above all other considerations and have come to reject MLK's dream.

With that in mind, it might not be terribly surprising to learn that in December 2023, a young Black woman was filmed pouring gasoline on the childhood home of MLK. With only moments to spare before the home was set afire, two retired NYPD officers intervened to stop the arsonist. MLK, whom history has identified as the most notable leader of the American Civil Rights Movement, and his dream are now persona non grata in the minds of Democrats.

Of course, when one considers the overall significance of an errant email invitation to a holiday party, it may seem rather trivial. However, just imagine the fallout if a mayor had been caught sending party invitations only to the White council members. I don't think it is an unreasonable standard to suggest that if it is improper to favor one group (e.g. White council members) then favoring any other group should be considered equally inappropriate. I believe MLK would agree.

> *"New York. This is a place where every day you wake up and you could experience everything from a plane crashing into our trade center to a person who celebrated a new business that's opened. This is a very, very complicated city, and that's why it's the greatest city on the globe."*

> –New York City Mayor Eric
> Adams, December 18, 2023

Adams was asked by a reporter how he would summarize 2023 in one word and why. The next day, Adams defended his answer by saying "I'm authentic. I'm going to talk the way New Yorkers talk."

> *"Some people who have children and families decide they want to go to a place where their children can play outdoors, larger green spaces, you want to see animals. You don't see animals except for rats in New York."*

> –New York City Mayor Eric
> Adams, December 21, 2023

Adams was explaining in a press conference why people were

leaving the city in droves. While this statement may be true, it is probably not the kind of thing a mayor should emphasize if he wants to promote his city to residents and visitors alike. Adams just doesn't come across as a very good advocate for living in the Big Apple.

"First thing they say, 'Oh, she's gonna play the race card now.' But no, God, isn't it them that's playing the race card when they only question one?"

–Fulton County (GA) District Attorney
Fani Willis, January 14, 2024

Willis made this comment during an address to a predominantly Black congregation at the Big Bethel AME Church in Atlanta. She was referring to Nathan Wade, who was one of three special prosecutors she had hired to prosecute former President Donald Trump and eighteen others, who were all charged with election interference in a criminal Racketeer Influenced and Corrupt Organizations (RICO) case.

One of the special prosecutors was a White woman, one was a White man, and one, Nathan Wade, was a Black man. Willis suggested that attacks against Wade and her were racially motivated.

Co-defendant Michael Roman asked the judge to disqualify Willis and dismiss the case, claiming that Willis attempted to defraud the public by concealing a romantic relationship she had with Wade that personally benefited her when he took her on lavish vacations to California, Florida, and the Caribbean. Both Wade (who received more than $650,000 from Fulton County for prosecuting Trump) and Willis testified in court that Willis repaid Wade in cash each time they traveled together. They also claimed that their romantic relationship did not start until after Wade was appointed special prosecutor. Cell phone records and witness testimony, however, contradicted their statements.

Lawyers for the defendants also noted that Wade was unqualified to serve as special prosecutor because his prior experience included primarily low-level criminal defense and personal injury cases. They argued that Willis hired him because of their romantic relationship and paid him a substantial salary which she then benefitted from through a series of kickbacks. They also dismissed her accusations of racism, claiming their focus on Wade was not based on his skin color but on the fact that he was the only one of the three special prosecutors known to be involved in an affair with the district attorney.

"Where's your manager?"

–California Governor Gavin
Newsom, January 31, 2024

Newsom was telling a story in which he witnessed a shoplifter at Target. He asked one of the employees, "Why didn't you stop him?" The employee responded, "The governor lowered the threshold, there's no accountability."

California Proposition 47 became effective on November 5, 2014, creating a new misdemeanor offense called shoplifting. The law, which was approved by 59% of California voters, effectively established an open invitation to shoplifters across the state. This offense includes any larceny at a commercial establishment where the value of the property taken does not exceed $950. Prior to this law, larceny with a property value of more than $400 was considered a felony. Making matters worse, district attorneys across California have decided either not to prosecute shoplifters or not to seek any jail time if they do.

Newsom, who supported the proposition in 2014, was incredulous when he was blamed by the Target employee for the crime crisis in

California. He said, "Why am I spending $380, everyone can walk the hell right out?"

Guess what, Governor? A lot of Californians are asking themselves that same question.

"Right now, we have, you know, young Black kids growing up in the Bronx who don't even know what the word computer is. They don't know, they don't know these things."

–New York Governor Kathy Hochul, May 6, 2024

Hochul was speaking to an audience in Beverly Hills, California, at the Milken Institute Global Conference. Her comment was met with widespread condemnation by residents of the Bronx. She later apologized, saying, "I misspoke, and I regret it. Of course, Black children in the Bronx know what computers are."

Her mea culpa was short-lived, however. On May 23, 2024, Donald Trump held a campaign rally in the Bronx. In spite of its long history as a deep blue community, Trump surprised many when an estimated 25,000 people attended the event.

In response, Kathy Hochul told CNN's Jake Tapper, "I'll tell you what won't make a difference at all, Jake, and that's for Donald Trump to be the ringleader and invite all his clowns to a place like the Bronx." Perhaps someone should remind Governor Hochul that the residents of the Bronx are her constituents, and she should probably stop insulting them.

Chapter 10

Allies and Advocates

"If you want a friend in Washington, get a dog."
–Harry S. Truman

"I don't regret setting bombs. I feel we didn't do enough."

–Professor of Education at the University of
Illinois at Chicago Bill Ayers, September 11, 2001

An unrepentant Ayers was referring to his role as founder of the domestic terrorist organization the Weather Underground. The Weather Underground began in 1969 with the goal to overthrow the US government, and officially declared war on the US government on May 21, 1970.

During the early 1970s, the group bombed numerous banks and government buildings, including the US Capitol, the Pentagon, the US State Department, and the New York City Police Department Headquarters. After the FBI was found to have used illegal tactics during their investigation into the Weather Underground, the Justice Department decided to drop pending criminal charges against the organization and its founder, Bill Ayers.

Incredibly, despite his criminal past, Ayers eventually became a professor of education at the University of Illinois. In 1993 Ayers founded the Chicago Annenberg Challenge (CAC). The CAC was supposedly established to improve Chicago's public schools but in reality, it did little to improve student performance and instead focused primarily on promoting radical political and social activism among students and parents.

In 1995, Barack Obama was appointed Chairman of CAC's Board of Directors. Obama remained on the board until 2001. Obama and Ayers lived in the same Chicago neighborhood, and Ayers hosted a kick-off fundraiser at his home for Barack Obama's first campaign for the Illinois Senate. The relationship between Obama and Ayers became a focal point during Obama's 2008 presidential campaign.

On October 15, 2008, during the final presidential debate between Barack Obama and John McCain, Obama tried to assure voters by saying, "Mr. Ayers is not involved in my campaign. He has never been involved in this campaign, and he will not advise me in the White House."

"No, no, no, not God Bless America, God Damn America. That's in the Bible."

–Reverend Jeremiah Wright, April 13, 2003

Wright made this statement during a sermon entitled "Confusing God and Government." When his comment surfaced on video in 2008, it made national news because he had been Barack Obama's pastor for twenty years at the Trinity United Church of Christ in Chicago.

Obama, who was running for president when the video made news, quickly distanced himself from Wright, just as he did when news arose of his relationship with former domestic terrorist Bill Ayers. Obama described Wright as "…like an old uncle who says things I don't always agree with." It's worth noting that according to ABC News, Wright married Barack and Michelle Obama, baptized their two children, and is even credited with coming up with the name for Obama's book, *The Audacity of Hope*.

According to Section 501(c)(3) of the Internal Revenue Code, churches are automatically considered tax-exempt. However, churches can lose their tax-exempt status if they violate the IRS code. In 1954, the code was amended to prohibit churches from engaging in political campaign activity. In 1987, it was amended again to prohibit statements opposing political candidates.

While the comment above made national news headlines, I find another part of that sermon by Wright to be just as interesting. At one point Wright said to his congregation, "Under Clinton, Blacks had an intelligent friend in the Oval Office. Oh, but government changed. The election was stolen. We went from an intelligent friend to a dumb Dixiecrat, a rich Republican who has never held a job in his life. Is against affirmative action, against education I guess he is, against health care, against benefits for his own military, and gives tax breaks to the wealthiest contributors to his campaign." Of course, Wright was referring to President George W. Bush, who was preparing for a second term at the time.

Wright's rhetoric sounds awfully political for a sermon, and one might wonder whether it violates the Internal Revenue Code. Whether it did or not never seemed to bother Barack Obama, as he said, "I don't think my church is actually particularly controversial."

"There's no one way to be a man. Men who get their periods are men. Men who get pregnant and give birth are men."

–American Civil Liberties Union
(ACLU), November 19, 2019, in a tweet
posted on International Men's Day

During a Senate hearing on July 12, 2022, Missouri Senator Josh Hawley questioned Khiara Bridges, a law professor at the University of California at Berkeley. Hawley asked the professor, "You've referred to people with a capacity for pregnancy, would that be women?" The professor responded, "There are also trans men who are capable of pregnancy as well as nonbinary people who are capable of pregnancy."

Moments later, the professor said to Hawley, "So I want to recognize that your line of questioning is transphobic, and it opens people up to violence." Hawley replied, "I'm opening people up to violence by asking whether or not women are the folks who can have pregnancies?…So we can't talk about it?"

Attempts like this by Democrats to silence opposing opinions have come to be known as *cancel culture*. The tactic has been widely used by social media platforms, news agencies, advocacy groups, schools, and, of course, politicians. This extreme behavior is seen by many as an open attack on free speech and symbolic of the radical change in Democrat party principles in recent years.

During her commencement speech at Wellesley College in 2017, Hillary Clinton made an interesting comment, "As the history majors among you here today know all too well when people in power invent their own facts and attack those who question them, it can mark the beginning of the end of a free society. That is not hyperbole. It is what authoritarian regimes throughout history have done. They attempt to control reality, not just our laws and rights and our budgets, but our thoughts and beliefs."

"In the primary, people would mock him, like, 'You think you can work with Republicans?' I'm not saying they're not a bunch of

f***ers. Mitch McConnell is terrible."

–Biden for President Campaign Manager
Jennifer O'Malley Dillon, December 15, 2020

Dillon was referring to congressional Republicans during an interview with *Glamour Magazine*. Ironically, Dillon claims she was trying to make a case for unity in the interview. Although she received much criticism for her comment, Joe Biden didn't appear to mind, as she soon transferred from serving on his campaign to serving as his incoming White House Deputy Chief of Staff.

"Shoot him!"

–Co-founder of the Lincoln Project
Steve Schmidt, February 12, 2021

Schmidt was referring to Jacob Chansley, also known as "the QAnon Shaman," after he peacefully walked through an open door and was led into the US Senate chamber with the help of Capitol police officers on January 6, 2021. The Democrat-led January 6 Committee had seen the footage of Chansley being led around by Capitol police but did not provide it to his attorneys to aid in his defense. Instead, he was described by US District Court Judge Royce Lamberth as the face of the January 6 "insurrection" and sentenced to forty-one months in prison.

"This was an insurrection."

–Harvard Law Professor Emeritus
Laurence Tribe, July 14, 2021

Tribe was referring to the actions of President Donald Trump's supporters on January 6, 2021. Following a rally led by Donald Trump on the Ellipse, many of his supporters, who like Trump questioned the integrity of the 2020 presidential election results, marched to the US Capitol building. Sadly, some in the crowd, which had been peaceful to that point, violently attacked Capitol Police Officers and forced their way into the building. Many other protesters entered the building as well to peacefully demonstrate their frustration over the election.

Instead of describing the event as a protest or even a riot, commentators in the media soon began using the term *insurrection*. While this may seem like a matter of semantics, it was actually a carefully scripted decision.

Section 3 of the 14th Amendment to the US Constitution notes: "No person shall be a Senator or Representative in Congress, or elector of President and Vice-President, or hold any office, civil or military, under the United States, or under any State, who, having previously taken an oath, as a member of Congress, or as an officer of the United States, or as a member of any State legislature, or as an executive or judicial officer of any State, to support the Constitution of the United States, shall have engaged in insurrection or rebellion against the same, or given aid or comfort to the enemies thereof."

Some observers claim that this provision of the 14th Amendment, which was ratified on July 9, 1868, is no longer applicable because it was specifically meant to address the issue of former Confederates serving in the US government. I reject that argument because I believe that unless it is amended, there is no expiration date on any component of the US Constitution. I have no problem with the concept that an insurrectionist should be barred from US government public office. This is why Tribe (and many other critics of Donald Trump) insisted on using the term *insurrection* to describe what happened on January 6. Their purpose was to establish a legal argument that Trump should not be allowed to serve again as President of the United States.

Many legal scholars, however, have challenged this premise because Trump has never been charged nor convicted of insurrection by a court of law. The counterargument is that the consequences of insurrection are self-enacting. This means that because of his involvement, Donald Trump should be automatically disqualified from serving as president even in the absence of a conviction.

If that were true, who exactly gets to decide what constitutes an insurrection? Who gets to decide if someone participated in an insurrection? Is there any burden of proof that must be met? If the media and political opponents get to label anyone they wish as an insurrectionist, this would diminish the impeachment provisions of the Constitution and could potentially lead to chaos. Imagine a game of political quid pro quo where for every blue State Supreme Court that bans Trump from their ballot, a red state Supreme Court reciprocates by declaring Biden an insurrectionist for his failure to secure the Southern border, leading them to ban him from their ballot. Where would it end? Is that the kind of pettiness we really want to open ourselves up to?

There must be some measure of procedural due process before a candidate can be banned from a state ballot. Unfortunately, at that moment, Trump's opponents seemed willing to stop at nothing to prevent him from winning a second term. According to their irrational logic, we must protect democracy by keeping those with whom we disagree off the ballot.

Sadly, on December 19, 2023, Colorado became the first state to express their intention to bar Trump from appearing on the state's ballot in 2024 after the Colorado Supreme Court cited the 14th Amendment in a four-to-three vote. When he was asked to comment on this issue, President Joe Biden had this to say: "He certainly supported an insurrection. There's no question about it. None. Zero."

DID I HEAR YOU RIGHT?

Fortunately, on March 4, 2024, the US Supreme Court ruled in a unanimous decision that "responsibility for enforcing section 3 [of the 14th Amendment] against federal officeholders and candidates rests with Congress and not the states." This effectively put an end to the issue.

"There is no such thing as learning loss. Our kids didn't lose anything. It's OK that our babies may not have learned all their times tables. They learned resilience. They learned survival. They learned critical-thinking skills. Then know the difference between a riot and a protest. Then know the words insurrection and coup."

–United Teachers Los Angeles President
Cecily Myart-Cruz, August 21, 2021

This comment was made in response to concerns about school closures during the COVID-19 pandemic. Following the recent release of the National Assessment of Educational Progress (NAEP) scores for 2022, the first administration of the test since the pandemic began, we learned just how detrimental school shutdowns during the pandemic were to student achievement. They showed the biggest drop in math performance in fourth and eighth grades since the testing program began in 1990.

Additionally, roughly a third of students in both grades were unable to read at the basic achievement level, the lowest level on the test. These results confirmed what was foreseen by parents across the country as they watched their children struggle to use online tools that were hastily adopted by schools and largely ill-equipped to serve as effective learning platforms for students. Even when COVID-19 cases diminished and pleas from parents to reopen schools grew louder, one influential coalition pressured public officials to keep them closed: teachers' unions.

As a former public school teacher, I ascertained the true nature of teachers' unions long ago. If there was still a doubt in anyone's mind that teachers' unions are entirely focused on the political and economic interests of their members and contribute absolutely nothing to student education, let their statements and actions during the pandemic remove such doubt forever.

"Larry Elder is a Black face on White supremacy."

–Professor and former Chair of the Department of
Pan-African Studies at California State University
Los Angeles Melina Abdullah, September 6, 2021

Professor Abdullah was referring to California Republican gubernatorial candidate Larry Elder during an event hosted by the African American Voter Registration, Education, and Participation Project (AAVREP).

Comments like this not only defy common sense, they cause observers to wonder just how low Democrats are willing to go in their pursuit of power. Responding to the attack, Elder stated "I anticipated that would happen. This is why a lot of people don't go into politics because of the politics of personal destruction."

"As these acts of malice, violence, and threats against public school officials have increased, the classification of these heinous actions could be the equivalent to a form of domestic terrorism and hate crimes."

–National School Boards Association President
Viola Garcia and Interim Executive Director
& CEO Chip Slaven, September 29, 2021

In a letter to President Joe Biden, the National School Boards Association (NSBA) claimed that individuals opposed to COVID-19 mask mandates and critical race theory were causing disruptions at school board meetings in several states. The NSBA's letter to President Biden asked for expertise and resources from the US Department of Justice, Federal Bureau of Investigation, US Department of Homeland Security, and the US Secret Service with its National Threat Assessment Center to focus on these "threats." They also asked the president to examine appropriate enforceable actions against these individuals using various federal laws, including the PATRIOT Act, which was passed by Congress shortly after the terrorist attacks on the US on September 11, 2001.

The PATRIOT Act provided the US government with "appropriate tools required to intercept and obstruct terrorism." Five days after the NSBA sent the letter to the president, Attorney General Merrick Garland issued a memo to the Director of the FBI and every US Attorney, directing them to discuss strategies for addressing these threats. I should clarify at this point that the so-called "domestic terrorists" referenced in the NSBA letter, are otherwise known as concerned parents.

"I wear a mask most of the time indoors. We took them off as people were having a hard time hearing us."

–American Federation of Teachers President
Randi Weingarten, November 6, 2021, in a tweet

On August 2, 2021, Weingarten said during an interview, "Masks stop transmission, so universal masking is going to be very helpful to keep kids safe, to keep the unvaccinated safe, and to keep schools open."

Weingarten's claim that universal masking will keep kids safe is laughable. Data showed that children are the least susceptible group when it comes to COVID-19. What Weingarten didn't say is that her union members demanded that students wear masks to make them feel safer in spite of evidence to the contrary. It's funny that a few months after calling for universal masking for students, Weingarten acknowledged that she removed her mask so she could be heard better. She doesn't seem to realize that if her audience can't hear well when someone speaks through a mask, the same might be true for students in a classroom. Teachers' Unions like the AFT have little regard for students and the negative impact mask-wearing had on them. Why should they? That's not who they represent, after all.

"I'm like, ugh. It's, like, triggering. This is, like, deeply unsafe. This is literally being weaponized against us, against the people we work with…If their organization and the people in it are being attacked and scrutinized at everything they do, that leads to deep burnout. That leads to deep, like, resistance and trauma."

–Black Lives Matter Global Network Foundation
Co-founder Patrisse Cullors, April 8, 2022

Ms. Cullors was upset after learning that the charitable organization she ran was required to disclose the organization's finances and activities on IRS Form 990 on an annual basis. Having not filed the required paperwork with the IRS, several states ordered her organization to cease raising money until it detailed what it had done with approximately $90 million collected in 2020. The organization reportedly purchased a 6,500-square-foot mansion in southern California for nearly $6 million in October 2020 that Cullors later described as a "haven, as a safe space." It was also reported that Cullors' organization had recently purchased four other homes totaling approximately $3.2 million.

DID I HEAR YOU RIGHT?

"I can't advocate on behalf of public education and the children of this city and educators in this city without it taking root in my own household."

—Chicago Teachers' Union Vice President
Stacy Davis Gates, April 19, 2022

Gates made this comment during an interview with *Chicago Magazine*. One month later, she became CTU's president. In September 2023, it was revealed that Gates had enrolled one of her children in a private Catholic high school. She explained that she made this decision for her son "so he could live out his dream of being a soccer player."

In a statement explaining her actions to her union colleagues, Gates said, "If you are a Black family living in a Black community, high-quality neighborhood schools have been the dream, not the reality... We aren't blessed with quality options blocks away from our home."

Interestingly, the next day the *Chicago Sun-Times* reported that there was a high-quality public high school with a soccer program only three miles from Gates' home. However, she chose to enroll her son in a private Catholic school nine miles from home.

For the record, I believe Gates, like any parent, should be free to send her child to any school she wants. That is the entire purpose behind the movement toward school choice. The American Federation for Children describes school choice as "any policy that allows families to take their children's education (tax) dollars to the approved education provider of their choosing—be it traditional public schools, public charter schools, private school, virtual learning, or homeschooling."

Gates' decision to send her son to a Catholic school would be far more understandable had she not been such an outspoken opponent of school choice. In August 2022, she posted a tweet saying, "School choice was actually the choice of racists." This appears to be a classic example of "rules for thee but not for me."

Gates' decision to send her son to a private Catholic school is essentially making the case for school choice but she appears to be too obtuse to see it. Unfortunately, low-income families don't have the flexibility to send their children to private schools like Gates can, which is why school choice advocates want families to have access to the tax dollars allocated for their child to attend a public school—so they can apply those funds to the school of their choice. The bottom line is that the status quo often forces low-income students to attend failing schools with no feasible alternative. School choice programs would reduce the control teachers' unions have over families and eventually diminish their influence. For now, however, the public schools remain firmly under the control of teachers' unions, and they will fight to preserve their power. What's best for the students is immaterial to their leaders.

> *"We have a student who came to America with Coyote, which is a group that helps people. This group gives you a time frame to make a payment of $5,000 to those who bring them to the states. Our student needs our urgent support to raise another $2,000."*

> –Assistant Principal of Mount Pleasant
> High School (Providence, RI) Stefani
> Harvey, January 26, 2023

Really, coyotes help people? They are human traffickers!

Harvey distributed this message in an email to teachers at her school. Her email raises many ethical questions. Did this administrator use her work computer for this email? Was the email sent during work hours? Could this email be viewed as a type of coercion by a supervisor to her staff? Is this a public declaration promoting state support not only for illegal immigration but for human rights violations like human trafficking?

One has to wonder given her description of a *coyote*; if this administrator is strikingly ignorant about the reality behind the many problems connected with illegal immigration or if she may be so ideologically motivated that she is willing to use her position to push forward a political agenda. One can only hope that this offensive request was simply a misguided attempt to help a student in need. As well-intentioned as that email might have been, our public officials at every level need to think before taking action that may be contrary not only to the law but to our country's collective interests.

"Our fear is that if an unqualified sonographer misdiagnoses a heart defect, an organ defect, spina bifida or an encephalopathic defect, that becomes a very local issue because our school budget will have to absorb the cost of a child in special education, supplying lots and lots of special services to children who were born with the defect."

–Chair of Framingham (MA) Democratic Committee Michael Hugo, February 7, 2023

Hugo made this comment during a Framingham City Council meeting, where a proclamation was being discussed about access to abortion. His remarks were met with widespread condemnation for suggesting that children with disabilities should be aborted. Disgusting!

"CEA believes that capitalism requires exploitation of children, public schools, land, labor, and/or resources. Capitalism is in opposition to fully addressing systemic racism (the school-to-prison pipeline), climate change, patriarchy, (gender and LGBTQ

disparities), education inequality, and income inequality."

–Colorado Education Association, April 22, 2023

This language was included in a resolution passed by Colorado's largest teachers' union. It declared its opposition to the economic system that led the United States of America to have the world's largest economy.

Compare those sentiments with an alternative description of capitalism featured on the website of US Congressman Chris Stewart, which notes, "The fruits of capitalism are many. It has increased access to education, driven up the value of labor over time, and allowed for an unprecedented level of economic mobility. The average modern person works fewer hours—in far better conditions—than their counterparts from earlier centuries and still enjoys a far better standard of living. American capitalism has led to innovations in health care, technology, and industry that have literally changed the world. These innovations have reduced infant mortality rates and increased life expectancy by decades. Rapid advances in technology during the Industrial Revolution and Digital Revolution have produced a standard of living that far exceeds that of our great-grandparents—with the opportunity for even further improvement. Capitalism—unlike socialism, Marxism or authoritarianism—rewards individual innovation and work ethic. Anyone can improve their station in life by hard work or coming up with a new idea."

"If you do a questionnaire, please make it a paper and pencil activity; any digital records are more permanent and may be requested under federal law."

–Jefferson County (CO) Education
Association, August 11, 2023

The practice of teachers surveying students to learn their preferred pronouns is legally unclear. As a result, school administrators in the Jefferson County School District (Colorado) have advised teachers to refrain from doing so. The local teachers' union, Jefferson County Education Association, however, issued an email to teachers encouraging them to do so but without making a digital trail. According to CBS Colorado, the union also advised teachers to "make your notations about students and not hold on to the documents." So obsessed are groups like this with the issue of gender identity in students that they will encourage legally dubious behavior in their members just to advance their cause.

"The President's first major bill signed into law has provided $10 billion in additional funding for law enforcement—and every Republican in Congress voted against that bill."

–Spokesperson for Biden-Harris 2024
Kevin Munoz, August 23, 2023

Munoz was referring to the $1.9 trillion American Rescue Plan Act, which was passed on March 11, 2021. Munoz's argument is a typical tactic of the Democrats. They put together a monstrous bill with hundreds of billions of dollars for their pet projects and then earmark a relatively small amount of money for worthwhile initiatives like public safety. They then criticize Republicans who vote against the bill by saying they don't support law enforcement.

Senate Minority Leader Mitch McConnell said it well. "Instead of working together to fight COVID-19, Democrats decided to exploit the crisis by jamming through unrelated liberal policies they couldn't pass honestly. A colossal missed opportunity for the American people."

"This is a win that will protect free speech in Denver for the years to come."

–Loevy & Loevy Law Firm Attorney
Elizabeth Wang, August 28, 2023

Wang made this comment following the unanimous decision by the Denver City Council to approve a $4.7 million settlement for arrests made by Denver police of individuals who violated a city curfew during their protests over the death of George Floyd in the summer of 2020.

Wang was the lead attorney for over 300 protestors who had filed a class action suit against the city. She went on to say, "In addition to compensation to protesters, the settlement prevents the city from enacting any curfew enforced against those engaged in protest activity in the future."

The curfew, which was established by Mayor Michale Hancock, was intended to prevent violence and destruction of property in the city. The plaintiffs argued that it was targeted unfairly against protesters, but the Denver City Attorney's Office denied that the city's curfew was unconstitutionally enforced.

Even as violent riots broke out in cities across the nation, many mainstream news outlets continued to describe them as "mostly peaceful." It is worth noting that during the George Floyd riots, dozens of people were killed and thousands of businesses were burned, looted, and vandalized.

According to *Axios*, "The vandalism and looting following the death of George Floyd at the hands of the Minneapolis police will cost the insurance industry more than any other violent demonstrations in recent history…US companies have learned the hard way that…most policies emphatically do cover riot-related losses."

In Denver and other cities, the majority of the criminal charges against the protesters were later dismissed, including all of those individuals who were arrested for curfew violations only. Apparently, the Denver City Council felt that wasn't enough and the protesters should actually be compensated for all their hard work.

"Learn to lose gracefully."

–National Women's Law Center President and
CEO Fatima Goss Graves, December 5, 2023

Graves made this comment as she discussed trans athletes competing in women's sports during a House Oversight Subcommittee on Health Care and Financial Services hearing, "The Importance of Protecting Female Athletics and Title IX." As she explained that trans athletes want to compete in sports for the same reasons women do, she also mentioned the need to "lose gracefully." Many observers believed this was a subtle critique directed toward outspoken female athletes who have argued that it is wrong to allow biological males to compete against females.

"It depends on the context."

–Harvard University President
Claudine Gay, December 5, 2023

Dr. Gay provided this answer when she was asked during a House Committee on Education and Workforce hearing whether calling for the genocide of Jews violated Harvard's code of conduct.

Apparently, based on Gay's testimony, there are acceptable and unacceptable ways to call for the genocide of Jews at Harvard. The presidents of the Massachusetts Institute of Technology and the University of Pennsylvania provided similar answers during their testimony as well. One can only wonder if their answers would be different if the words Latino, Black, gay, or trans were substituted for the word Jews. These are campuses that treat misgendering a fellow student as a serious offense but for some reason seem to have trouble condemning the genocide of Jews.

Gay was widely ridiculed for her comment, and several Republican lawmakers publicly called for her dismissal. Nevertheless, more than 600 Harvard faculty members signed a petition calling for her to keep her position. In response to calls for her termination, Harvard's governing board announced that they "unanimously stand in support of President Gay."

If a kindergartener were asked whether calling for Jews to be killed was a bad thing, they would unequivocally answer yes. It's pathetic that the president of what was once considered the country's most esteemed university couldn't do the same.

On December 13, 2023, the House of Representatives passed House Resolution 927. The resolution condemned antisemitism on university campuses and the testimony of those university presidents who testified before the House Committee on Education and the Workforce.

Not surprisingly, 125 Democrats voted against the resolution. On numerous occasions in recent months, fliers of Jewish civilians taken hostage by Hamas have been vandalized or removed at Harvard. However, according to reports by the *Daily Wire*, starting in April 2024 Harvard hired 24/7 security to guard an anti-Israel Apartheid Wall that features anti-Israel art and a quote from an infamous Palestinian terrorist.

In a strange twist to this story, soon after Dr. Gay's testimony before Congress, reports began to surface that she had plagiarized portions of her 1997 Ph.D. dissertation as well as other papers. Soon, approximately fifty examples of plagiarism throughout the course of Dr. Gay's career were identified.

On January 2, 2024, Dr. Gay resigned as President of Harvard University after just six months in the role. Dr. Gay and her supporters claimed that she had been sloppy, but she had not actually committed academic plagiarism. The day after her resignation, she wrote in an op-ed for *The New York Times,* "My critics found instances in my academic writings where some material duplicated other scholars' language without proper attribution."

Plagiarism is defined as "An act or instance of using or closely imitating the language and thoughts of another author without authorization and the representation of that author's work as one's own, as by not crediting the original author." This definition sounds an awful lot like what Dr. Gay said she did. I wonder if she copied that language too.

"It will cost $50 billion and three cents. And so what? That's audacity."

–Chicago Teachers' Union President
Stacy Davis Gates, March 5, 2024

Gates was referring to her union's collective bargaining proposal to the city of Chicago. The contract proposed by the union features more than 700 demands, including an annual wage increase of 9% and free abortions for union members. It has yet to be explained how free abortions for union members will lead to an increase in student achievement.

To put this outrageous proposal in context, the budget for the Chicago Public Schools is roughly $9 billion and it is currently dealing with a $400 million deficit. Moreover, the tax revenue for the entire state of Illinois was approximately $50 billion in 2023. It's also worth noting that Chicago Mayor Brandon Johnson was previously employed as Legislative Coordinator for the Chicago Teachers' Union. CTU also contributed approximately $2.6 million to Johnson's mayoral campaign. With all of that going for them, Gates and her colleagues may just pull off this scam.

"The threat Trump poses to our democracy has never been greater. He is running an increasingly unhinged campaign of revenge and retribution."

–Biden-Harris Campaign Statement,
May 30, 2024, in an X post

This post was written on the day Donald Trump was found guilty by a New York City jury of falsifying business records in what many observers on both the Left and Right believed was a politically motivated prosecution. Here we have a Democrat prosecutor with strong ties to the Biden administration, a Democrat judge who donated to the Biden campaign, and a jury from an overwhelmingly Democrat jurisdiction convicting former President Trump of thirty-four felony counts. Yet somehow we simpletons are supposed to believe the Biden campaign when they tell us that Trump is the one who is out for revenge and retribution.

*"You have no right to be here, you Nazi piece of s***."*

–Melissa Cohen-Biden, June 4, 2024

Cohen-Biden is married to Joe Biden's son, Hunter. She directed this comment to former Trump White House aide Garrett Ziegler in a hallway outside of the courtroom where Hunter Biden was on trial for lying on a federal form to purchase a firearm.

Ziegler was reportedly among those in the Trump administration who called for the contents of Hunter Biden's infamous laptop to be made public. Following the encounter, Ziegler told NBC News, "For the record, I'm not a Nazi. I'm a believer in the US Constitution. I haven't said one thing to them." It's worth noting that Hunter Biden's trial is being held in a federal courthouse and members of the public are allowed to attend federal judicial proceedings—even Trump allies.

***

I'd like to end this book by sharing one final quote:

"Politicians and diapers must be changed often, and for the same reason."

–Mark Twain

www.ingramcontent.com/pod-product-compliance
Lightning Source LLC
Chambersburg PA
CBHW052120270326

41930CB00012B/2696